MAJ. GENERAL JOHN SULLIVAN

THE

MILITARY SERVICES

AND

PUBLIC LIFE

OF

MAJOR-GENERAL JOHN SULLIVAN,

OF THE AMERICAN REVOLUTIONARY ARMY.

BY

THOMAS C. AMORY.

BOSTON:
WIGGIN AND LUNT.
ALBANY, N.Y.: J. MUNSELL.
1868.

Entered according to Act of Congress, in the year 1868, by
THOMAS C. AMORY,
In the Clerk's Office of the District Court of the District of Massachusetts.

CAMBRIDGE:
PRESS OF JOHN WILSON AND SON.

TABLE OF CONTENTS.

		PAGE
	PREFACE,	3
1740	Birth	8
1774	Member of Provincial Assembly	10
	Delegate to Continental Congress	10
	Attack on Fort at Newcastle	10
	Address to Governor	13
1775	In Congress	14
	Appointed Brigadier-General	15
	Siege of Boston	15
	Letter on New-Hampshire Constitution	17
	Letter to John Adams	21
1776	Command in Canada	23
	Address of Officers	23
	Promotion to Major-General	24
	Battle of Long Island	24
	Taken Prisoner	29
	Lord Howe's Letter	29
	Interview with Congress	29
	Exchange for General Prescott	31
	In Westchester	36
	Capture of Lee	36
	Battle of Trenton	36
1777	Battle of Princeton	37
	Descent on Staten Island	38
	Letter to Congress	41
	Battle of Brandywine	43

CONTENTS.

		Page
1777	Letter to Congress	47
	Letter to John Adams	54
	Battle of Germantown	57
	Letter to President Weare	57
1778	Valley Forge	65
	Command in Rhode Island	67
	Letter to Pigott, April 27	68
	Letter to Pigott, June 4	69
	Letter to Congress, May 3	70
	Letter of Lafayette	73
	Crosses on to the Island	74
	Address to D'Estaing	77
	Letter to Washington	79
	Battle of Rhode Island	81
	Letter to Congress	84
	Letter of General Greene	89
1779	Expedition against the Six Nations	96
	Letters to Washington	98
	Letter to Governor Clinton	103
	Washington's Instructions	104
	Letter to Congress	109
	Letter of Colonel Pickering	113
	Letter of Washington	114
	Letter to Washington	117
	Clinton joins him	117
	Battle of Newtown	119
	Letter to Congress	121
	Requests troops to be content with half-rations	125
	Address to Oneidas, Sept. 1	127
	Response	128
	Letter to Congress, Sept. 30	130
	Address to Oneidas	140
	Response	141
	Letter to Congress, Oct. 2	142
	Iroquois	145
	Thanks of Congress	151
	Address of the Jersey Brigade	152
	Resigns	153
	Letter to Washington, Nov. 6	153

CONTENTS.

		PAGE
1779	Letter to Washington, Dec. 1	155
	Reply of Washington, Dec. 15	156
	Qualifications as a General Officer	158
	Criticisms	164
1780	Delegate to Congress	171
	Hampshire Grants	172
	State of Affairs	174
	Committee of War	175
	Letter of Washington, Nov. 20	176
	Letter of Washington, Nov. 25	178
	Address to the States	178
	Committee on Finance	179
1781	Committee on Mutiny in Pennsylvania Line	180
	Letter of Lafayette, Jan. 9	180
	Letter to Minister of France, Jan. 13	180
	Choice of Superintendent of Finance	181
	Letter of Washington, Feb. 4	184
	Articles of Confederation, March 1	187
	Measures of Finance	187
	Thomas Burke	191
	Jersey Hulks	191
	Depreciation of Currency	192
	Attorney-General of New Hampshire	192
1782	Disturbances at Keene	192
1783	Society of Cincinnati	197
	State Constitution	198
1784	Major-General	198
	Member of the Council	200
	Refugee Loyalists	201
	Organization of State Militia	201
1785	Presidential Canvass	204
	Vindication	205
1786	President of New Hampshire	209
	Allen Claim	209
	"New-Hampshire Spy"	211
	Inaugural Address	212
	Insurrectionary Movements	215
	Address to the People	218
	Address to Legislature	228

b

CONTENTS.

		PAGE
1786	Plan for paying Federal Debt	222
1787	Re-elected President	225
	Letter from Gen. Knox	227
	Federal Constitution	229
1788	Convention for Ratification	229
	Fast Proclamation	231
	Ratification	236
1789	Federal Offices	240
	Re-elected President	241
	Judge of Federal Court	241
	Washington's Visit	241
	Thanksgiving Proclamation	243
	Returns from Presidency	244
	Opens his Court	244
	Health undermined	245
1795	Death	246
	Character and Services	246

APPENDIX.

Parentage 263
Early Life 291
Attack on Fort 295
Durham Military Association 297
Gen. Scammell's Letter 298
Letter from Officer in Canada 300
Livius's Letter 301
Military Organization 307
Washington's Visit 319

ERRATA.

Page 10, line 19, for "12th," read "17th."
„ 26, line 2, for "on," read "to."
„ „ line 3, for "to," read "by."
„ 209, line 19, for "sons," read "grandsons;" and for "who," read "and John Tufton Mason, son of Robert."
„ 249, line 7, for "like him," read "not for so long a period."
„ 279, line 24, for "3," read "4."
„ 280, line 3, for "4," read "3."

PREFACE.

The prominent position held for nearly a quarter of a century by General Sullivan, in civil and military life; the important epoch and events with which he was associated; the mass of material of interest to students of American history, that can in no other way be so intelligibly placed before the public, — indicate an obligation somewhere to prepare his biography. Such a work should be less the history of the individual than of his times, — of New Hampshire in the Revolution and the periods that followed it; her social, professional, and political life while he was engaged in her service. Whatever incidents he was conspicuously connected with, shedding light on the course of public affairs, or serving to illustrate the personages who shared with him in their management, would come within its scope.

Whilst many other distinguished characters remained uncommemorated, those whose duty it was to cherish his memory felt under no constraint to call attention to his public services. But now that those services have been made subject of misrepresentation and erroneous impression, for want of information at hand to correct them, this should no longer be delayed.

With profound distrust of his own ability to meet this obligation, the writer has, for many years, been diligent in collecting materials, in the expectation that some one would be found better qualified and more favorably placed for the preparation of a suitable biography. He is now himself reluctantly persuaded to proceed with the work; and would be grateful to whoever possesses what will add to its value, to permit him the use of it for his purpose. Pamphlets, newspapers, public documents, correspondence, or personal anecdotes would be acceptable. This request is addressed to gentlemen in all parts of the country, who are disposed to render their aid; but especially to those of New Hampshire, who best know how much there remains that is generally interesting, connected with the official and professional life of General Sullivan, which must perish or be lost to the public, if not recorded in print.

Towards the close of the year 1866, appeared a publication with many perversions as to his services in the war, which was promptly responded to in the December number of the New-York "Historical Magazine;" and also in a paper, read the same month before the Massachusetts Historical Society at their meeting, and published in their recent volume of "Proceedings." Our design was simply to place that paper within reach of readers to whom the volume itself was not readily accessible. But it has grown in the press much beyond its original dimensions, and now embraces a full account of the campaigns in Rhode Island, in 1778, and in New York, in 1779, with the events of his subsequent career in Congress, and of his official life in New Hampshire. Many documents procured from the State and National Archives, not heretofore given to the public, and a few of his writings are added. It still is not so much a biography as a vindication, and we hope to be encouraged to extend and improve it.

It is not to be hoped that any refutation in our power to make, however conclusive, will follow a work of established popularity, circulating abroad as well as at home. The wrong done is not to be repaired. Life and reputation are held on a precarious tenure, both alike at the mercy of the unscrupulous. To many minds, to censure is to condemn. All that can be hoped is to rescue the military character of General Sullivan from misapprehension amongst our own people, and to spread as widely as possible evidence to remove the aspersions cast upon it. He did his best; was indefatigable in the service of his country; devoted the best years of his existence to the establishment of her independence, liberties, and social order on secure foundations; was honest, generous, and self-sacrificing; loyal to every obligation, public and private; and it is confidently believed that now, as when in the Revolution he was occasionally subjected to unfriendly criticism, he will gain a higher place in the estimation of his countrymen, from having been unjustly maligned.

BOSTON, November 1, 1868.

THE MILITARY SERVICES

OF

MAJOR-GENERAL JOHN SULLIVAN.

IN a recently published volume by George Bancroft, the ninth of a work entitled "History of the United States," and the third of that portion of it devoted to the American Revolution, certain errors are found which require correction. These reflect upon the character and conduct of several of our most honored Revolutionary officers, — in part being, it is conceived, mistakes of judgment; in other instances, misapprehensions of fact. The present object is to set right those that relate to Major-General John Sullivan, of New Hampshire.

It is unfortunate for his fame, that, with the exception of the brief memoir in the Third Volume of the Second Series of Sparks's "American Biography," no separate account has been given either of his civil or his military career. The hope had been indulged, that some citizen of New Hampshire, familiar with the part taken by that State in the war, and with the character and services of its historical personages who co-operated with Sullivan in his labors, would have felt called upon to become his biographer. But this hope has been disappointed.

His immediate descendants, incessantly employed in public or professional labor, have had neither the leisure nor the disposition to determine what place he should occupy among the patriots who founded the republic. Much as they revered his memory, the obligation to secure for him his just reward in the grateful remembrance of his countrymen, did not rest upon them. If, at a crisis fraught with the destinies of America, he had fortunately been instrumental in establishing its independence and national existence on firm foundations, it was for the public whom he served to make acknowledgment. But when, without a shadow of reason or particle of proof, his discretion and generalship are subjected to obloquy, it becomes their sacred duty, as their right, to vindicate them. It is incumbent upon whoever is familiar with the evidence, and detests historical injustice, to help in protecting his fame from undeserved disparagement.

It might well have been wished, that some abler writer had assumed the task. But the materials for the purpose are widely distributed, the story of the Revolution has been of late often repeated, and the most favorable time has not perhaps yet arrived for a detailed account of his active and eventful life. In submitting with diffidence to the candor of the public this vindication of his military character from reproaches unwarranted by contemporary evidence, and at variance with the opinion entertained of his qualifications for command by the best and ablest of his brother officers, confidence is indulged that judgment will be reserved until both sides have been heard.

Although the name of General Sullivan and his services are generally familiar to students of American history, a brief recital of the principal incidents of his career is indispensable to a clear view, or just estimate of so much of it as has been subject for misrepresentation. He was born at Somersworth, in New Hampshire, on the opposite side of the river from Berwick, in Maine, which was his early home,

18th February, 1740, receiving from his father, who had himself enjoyed the advantages of a liberal culture in Europe, a good education.* After a voyage to the West Indies, he became a member of the family of the Hon. Isaac Livermore, a lawyer of Portsmouth, in extensive practice, and, under his instruction, prepared himself for his profession. He early exhibited ability of a high order; gained the respect and encouragement of his instructor; and soon attained, by his industry, learning, and eloquence, a distinguished position at the bar of New Hampshire. Such was his professional success, that, soon after his marriage at the age of twenty, he purchased the commodious dwelling at Durham, still in good preservation, which continued to be his abode for the remainder of his life, and that of his widow till her death in 1820.

For the next ten years, he was constantly employed in lucrative causes, taking an elevated rank as an able advocate and judicious counsellor. He enjoyed the friendship of the Wentworths and the Langdons, as well as that of Lowell, Adams, and Otis, leading members of the Massachusetts Bar. He early promoted the introduction into New Hampshire of that manufacturing industry to which she owes so large a portion of her present prosperity, establishing cloth and fulling mills at Durham, and, before the breaking out of the war, had accumulated, if not wealth, a handsome competence.

Of a robust constitution and active spirit, he had a natural taste for military life; and although, with the exception of uniting with his father and brothers in the defence of Berwick from occasional attacks by the Indians, he had, before our Revolutionary period, no actual experience of warfare, heroes of Louisbourg abounded in his neighborhood, inciting emulation. He is said to have devoted, in his historical studies, particular attention to military movements and en-

---

* See Appendix.

2

gagements, and to have been able accurately to describe most of the great battles of ancient and modern times. In 1772, at the age of thirty-one, he held a colonial commission as major, and improved every opportunity to become acquainted with the practical details, as well as the rudiments, of military science.

His ardent nature and his abhorrence of oppression, his contributions to the political press, and his extended influence and popularity, marked him early as a leader in the impending struggle. In the spring of 1774, he was a member of the Provincial Assembly of New Hampshire, and, in September of the same year, was sent to Philadelphia as one of the New-Hampshire delegation to the Continental Congress. His name appeared on many of the most important committees of the latter body; he took his part in its deliberations, prepared several of its important papers, and stood well with his associates.

Soon after his return home, he planned, with Thomas Pickering and John Langdon, an attack, on the night of the 12th of December, upon Fort William and Mary, at Newcastle, in Portsmouth Harbor, — one of the earliest acts of hostility against the Mother Country; and, by the aid of a portion of a force he had been for some months engaged in drilling in their military exercises, in preparation for the anticipated conflict, carried ninety-seven kegs of powder and a quantity of small arms, in gondolas, to Durham, where they were concealed, in part, under the pulpit of its meeting-house. Soon after the battles of Lexington and Concord, in April, had aroused the people to a realizing sense that they were actually engaged in hostilities, these much-needed supplies, or a portion of them, were brought by him to the lines at Cambridge, where he marched with his company, and were used at the battle of Bunker Hill.*

---

* See Appendix.

In order to justify to public opinion, not only in the province, but throughout the country, the motives actuating this first directly overt act of hostilities, he published through the press, on the 24th of December, — not many days after it occurred, — the following address to the inhabitants of British America. This address has a sufficiently close relation to the main object of this publication, to warrant its introduction. It will, moreover, serve to show the resolute and uncompromising spirit in which the patriots put at risk their lives and fortunes in entering into rebellion; it indicates the elevated principles that governed them, as well as the ability and good temper with which they vindicated their course. It reads: —

FRIENDS AND COUNTRYMEN, — At a time when ministerial tyrants threaten a people with the total loss of their liberties, supineness and inattention on their part will render that ruin, which their enemies have designed for them, unavoidable. A striking instance of this we have in the history of the Carthaginians. That brave people, notwithstanding they had surrendered up three hundred hostages to the Romans, upon a promise of being restored to their former liberties, found themselves instantly invaded by the Roman army. Roused by this unexpected procedure, they sent deputies to demand an explanation. They were told, that they must deliver up all their arms to the Romans, and then they should peaceably enjoy their liberties. Upon their compliance with this requisition, Marcius, one of the Roman consuls, thus addressed them: "We are well pleased with these first instances of your obedience, and therefore cannot help congratulating you upon them. I have now but one thing more to require of you, in the name of the Roman people. I will therefore, without further preamble, plainly declare to you an order, on which the safety of your republic, the preservation of your goods, your lives, and liberties, depend: Rome requires that you abandon your city, which we are commanded to level with the ground. You may build yourselves another where you please, provided it be ten miles from the sea, and without walls or fortification. A little courage and resolution will get the better of the affection which attaches you to your old habitations, which is founded more in habit than in reason." The consternation of the Carthaginian deputies, at hearing this treacherous speech, is not to be expressed. Some swooned, others burst into cries and lamentation; nor were even the Roman soldiers, who were present, unmoved at the affecting scene. "This sensibility," said the inhuman consul, "will wear off by degrees. Time and necessity teaches the most unfortunate to bear their calamities with patience: the Carthaginians, when they recover their senses, will choose to obey."

Although the Carthaginians, after this, made a noble and manly resistance, yet the surrender of their arms proved the destruction of that city which had so often contended with Rome for the empire of the world.

Equally inexcusable with the Carthaginians will the Americans be, if they suffer the tyrants, who are endeavoring to enslave them, to possess themselves of all their forts, castles, arms, ammunition, and warlike stores. What reason can be given by them for such cowardly and pusillanimous conduct? Perhaps it may be said that there yet remains some gleam of hope that the British Ministry may do us justice, restore to us our liberties, and repeal those oppressive acts which now hang over America. Were this even probable, it would hardly justify such a course. But what foundation have we for such hope? If this be the intention of the ministry, is a formidable fleet and numerous army necessary to bring it about? Could they not have given up their plan for enslaving America, without seizing all the strongholds on the continent, upon all the arms and ammunition, without soliciting, and finally obtaining, an order to prohibit the importation of warlike stores into the colonies? Does this speak the language of peace and reconciliation? or does it not rather speak that of war, tumult, and desolation? And shall we, like the Carthaginians, peaceably surrender our arms to our enemies, in hopes of obtaining in return the liberties we have so long contended for?

Be not deceived, my countrymen: should the Ministry ever prevail upon you to make that base and infamous surrender, they will then tell you, in the language of the haughty and inhuman Marcius, what those liberties are which they will in future suffer you to enjoy; and endeavor to persuade you, that, when you have recovered your senses, you will choose to obey. Is it possible that any person among us thinks of making a submission to the several powers which now claim a right to rule over us? If so, let him take a view of the situation he and his American brethren must then be in. We all acknowledge our submission to the authority of our Provincial legislature, in the same manner as the people in Great Britain acknowledge the power of Parliament over them; because the Assemblies here and Parliament there are composed in part of persons elected by the people, and who are liable, for any misconduct, to be excluded by them from ever acting again as their representatives; and, where the people have this constitutional check upon their rulers, slavery can never be introduced. "But," says the famous Mr. Locke, "whenever a power exists in a state over which the people have no control, the people are completely enslaved." If this be the case, what shall we say to the claim of Parliament to legislate for us in all cases whatsoever, — to the mandates of a minister of state, which so often have superseded the laws of the Colonial legislatures, although assented to by his Majesty? or to the late order of the King and Council prohibiting the importation of warlike stores into the Colonies; and who, by the same color of right, may, whenever they please, prohibit the importation of any, or even every, other article? These are undoubtedly such powers as we have no check upon or control over, — powers similar to those which have spread tyranny and oppression over three quarters of the globe; and, if we tamely submit to their authority, will soon accomplish that slavery which they have long been endeavoring to bring upon America.

I am far from wishing hostilities to commence on the part of America; but still hope that no person will, at this important crisis, be unprepared to act in his own defence, should he by necessity be driven thereto. And I must here beg leave to recommend to the consideration of the people on this continent, whether, when we are by an arbitrary decree prohibited the having arms and ammunition by importation, we have not, by the law of self-preservation, a right to seize upon those within our power, in order to defend the liberties which God and nature have given to us; especially at this time, when several of the Colonies are involved in a dangerous war with the Indians, and must, if this inhuman order have the designed effect, fall a prey to those savages and barbarians, who have so often deluged this land in blood.

The following month, at a convention of the Province at Exeter, he drafted its address to the Governor, Sir John Wentworth, which, while preserving the forms of loyalty, plainly intimates a determination to maintain their rights.

We, the delegates of the several towns of this Province, assembled in Congress at Exeter, on the twenty-fifth day of January, 1775, avowing our loyalty to his Majesty, and regard for the peace and tranquillity of this Province, beg leave to address your Excellency in behalf of the people, whose steady adherence to the law, and submission to legal authority, have been often acknowledged by your Excellency, and confessed by the Ministry in Great Britain.

Permit us to remind your Excellency, that, for nearly ten months past, the inhabitants of the Province, by a dissolution of their late Assembly, have been deprived of the constitutional right of having a share in their own government; and that, during the before-mentioned space of time, the whole power of government has been lodged with your Excellency and the Council, each appointed by the Crown, and holding your commissions during pleasure.

We are fully sensible that the power of dissolving the Assembly of the people is, by the constitution, vested in the Crown; yet we apprehend that this, like any other prerogative, may, by an undue exercise thereof, become grievous and oppressive.

For if the prerogative can be extended to dissolve one Assembly after another, merely because the members differ in sentiment from his Majesty or his representative, the people cannot participate in their own legislative council unless permitted by the Crown, and must expect a dissolution of their members whenever they are represented by persons who have virtue and firmness enough to act their own judgment.

Immediately after the attack on the fort, the Governor of the Province had issued a proclamation, declaring the offenders guilty of treason, and offering a reward for their apprehension. In open defiance of his authority, Major Sullivan, Lieutenant Adams, and other citizens of Durham holding civil or military commissions from the king, assembled at the Adams tavern, and, with Sullivan at their head, moved in procession to the Common, near the meeting-house, where they kindled a bonfire, and, in the presence of a large number of persons, burned their commissions, uniforms, and all other insignia which in any way connected them with the royal government.

Resuming his place, on the 10th of May, in the Congress, he was placed on many of its most important committees, and of that of war was chairman. When, soon after, Dickinson moved a second address to the king, John Adams says Sullivan opposed it in a strain of wit, eloquence, and fluency, unusual even for him, filling with dismay those who favored reconciliation.

In June, when Washington was elected commander-in-chief, Sullivan, appointed one of the eight brigadiers, went with him to Cambridge, where his brigade, posted at Winter Hill, with that of Greene, formed Lee's division, the left wing of the army investing Boston. He was twice detailed to the eastward to fortify against British cruisers; was active and zealous in procuring re-enforcements, rendering the war popular, and harassing the enemy; and won the affection and respect of Washington and his brother officers. Various attempts were made to draw on an engagement, some of which were planned by Sullivan, whose post at Winter Hill approached very nearly the advanced lines of the enemy at Charlestown. The following letter to the New-Hampshire Committee of Safety relates an incident entitled to mention in the annals of such a war, and which proves masked batteries no recent invention: —

WINTER HILL, July 29, 1775.

I was preparing, when the gentleman you sent me arrived, on Saturday, to take possession of the Ploughed Hill, near the enemy's encampment at Charleston. This was done Saturday night; and, on Sunday morning, a heavy cannonading ensued, which lasted through the whole day. The floating batteries and an armed vessel attempting to come up and enfilade us as expected, a battery, which had been prepared on purpose, was opened upon them, cutting away the sloop's foresail, and making her shear off; disabling one floating battery, and sinking another. Yesterday, they sent a man-of-war to Mystick River, drew their forces from Boston, formed a long column, and prepared to come out; but, finding our readiness to receive them, declined the combat. Last evening, they began to throw bombs, but have as yet done no damage. Their cannon have been more successful, having killed three or four.

A few days later, on the 5th of August, he alludes, in another letter to the Committee, to the dismay of the besiegers, occasioned by the discovery that their powder was nearly exhausted: —

General Washington has, I presume, already written you on the subject of this letter. We all rely upon your keeping both the contents of his letter and mine a profound secret. We had a general council the day before yesterday, and, to our great surprise, discovered that we had not powder enough to furnish half a pound a man, exclusive of what the people have in their horns and cartridge-boxes. This situation we are reduced to by the Massachusetts Committee making a return to General Washington of four hundred and eighty-five quarter-casks on his arrival, which he supposed were then on hand. To his surprise, he found that it was what was provided last winter, and that there is now on hand but thirty-eight barrels; which, with all the powder in the other magazines, will not furnish half a pound per man. The General was so struck, that he did not utter a word for half an hour. Every one else was also astounded.

Messengers are despatched to all the Southern Colonies to draw in their public stocks; and I must entreat you to forget all colony distinctions. Consider a Continental army devoted to destruction, unless immediately supplied; and send us at least twenty barrels of powder with all possible speed. Should this matter take air before a supply arrives, our army is ruined. You, gentlemen, will need no words from me to induce an immediate compliance with this request. You can have no necessity of powder in the country: there is not the most distant probability, or even possibility, of an attack upon you.

While busily engaged in camp, he wrote his friend Meshech Weare, then at the head of affairs in New Hampshire, the following response to a request for his opinion as to what frame of government should be adopted by the Province upon its re-organization. If his views are not particularly profound or philosophic, this letter evinces the practical good sense that distinguished the popular leaders. It exhibits the objects for which they were contending; is fraught with suggestions that can never grow old; and affords abundant proof, if any is needed, that Sullivan merited the esteem in which he was held.

WINTER HILL, Dec. 11, 1775.

DEAR SIR, — Though continually involved in those difficulties which necessarily attend a military life, I can by no means forget the duty I owe to that Province, whose generous favors I have so often experienced. Deeply impressed with gratitude to that truly patriotic Colony, and fully sensible that the remaining part of my life ought to be devoted to the interest of my country in general and that Province in particular, I have stolen a few moments from the busy scenes of war to offer you my thoughts upon a matter, which I deem essential to the future welfare of my truly spirited and deserving brethren within that government.

I hear that the Continental Congress has given our Province power to assume government; but the contents of their letter to the Provincial Congress having never transpired, and my friends at the Continental Congress having never informed me, but in general terms, that we had liberty to assume government, I must conclude that liberty is given to set up and establish a new form of government. For as we were, properly speaking, a king's government before, the giving us power to assume government would otherwise be giving us a license to assume a form not within our control. Taking it, therefore, for granted that the Congress has given us liberty to set up that form of government which will best answer its true end and design, I shall beg leave to offer you my thoughts upon the subject, leaving you to make such use thereof as your wisdom shall direct.

And, as my ideas of government may, in some measure, differ from those of others, I shall beg leave to premise, that all government is, or ought to be, instituted for the good of the people; and that form of government is most perfect where that design is most nearly and effectually answered. Secondly, that government which admits of contrary and conflicting interests, is imperfect, and must work its own ruin, whenever one branch has gained a power sufficient to overrule or destroy the other; and the adding a third, with a separate and distinct interest, in imitation of the British Constitution, so much celebrated by those who understand nothing of it, is only like two contending powers calling in a third, which is unconnected in interest, to keep the other two in awe till it can gain power sufficient to destroy them both. And I may almost venture to prophesy, that the period is now at hand when the British nation will too late discover the defects in their much-boasted Constitution, and the ruin of that empire evince to the world the folly and danger of establishing a government consisting of different branches, whose interest must ever clash with each other.

Thirdly, That no danger can arise to a state from giving the people a free and full voice in their own government; and that what are called the prerogatives of the Crown, or checks upon the licentiousness of the people, are only the children of ambition or designing men, not at all needed: for, though many states have been overturned by the rage and violence of the people, yet that spirit of rage and violence has ever been awakened in the first place by the misconduct of their rulers. Whenever this has been carried to dangerous heights, so far from being attributable to too much power being lodged in the hand of the people, it has clearly been owing to their having too small, and their rulers too extensive, a power. Thus we find Rome enjoyed its liberties till their Dictators and others were clothed with power unknown before, and made, in some sort, independent of the people; and to the authority so inconsiderately given should be charged all the tumults at Rome and the final ruin of that empire. This uncontrollable power, so much sought after by designing men, is made use of to enslave the people, and either brings about that event or raises the just indignation of the people to extirpate the tyrant thus seeking their ruin. And it sometimes happens that this resentment is so far carried, by the fury of an enraged populace, as totally to destroy the remains of government, and leave them in a state of anarchy and confusion; and too often have designing persons taken advantage of this confusion, and established tyranny in its place. I am well convinced that people are too fond of their own ease and quiet to rise up in rebellion against government, unless where the tyranny of their rulers becomes intolerable; and their fondness for government must clearly appear from their so often submitting to one tyrant after having extirpated another, rather than live in a state of anarchy.

I would therefore advise to such a form of government as would admit of but one object to be kept in view of the governor and the governed, namely, the good of the whole; that one interest should unite the several governing branches, and that the frequent choice of the rulers by the people should operate as a check upon their conduct, and remind them that a new election would soon honor them for their good conduct, or disgrace them for betraying the trust reposed in them. I by no means object to a Governor, but would have him freely appointed by the people, and dependent upon them; and his appointment not to continue for a long time, unless re-elected, — at most, not exceeding three years; and this appointment to be made by the freeholders in person, and not by their representatives, as that would be putting too dangerous a power in their hands, and possibly a majority of designing men might elect a person to answer their own particular purposes, to the great emolument of themselves and the oppression of their fellow-subjects; whereas we can never suppose the people to have any thing but the true end of government, their own good, in view, unless we suppose them idiots or self-murderers.

I am likewise much in favor of a Council and House of Representatives, but would have them likewise chosen by the people, and by no means for a longer time than three years. This mode of election would effectually guard against that pernicious tendency of governors, — to throw aside persons whom they find will not join them in enslaving the people. The late conduct of Bernard and Hutchinson, and the present unhappy state of the Province I am now in, are striking witnesses of the justice of this observation; nor can I see the least reason for a Governor having the power to negative a Speaker of the House.

I would have some rule established for rendering persons incapable of holding either of the above offices, that should, either before or after election, bribe or treat the voters, with intent either to procure an election or reward the electors.

Having chosen him, accusation against the Governor should be tried by the two Houses: if against either of the other members, by the Governor and the other members of both Houses, he having only a vote equal to any other member; and, in case judgment should pass against the newly elected Governor, the old one to remain till another election be had, and, in case he be the same person previously elected, the President of the Council to supply his place till an election can again be made. The President should be appointed by free vote of the members of Council, at their first meeting.

The infamous practice of bribing people in Great Britain to sell their votes, and consequently their liberties, must show the danger of permitting it to be introduced under our constitution. To prevent it, and to guard against the undue influence of persons in power over voters, I would recommend the said Pennsylvanian method; viz., that every vote should be rolled up, and sealed; on the back thereof should be noted that it is a vote for a Governor, which should be deposited in a box prepared for the purpose; and a vote for Councillors and Representatives, likewise sealed up, and noted on the back, should be brought in like manner and deposited in separate boxes provided for that purpose; that all voters, having once given in their votes, should pass out, and care be taken that they should not come in again till the voting is over. Or, if thought more expedient, let the clerk of the meeting have a perfect list of all the voters, with columns ruled against their names, — one marked for a Governor, one for a Representative; and, when a person brings in his vote for one of them, let a mark be made against his name in that column; and, if he brings in for all three at the same time, a mark be made in each column: which, I think, will effectually prevent any fraud in voting. The Representative's box should be examined in the meeting, and the election declared; the votes given for a Governor and Council to be sealed up by the clerk, and forwarded by him to the capital of the Province, where, all the votes being had together, a sworn committee should examine the whole, and declare the elections. This method, though it may appear somewhat troublesome, will not prove to be so on trial. It is the most effectual method to secure the freedom of voting, and prevent every species of fraud.

Any persons who offer themselves as candidates for office, may, agreeably to the method practised in Pennsylvania, publish their design in the newspapers, or communicate it in any other method they may think proper, or leave the people to find out persons of merit, and nominate for themselves. All civil officers should be appointed by the three branches; and all military officers by the Governor and Council, and never superseded in commission, but by the same power which created them. All laws negatived by a Governor, if revived afterwards, and passed, by a new House and Council, to be assented to by him at all events; as it would be unreasonable to suppose two Houses of Representatives, and two sets of Councillors, possessed of less wisdom, or to have less understanding of the true interests of the people, than a single person, after time for reflection and to consult their constituents.

And here I must beg leave to observe, that, however high other people's notions of government may run, and however much they may be disposed to worship a creation of their own, I can by no means consent to lodging too much power in the hands of one person; or suffering an interest in government to exist separate from that of the people; or any man to hold an office, for the execution of which he is not, in some way or other, answerable to that people to whom he owes his political existence. Time will not permit me to go more largely into the subject, but I must leave you to weigh these hints, and make such improvements thereon as your wisdom shall direct; and, though my notions of government are something singular, yet I think this plan will be an improvement on the constitution, — by far the best that I know. Where I have supposed a defect in that constitution, I have taken the freedom to borrow from that of Pennsylvania and of other governments, to supply it, and, in some instances, have added my own thoughts, which, if they have the force of reason in them, will have their weight.

His correspondence has much of it perished: what remains is widely dispersed; but a letter to John Adams is selected from what are accessible, which shows how actively he was engaged: —

CAMP ON WINTER HILL, Dec. 21, 1775.

DEAR SIR, — Did not the hurry of our affairs prevent, I should often write you respecting the state of our army; but it has been my fortune to be employed almost night and day. When I had Winter Hill nearly completed, I was ordered to Ploughed Hill, where for a long time I was almost day and night in fortifying. Twice have I been ordered to the Eastward, to fortify and defend Piscataway Harbour; but unfortunately was obliged to return without an opportunity of proving the works I had taken so much pains to construct. This being over, I was called upon to raise 2,000 Troops from New Hampshire, and bring them on the lines in ten days; this I undertook, and was happy enough to perform; otherwise the desertion of the Connecticut Troops might have proved fatal to us. I might add that 3,000 from your Colony arrived at the same time to supply the defect. This, with the other necessary business in my Department, has so far engaged my time and attention that I hope you will not require an apology for my not writing. I have now many things to write, but must content myself with mentioning a few of them at present, and leave the residue to another opportunity. I will in the first place inform you that we have possession of almost every advantageous post round Boston, from whence we might, with great ease, burn or destroy the town, was it not that we fail in a very trifling matter, namely, we have no powder to do it with. However, as we have a sufficiency for our small arms, we are not without hope to become masters of the town. Old Boreas and Jack Frost are now at work building a bridge over all the rivers and bays, which once completed, we take possession of the town, or perish in the attempt. I have the greatest reason to believe I shall be saved, for my faith is very strong. I have liberty to take possession of your house. Mrs. Adams was kind enough to honor me with a visit the other day in company with a number of other ladies and the Rev. Mr. Smith. She gave me power to enter and take possession. There is nothing now wanting but your consent, which I shall wait for till the Bridge is completed; and, unless given before that time, shall make a forcible entry, and leave you to bring your action. I hope in less than three weeks to write you from Boston.

The prisoners taken in our privateer are sent to England for trial, and so is Col. Allen. This is poor encouragement for our people to engage in the service when the prisoners of the enemy are treated with so much humanity and respect, and the law of retaliation not put in force against them. I know you have published a declaration of that sort; but I never knew a man to feel the weight of chains and imprisonment by mere declarations on paper; and, believe me, till their barbarous use of our prisoners is retaliated, we shall be miserable. Let me ask if we have anything to hope from the mercy of His Majesty or his Ministers? Have we any encouragement from the people in Great Britain? Could they exert themselves more if we had shaken off the yoke and declared ourselves independent? Why, then, in God's name, is it not done? Whence arises this spirit of moderation? — this want of decision? Do the members of your respectable body think that the enemy will throw their shot and shells with more force than at present? Do they think the fate of Charlestown or Falmouth might have been worse, or the King's Proclamation more severe, if we had openly declared war? Could they have treated our prisoners worse if we were in open and avowed rebellion, than they now do?

Why, then, do we call ourselves freemen, and act the part of timid slaves? I don't apply this to you — I know you too well to suspect your firmness and resolution. But let me beg of you to use those talents I know you possess to destroy that spirit of moderation which has almost ruined, and, if not speedily rooted out, will prove the final overthrow of America. That spirit gave them possession of Boston, lost us all our arms and ammunition, and now causes our brothers which have fallen into their hands to be treated like rebels. But enough of this. I feel too sensibly to write more upon this subject. I beg you to make my most respectful compliments to Mr. Hancock and your brother delegates, also to Col. Lee and those worthy brethren who laboured with us in the vineyard, when I had the honor to be with you in the Senate. You may venture to assure them that when an opportunity presents, if I should not have courage enough to fight myself, I shall do all in my power to encourage others.

It is not proposed to present any detailed account of his services at the siege. In the archives of New Hampshire, at Concord, are to be found numerous other communications from him to the Assembly and Committee of Safety. They prove him to have been busily employed in the performance of the duties assigned him. When, at a later period, unjustly censured, as again now, that four thousand men did not defeat thrice their number at Brandywine, he alludes, as will be seen in the sequel, to some of the services he rendered.

After the evacuation of Boston, 17th March, 1776, he took command of the army in Canada, conducting the retreat beginning with the fall of Montgomery at Quebec, and, in this arduous service, displayed skill, prudence, and energy, to the satisfaction of Washington and of Congress. When his command had been extricated from the perils, to which disease and the great superiority of the enemy's forces in Canada had exposed them, Gates was appointed to the northern army. On the 12th of July, 1776, Sullivan took leave of his officers, and they presented him an address on the occasion, which evinces their sensibility to the dangers they had escaped, and the esteem in which he was held by them.

WE the field officers of the several regiments composing the army of the United Colonies in the northern department having been informed of your Honors intended departure from hence esteem it would be unpardonable in us to forego this opportunity of rendering the homage due to him, who upon the late trying occasion has comforted supported and protected the shattered remains of a debilitated army and with unwearied care watchfullness and attention has landed the public stores of every kind without the least diminution safe at this place. It is to you Sir the public are indebted for the preservation of their property in Canada It is to you we owe our safety thus far. Your humanity will call forth the silent tear and grateful ejaculation of the sick; your universal impartiality will force the applause of the wearied soldier. Permit us then worthy Sir to take our leave wishing you every happiness and success your most sanguine inclinations can suggest, or our most fervent prayers procure.

[Signed by] John Moore, Joseph Celty, Enoch Poor, Matthew Ogden, Nathan Fuller, William Bond, William de Haas, Israel Shrieve, Elisha Porter, Moses Hazen, John McDuffee, T. Alden, Seth Reed, Anthony Wayne, John Stark. James Reed, John Greaton, William Maxwell, Abner Morgan, Edward Antill, Thomas Poor, Charles Burrell, Joseph Vose, John Patterson, Arthur St. Clair, David Rhea, Jonathan Loring.

The names signed to this address are appended, as among them will be recognized many distinguished in the subsequent campaigns, nearly all of them familiar to readers of its annals. With most of these officers, he ever afterwards maintained the most intimate and friendly relations; and their frequent expressions of affection and respect, at subsequent periods of the war, indicate how high he stood in their estimation.

In the early part of August, he was promoted to the rank of Major-General, and joined the main army under Washington, at New York. A British force, over thirty thousand strong, had recently arrived from Halifax; and, on the 22d, General Howe landed fifteen thousand troops on Long Island, increased by the 27th, the day of the battle, to twenty-four thousand, besides which he had, to his great advantage, as they were familiar with the country, a body of Loyalists, under De Lancy. His object was the city of New York, then occupied by the American army. Our success in compelling the evacuation of Boston, and the recent intelligence of Lee's good fortune in repulsing the British at Charleston, tended to encouragement, though neither in numbers, organization, nor equipments were we at all equal to the enemy.*

As possession of the westerly portion of Long Island was

---

* See Appendix.

indispensable to any effective operations against the city, it was probable that that would be the first point of attack. Washington occupied it with about nine thousand men,— as many as he could prudently spare from his main force,— and had caused lines of intrenchment to be constructed for their protection.

Where Long Island approaches nearest to the city, there is a neck of land, about two miles and a half long, and containing about fifteen hundred acres, which is capable of being defended, on its eastern front, by works a mile and a quarter in length. Two miles in front of these lines is a range of hills, at points two hundred feet in elevation, somewhat irregular in their general course from north to south, and intersected by defiles, through which, here and there, were roads running from the shore to the neighboring villages. As these heights commanded the interior lines about Wallabout Bay, it was necessary, for any effective defence, that they should be occupied. Greene had been in command, and, with Sullivan and Stirling, engaged in fortifying them, when he was taken ill of a fever, and compelled, on the 24th, to leave the island. Sullivan succeeded; but, as there were indications of an impending conflict with the enemy, to Putnam, whose age as well as seniority of commission was considered to constitute a claim to the position next in responsibility to that of the commander-in-chief, was confided the direction of our forces on the island.

While, if an effort were to be made to retain possession of New York, it was important to oppose the approach of the enemy at Brooklyn, his landing on the island might be used as a feint merely to lure our forces thither, and, by the aid of his fleet, the city be taken. This compelled the separation of our army by the straits between the islands, and explains why a force so inadequate was exposed.

While the British were concentrating their forces, the heights were occupied by several of our regiments; and skirmishes occasionally occurred. But as the line of hills to be guarded, extending from Yellow Hook, on the Jamaica road, to what is now Greenwood Cemetery, was nearly six miles in length, the force employed for the purpose was wholly insufficient. What force we had, from some oversight of Putnam, who disregarded the injunctions of Washington and the advice of Sullivan, was not wisely distributed. Stirling, as Sullivan says, was to have commanded outside the lines; while to him was assigned the command, under Putnam himself, of the five thousand within. As Putnam had reason to believe the enemy would advance by the shore and the Gowanus road, at half-past three, on the morning of the 27th, he awoke Stirling in his tent, and sent him to oppose them. Sullivan went out to the heights, in front of Flatbush, where Hurd's, Parsons's, Hand's, and Miles's regiments were stationed, — General Woodhull, with a force of Long-Island militia, keeping guard on the extreme left.

When he reached the front, he called for volunteers to ascertain the position of the enemy, but, out of twelve selected for the purpose, not one returned. In the plain at Flatbush, Van Heister kept his attention occupied by his artillery and occasional attacks in line. Meanwhile, Howe, Clinton, Cornwallis, and Percy — who, with the principal portion of the British army, had, the evening before, fallen back to Flatlands, and thence made a circuit of several miles during the night, sawing down the trees that obstructed their march, lest the sound of the axe should betray their design — had interposed themselves between the heights and our interior lines, two or three miles in our rear. By cutting off all our patrols and detachments, they accomplished their object without our knowledge; and when, at half-past eight, we discovered them, it was too late to escape.

Of our force on the island, in all about nine thousand, probably four thousand, including the fifteen hundred under

Stirling, were on the Heights. Sullivan, when he found his earlier anticipation fulfilled, and that his position was surrounded, made a reconnoissance with four hundred men; and, as he was returning, found himself between Van Heister, who was pressing up from Flatbush, and Clinton at Bedford. His small force fought well, in the woods, from half-past nine till twelve, by which time they were killed or scattered, and he himself was taken prisoner.

Mr. Bisbee, who was with Sullivan in the battle, states that when his men, finding further resistance useless, dispersed, Sullivan, intending to sell his life as dearly as possible, rode toward the enemy, with the expectation of sharing the fate of so many of his soldiers who had received no quarter. As he approached, several Hessians, instructed in capturing prisoners, contrived to arrest his course, render useless his weapons, and lift him from the saddle.

Bancroft states (p. 91) that Sullivan's party fired with nervous rapidity. Is it not possible the authority on which this statement is made was that of the British officer, who, in relating what occurred on the afternoon of the day before, says that the force with which he was connected opposite Flatbush, experiencing loss from the American batteries on the heights, quietly withdrew into the woods behind the inequalities of the ground, the shot striking the trees over their heads?

The Americans underrated the force opposed to them, — some six times their number, — or they would have withdrawn earlier within the lines. Howe over-estimated the American force, or he would have proceeded at once to take their lines by assault. The vigorous resistance by Stirling on the right, and the desperation with which the left, as they retired, disputed the ground with the Hessians, who gave no quarter, led the British general, who remembered the loss sustained in attacking our lines at Bunker Hill, to make regular approaches. After two rainy days, Washington withdrew his army on the 29th, leaving on the mind of the enemy the impression, that, though we might be defeated, we could not be easily conquered.

Our loss was heavy, but not so great as might have been expected under the circumstances, from the vast superiority of the enemy and the mode in which we were surrounded. Congress and public opinion alike demanded that Howe should be resisted, it being deemed more judicious to sustain a partial defeat than abandon New York without an effort. The Island shore was high, and commanded the city. But the force that could be spared to keep possession was wholly inadequate to guard any such extent of country, or prevent the British, many times their number, from effecting their objects. The inhabitants were loyalists, many of them in the British camp; pickets and patrols were easily cut off; and twenty-four thousand veterans, under accomplished officers, — such as Howe, Cornwallis, Clinton, Erskine, Grant, Percy, and Van Heister, — could find no great difficulty in environing and defeating four thousand, if these ventured to oppose them. That their resistance was creditable, — Sullivan's was declared by the enemy to have been "gallant and persistent," Stirling's by all admitted to have been brave to the point of heroism, — is proved by the hesitation of Howe to follow up his advantage.

There were reasons enough for the result, without ascribing it to neglect to guard the Bedford road, — which both Washington and Sullivan had repeatedly urged upon the attention of Putnam, and which had in reality been provided for, as well as the means at our disposal admitted, and in part by the force of Woodhull, — or casting reproach upon honorable men, who were risking life on the field and scaffold to maintain the rights and liberties of their countrymen. Sullivan certainly was vigilant, paying for some nights fifty dollars from his own resources, to procure intelligence of the enemy's movements.

When candid minds remember, that it was no disgrace to yield to superior numbers, arms, and artillery, it will seem hardly worthy of an American historian to go out of his way to assign imaginary reasons, why this and so many of our Revolutionary battles, where the odds were fourfold against us, resulted as they did. The Americans effected all, and more than all, that could have been expected under the circumstances; but, in the excited state of the public mind, it was human to attach blame to some one, in order to explain defeat. It was much to the honor of General Washington that he never condescended to such injustice, or sought to build up his own reputation by creating prejudice against his subordinates. It would be creditable to modern historians, eager to attract attention to their books, if they were equally conscientious, and exhibited more of the fairness and candor that distinguished Judge Marshall, in his earlier and more reliable relation of the events of the Revolution.

Sullivan and Lord Stirling were taken, as prisoners, on board the "Eagle," the flagship of Lord Howe, the British admiral, who courteously received them. He agreed at once to their exchange, Sullivan for General Prescott, who was then at Philadelphia, where Congress was in session. The conversation of the Admiral with his prisoners was frank and friendly, expressing his wish, that such mutual concessions might be made as would adjust the dispute. The previous efforts of himself and his brother, the General, to open negotiations, had been defeated at the threshold, as his instructions forbade his recognition of the Congress; and it was now proposed, that their desire for a conference should be informally communicated by Sullivan, who was to be released on parole to effect his exchange.

Before consenting to communicate to Congress the proposition of Lord Howe, Sullivan consulted Washington, who gave his approbation. This appears from the following note of Lord Howe, addressed to Sullivan from on board the "Eagle," 30th August, 1776, in which he says: —

Understanding, by your letter, that the only doubt of the propriety of your going to Philadelphia is, by your conversation with General Washington, removed, I do not see occasion to give you further trouble, but to recommend the prosecuting of your journey as you were pleased on that condition to propose.

Sullivan proceeded to Philadelphia; and, on Monday the 2d of September, Congress, being informed that he had come with a design of communicating a message from Lord Howe, ordered that he should be admitted, and, after a verbal communication, he was desired to reduce it to writing. Its purport, as submitted the following morning, was, that Lord Howe could not at present treat with Congress as such, yet was very desirous of having a conference with some of its members, whom he would consider, for the present, only as private gentlemen, and meet them himself in that character, at any place they should appoint; that he, in conjunction with General Howe, had full powers to compromise the dispute between Great Britain and America, upon terms advantageous to both, the obtaining of which had delayed him two months in England, and prevented his arrival before the declaration of independence. That he wished a compact might be settled at this time, when no decisive blow had been struck, and neither party could say that they were compelled to enter into such agreement. That, in case Congress were disposed to treat, many things, which they had not yet asked, might and ought to be granted them; and if, upon the conference, they found any probable ground of accommodation, the authority of Congress must be afterwards acknowledged, otherwise the compact would not be complete.

On Thursday, Congress — resuming the consideration of the report of the Board of War, of which Mr. John Adams was chairman, and to which the communication would seem to have been referred — resolved, that General Sullivan be requested to inform Lord Howe, that the Congress, being the representatives of the free and independent States of America, cannot with propriety send any of its members to confer with his lordship in their private characters; but that, ever desirous of establishing peace on reasonable terms, they would send a committee of their body to know whether he had any power to treat with persons authorized by Congress for that purpose, in behalf of America, and what that authority was, and to hear such propositions as he should think fit to make respecting the same.

It was further resolved, that the President be desired to write to General Washington, that it is the opinion of Congress no proposals for making peace between Great Britain and the United States of America ought to be received or attended to, unless the same be made in writing, and addressed to the representatives of the said States in Congress, or persons authorized by them; and, if application be made to him by any of the commanders of the British forces on that subject, that he inform them, that these United States, which had entered into the war only for the defence of their lives and liberties, would cheerfully agree to peace on reasonable terms, whenever such should be proposed to them in manner aforesaid.

His exchange for General Prescott, and that of Lord Stirling for Brigadier-General McDonald, having been assented to on the previous day, Sullivan was requested to convey to Lord Howe the first resolution. On Friday, Dr. Franklin, John Adams, and Mr. Rutledge were elected a committee to "be sent to know whether Lord Howe had any authority to treat with persons authorized by Congress for that purpose in behalf of America, and what that authority is, and to hear such propositions as he shall think fit to make respecting the same." The conference was held on the following Wednesday, Sept. 11, on Staten Island, opposite Amboy; and the report of the committee, submitted on the 17th, states at length what took place. The only explicit proposition was, that the Colonies should return to their allegiance: the rest consisted of assurances that the offensive Acts of Parliament should be revised, and instructions to governors reconsidered. They had replied, that it was then too late; that they had been patient under the tyrannical government, till the late Act of Parliament had declared war against them, and they had declared their independence: the Colonies now considered themselves independent states, and it was not in the power of Congress to agree for them that they should return to their former dependent state; and that General Howe might more readily obtain fresh powers from home to treat with them as independent states, than they could any authority from the several Colonies to consent to submission.

The conference resulted as might have been expected; but it by no means follows that the proposition by Howe for holding it should not have been entertained. Many gentlemen, — in wisdom and services as efficient in the field, as either of the committee in the Congress, in securing independence, — and among them Washington and Greene, approved both of the course of Sullivan in making the communication, and of that taken by Congress in disposing of it. Had Lee been captured at Antietam or Gettysburg; and the Federal Administration suggested in confidence to him, upon his exchange, a proposition to the Confederate Congress for such a conference as took place in the winter of 1865, — it would not only have been far from derogatory for Lee to have communicated it, but culpable in him to have declined.

Mr. Bancroft — in his severe denunciation of what was a very simple and natural thing to do, for any one who was a prisoner in a civil war — loses sight, not only of what is just, but of what is dignified. It does not matter much now to General Sullivan, nor will it affect his historical position among those who are familiar with the events and characters of the Revolution, what Mr. Bancroft may think of his discretion. The majority of sensible readers will be puzzled to recognize any logical connection between the terms and the facts, and will conclude, upon the whole, that after a serious defeat, with a victorious army against us of double the strength of any we had to oppose to it, the chance of establishing independence was not so great as it had been; and that, if we could make peace upon the terms we had always before the war insisted upon, — namely, allegiance to the Crown, chartered rights inviolate, independence of Parliament, — it was worthy of consideration. At all events, time was gained to recover our vigor, discouraging by negotiation the activity of the enemy, and obtaining recognition as belligerents, which, in the event of disaster, might have saved even Washington himself from the scaffold.

That Lord Howe did not divulge any such powers at the subsequent conference with Adams, Franklin, and Rutledge, the Committee of Congress appointed in pursuance of his overture for negotiation, is neither reason nor argument that he did not possess them. As the committee insisted throughout upon independence as the only admissible basis of negotiation, there was no occasion to do so. If the control of Parliament over any adjustment was likely to be paramount, it must be remembered, that Magna Charta and the settlement of 1688 had always been constitutionally regarded as concessions from the prerogative, that the treaty-making power vested in the Crown, and that, if terms had been concluded under the powers lodged with the Howes by the king and his cabinet, upon the principle that legislation and representation, in all cases whatsoever, should go together, or upon such a system of government as that, at this time, proposed to be carried out in the Canadas, Parliament would probably have assented or acquiesced. It was, therefore, no indiscretion in Sullivan to repose the most implicit confidence in the assurances given him, that adequate powers were possessed by the Howes to effect an accommodation; or inconsistency in them to intimate as much on board the "Eagle," in confidential intercourse, and yet not make their full powers to treat known when the formal conference took place.

As it was simply intended, that Sullivan should communicate, in an informal manner, an *overture* for negotiation through such conference, only to be held if sanctioned by Congress, it was wholly unnecessary that he should have received any written instructions; indeed, instructions were wholly out of the case. He, as one of the acting parties, was receiving himself a proposition, affecting his associates as well as himself, and compromising no one, upon which he merely consented to consult. To deny the propriety of such a course in civil war, would be to close the door to all negotiation; and, if our affairs had been as desperate as they looked at that particular crisis, with thirty thousand men in the field against half that number, in the event of further disaster, it would have subjected all concerned in the rebellion to the mercy of the conquerors upon unconditional surrender.

In the freedom of confidential intercourse with his old associates of the Congress, not probably more than forty in number, General Sullivan stated with entire frankness all that had occurred on board the vessel, as no doubt it was the wish of Lord Howe, and his manifest duty as an officer appointed under their authority, that he should. When requested to commit to writing what he understood Lord Howe to propose, he was cautious and guarded, and no exceptions were or could be taken to his words. Subsequently, at the conference, Rutledge, in repeating from recollection, gave a force and color to what Sullivan had said several days before in his oral communication, which Howe claimed was beyond the natural import of his language. Of course, he meant if Sullivan had been correctly reported; but any fair and generous mind, knowing how easily expressions may be misinterpreted or erroneously recalled, would never think of impeaching character or impugning veracity on grounds so unsubstantial.

It should be borne in mind, that recourse was had to this indirect mode of opening communications, always of advantage to belligerents, and especially in civil war, in consequence of the prohibition of the British Government to the Howes to recognize the Congress. General Washington knew what was intended, and did not consider it proper that the military authority should prevent an appeal to the civil power. It would not only have been churlish towards Howe, to decline communicating what was a mere overture for a conference; but it would have been an imprudent oversight to have neglected so valuable an opportunity of ascertaining the extent of the boasted powers of the Commissioners, as well as a reflection upon the ability and wisdom of Congress to decide what their public duty demanded. They concluded to accept the proposition, and improved it to disabuse their constituents of any expectation of satisfactory concessions, thus gaining time needed for re-organization after defeat, and inspiring a more determined spirit to persevere in the contest.

All condemn, now, the want of wisdom of the Confederate leaders in declining, at Fortress Monroe, the terms proposed by Mr. Lincoln. In numerous wars, and especially those of a civil character, peace has been brought about by informal propositions. Humanity demands that no reasonable means should be neglected to stay the useless effusion of blood. Sullivan had been a respected member of the Congress. Settlement of the difficulty was as much an affair of New Hampshire as of Massachusetts. John Adams, fearing re-action, might have said, that he wished a bullet had passed through the brain of the emissary, as Mr. Bancroft courteously calls him. But this was simply his mode of expressing his extreme unwillingness to enter into any negotiation with the British Government, rather than an indication of an impaired confidence in the integrity or patriotism of that emissary. His relations with Sullivan, then and throughout the war, seem to have been respectful and friendly; and, a few days later, he himself was not unwilling to go with Franklin and Rutledge to confer with Howe on the same business, though as much convinced when he went, as before or afterwards, that no propositions would be made which were based on the independence of the States. Besides, a few years later, he writes that he would gladly exchange all prospects of success in the war for the condition existing before the commencement of hostilities. We think, therefore, that the whole passage in Mr. Bancroft's volume, to which we have referred, betrays an unreasonable prejudice on the part of the writer against General Sullivan.

In October and November, Sullivan was with Washington, in Westchester County; and, after the army crossed the Hudson, he was placed under the orders of Lee. When the latter was taken prisoner, on the 13th of December, Sullivan forthwith obeyed the orders of Washington to join him at Newtown, opposite Trenton; and, having crossed the Delaware at Easton, he effected, on the 20th, a junction with the main army. The same day, Gates arrived with five hundred men, — all that remained of four New-England regiments. Immediate measures were taken for the surprisal of Rahl at Trenton; and on the 25th, at three o'clock, with twenty-four hundred men, — one-half of his whole army, — Washington marched to MacKonkey's ferry, and, by three o'clock in the morning of the 26th, had crossed the river. It was bitterly cold; and a storm of snow and hail set in as they started for a nine-miles' march to Trenton. Sullivan commanded the right wing, on the river-road; Greene, the left: and both reached Trenton nearly at the same moment, — at eight o'clock. The surprise was complete. Rahl was defeated and mortally wounded; and Washington recrossed the Delaware, with nine hundred prisoners.

When, on the 30th, Washington again crossed the Delaware into Jersey, taking post at Trenton, and found Cornwallis in his front, too strong to attack with any reasonable chance of success, he moved, in the night of the 2d of January, towards

Princeton. On his way, several British regiments were encountered, General Mercer, one of our most promising officers, was fatally wounded, Colonel Mawhood was repulsed by Washington in person, and the Fortieth and Fifty-fifth were pursued by Sullivan to the College, whence, after slight resistance, they fled to Brunswick, nearly two hundred (194) of them being taken prisoners.

During the next six months, Sullivan was busily engaged in front of the main army, which lay during the winter at Morristown; and at that season, incessantly vigilant, he kept the British at Brunswick and Amboy, many times his number, from marauds.

In a spirit of rivalry in the army,—falling far short of any bitterness of feeling, though not always so in Congress,— the palm of valor was disputed between the South and the North. In a letter of this period, Feb. 13, 1777, to Meshech Weare, President of the Assembly of New Hampshire, he writes, "You may want to know how your men fight. I tell you, exceedingly well, when they have proper officers. I have been much pleased to see a day approaching to try the difference between Yankee cowardice and Southern valor. The day, or rather the days, have arrived. . . . General Washington made no scruple to say, publicly, that the remnant of the Eastern regiments were the strength of his army, though their numbers, comparatively speaking, were but small. He calls them in front when the enemy are there; he sends them to the rear when the enemy threatens that way. All the general officers allow them to be the best of troops. The Southern officers and soldiers allow it in time of danger, but not at all other times. Believe me, Sir, the Yankees took Trenton before the other troops knew any thing of the matter. More than that, there was an engagement; and, what will surprise you still more, the line that attacked the town consisted of but eight hundred Yankees, and there were sixteen hundred Hessians to oppose them. At Princeton, when the Seventeenth regiment had thrown thirty-five hundred Southern militia into the utmost confusion, a regiment of Yankees restored the day. This General Mifflin confessed to me, though the Philadelphia papers tell us a different story. It seemed to have been quite forgotten, that, while the Seventeenth was engaging these troops, six hundred Yankees had the town to take against the Fortieth and Fifty-fifth regiments, which they did without loss, owing to the manner of attack. But enough of this. I do not wish to reflect, but beg leave to assure you, that newspapers, and even letters, do not always speak the truth."

As the summer advanced, the British general, after various efforts to cross through New Jersey, which were as often disconcerted, embarked twenty thousand men for a destination for several weeks conjectured, but not known. Sullivan lay at Hanover, about twenty miles from Staten Island, whence frequent forays had been made by the enemy on the main. Earlier in the spring, an expedition, sent from New York against Danbury, in Connecticut, had been very destructive; the banks of the Hudson frequently harried; and New Jersey visited by marauding parties, and peaceable citizens plundered or carried off. Ascertaining, that, while sixteen hundred European regulars were at the northerly end of the Island, about eight miles off, near New Brighton, one thousand loyal militiamen were scattered at different posts along the shore, he arranged with his officers an expedition to capture the latter.

Ogden says the plan was well concerted, and perfectly consistent. The enemy were put to rout, and many prisoners were taken, with little loss. From a mistake of Smallwood's guide, who led him, in the obscurity of the night, in front, instead of to the rear, of one of the regiments, the regulars became aware of their presence on the island; and, following them to the boats, attacked the rear guard left to pick up stragglers from the ranks. The guard "sold themselves dear," it is said, and, after vigorous resistance and some loss, about two hundred were compelled to surrender. Sullivan brought away with him from the island twenty-eight civilians, in retaliation for similar treatment, as above mentioned, towards the friends of independence.

Judge Marshall says, " The enterprise was well planned, and, in its commencement, happily executed;" "but the boats were insufficient." The boats that carried the force to the island were certainly capable of bringing them back, and would have done so in safety, had it not been for a laxity of discipline on the part of his subordinates, which Sullivan, by the strictest orders, had done what he could to prevent. Moreover, Ogden had taken possession of a small vessel, upon which were placed his prisoners; and their red uniforms led the boatmen to suppose her an armed vessel of the enemy, and to keep off. Similar enterprises, some attended with the happiest results and consequently familiar, others baffled and forgotten, were constantly occurring; and, if ever likely to prove successful, it was at that very conjuncture, when the British army was at sea.

When the expedition was subsequently subjected to investigation, the Court of Inquiry, composed of Generals Stirling, MacDougall, and Knox, Colonels Spenser and Clark, held Oct. 12, were unanimously of opinion, —

"That the expedition against the enemy on Staten Island was eligible, and promised great advantage to the cause of America;

" That it was well concerted, and the orders for the execution proper; and would have succeeded, with reputation to the general and his troops, had it not in some measure been rendered abortive by accidents, which were out of the power of the general to foresee or prevent;

" That General Sullivan was particularly active in embarking the troops to the island, and took every precaution in his power to bring them off; That he made early provision at

Elisabethstown for refreshing the troops of his division, when they returned to Jersey;

"And, upon the maturest consideration of the evidence in the possession of this Court, General Sullivan's conduct, in planning and executing the expedition, was such, that, in the opinion of this Court, he deserves the approbation of the country, and not its censure.

"The Court, therefore, are unanimously of opinion, that he ought to stand honorably acquitted of any unsoldierlike conduct in the expedition to Staten Island."

This decision was signed by all the members of the Court; and Congress resolved that the result, so honorable to General Sullivan, was highly pleasing to themselves, and that the opinion of the Court should be published in justification of that injured officer.

Had the result been, as might have been reasonably anticipated, the capture of the thousand loyal militiamen, it would have been considered a very sensible enterprise. Our general officers were encouraged to activity, and to embrace all similar occasions of inflicting loss on the enemy, by the leading men of the time; and the letter of John Adams to Sullivan, given in his Biography (Works, i. 259), probably made him emulous to do all in his power.

The mischances of the night were not to be guarded against, and ought not to work to the prejudice of Sullivan. He had taken part in an expedition of a similar character, eight months before, at Trenton, which had redounded to the honor of all who were engaged, proving of infinite advantage to the cause for which we were contending. It also bore many points of resemblance to his first exploit, the attack on Fort William and Mary, at Portsmouth, in December, 1774, — by many considered as the earliest hostile proceeding against the Crown. Bunker Hill, Dorchester Heights, Trenton, Princeton, Germantown, were similar night movements, suggested by opportunity, and depending on secrecy for success; and, had this been attended with the good fortune reasonably to have been anticipated, it would have redounded as much as Trenton to the credit of our arms.

The following letter to Hancock explains, in a measure, the malign spirit with which he had to contend in the discharge of his duty: —

CAMP ON METUCHIN HILLS, Oct. 17th, 1777.

DEAR SIR, — I do myself the honor to enclose Congress a copy of the result of a Court of Inquiry, respecting my conduct on Staten Island, after perusing which and examining the evidence sent by me in a former letter, Congress must be at some loss, to know how it was possible for Lt. Col. Smith, and Major Taylor, to write so warmly against me, to their friends in Congress when there was no colour for it. I shall now give Congress the key to it, and it will no longer remain a mystery. On the 13th August, last, when my Division lay at Hanover, these two gentlemen attacked Major Sherburn who acted as Deputy Adjutant-General, on the Public Parade, before all the soldiers, about the severity of the duty, averring that there was no necessity of picquets, or out-guards, as we were in a friend's country and the enemy at such a distance. This was said with heat on the one side, and replied to with as much warmth on the other; I was much surprised at hearing so dangerous a doctrine had been advanced by field officers before the soldiers of my Division. I knew it was an established rule among military men to use the same precautions in a friend's country, as in an enemy's; for a relaxation or neglect of duty has proved the destruction of many armies. The fate of Hannibal after his troops had tasted the delights of Capua, was a striking instance of the evil tendency which follows such neglect. I therefore on the next day, issued orders to my Division, which you have, enclosed. This matter being known throughout the division, it was early perceived against whom they were pointed. This was by them deemed unpardonable, and, I suppose, retaliation determined upon.

But no opportunity offered till the affair of Staten Island. They immediately began to make a party against me, in which they were warmly seconded by General de Borre. This, Sir, was the foundation of all the clamor raised against me; and every engine was set at work to raise a report throughout the country, that my officers in general were dissatisfied with my conduct. This report coming to the hearing of the officers, they have met on the occasion, and the regiments have many of them delivered in, and the others are making out papers, similar to the one you have, enclosed, from Col. Ford's. I believe some officers in Hazen's will not do it; but many of them have, and some conclude by saying that if they were as happy with the field officers of his regiment as with me, they would be as happy as they could wish. I hope, after having dealt thus openly with Congress, and laid every thing before them, the party who have arisen up against me, will at least be sensible that they have injured me without cause. I am happy that my conduct in military life thus far will bear the strictest scrutiny, and every inquiry into it will redound to my honour. But I am far from expecting this always to be the case. I well know that I am in common with the rest of mankind liable to errors, and it must be a miracle if I escape them all. At the same time, though at a distance from the Senate, I know there is a party who would improve the first [opportunity?] to work my ruin. This was the only motive that induced me to ask to retire from the army. It was not because I was weary of serving my country, but to rescue my reputation from ruin. It is exceedingly hard for me to fight against the enemies of my country, and at the same time combat with the very persons I am fighting for. The last action took off half of my [military] family, perhaps the next may sweep the residue, and involve me in their fate; and, what is still more deplorable, my reputation may unjustly perish by my side. This is a poor encouragement to sacrifice that life which I have often ventured in my Country's cause, and to exchange domestic ease for the dusty field of Mars. But as every American looks up to Congress, for justice, I cannot persuade myself that it will refuse, either to approve my conduct publicly, or grant me leave to retire from the army.

The following is the account of the expedition by Marshall:—

"The force of the enemy on the island amounted to between two or three thousand men, of whom nearly one thousand were Provincials, who were stationed at different places on the coast, opposite the Jersey shore. The British and German troops, amounting to sixteen hundred men, were in a fortified camp, near the Watering Place. General Sullivan thought it practicable to surprise and bring off the Provincials before they could be supported by the European troops; and he was the more stimulated to make the attempt by their occasional incursions into Jersey. In one of these, very lately made, they had carried off a number of cattle and about twelve individuals noted for their attachment to the American cause. This expedition was undertaken with the select troops of his division, aided by a few Jersey militia, under Colonel Frelinghuysen.

"They had to march about twenty miles to the place of embarkation, where only six boats had been procured. Three of these were allotted to Colonel Ogden, who commanded one detachment intended to attack Colonel Lawrence, who lay near The Old Blazing Star ferry, and Colonels Dungan and Allen, who lay about two miles from each other, towards Amboy. The other three were taken by General De Borre, who was accompanied by Sullivan in person, and who was to attack Colonel Barton, near The New Blazing Star ferry, and having secured that party, to assist Ogden. General Smallwood was to cross at Halsey's Point, and attack Buskirk's regiment, which lay near Decker's Ferry. All the troops crossed over into the island, before day, without being perceived by the enemy. From being misconducted by his guides, Smallwood began his attack on a different point from that which he intended, in consequence of which the regiment he attacked made its escape; but Ogden and De Borre succeeded in a very considerable extent. Lawrence and Barton were completely surprised; and both of them, with several of their officers and men, were taken.

"The alarm being given, it was necessary to use the utmost dispatch in drawing his forces off the island. It had been impracticable to obtain a sufficient number of boats to embark them all at the same time; and some confusion appears to have prevailed in this part of the business. General Campbell, with a considerable force advanced upon them; and the rear-guard (about two hundred) after defending themselves for some time with great gallantry, finding the boats could not be brought back to take them over the channel, were under the necessity of surrendering prisoners of war. The enterprise seems to have been well planned, and, in its commencement, to have been happily executed. Its disastrous conclusion is most probably attributable to the want of a sufficient number of boats, without which the expedition ought not to have been undertaken." — *Life of Washington.*

Mr. Bancroft says, disingenuously, that Sullivan could not, in consequence of the descent on Staten Island, obey the orders which met him on his return, to join Washington with all speed. In a week, he moved three thousand men from Hanover to the Elk, — one hundred and thirty miles, probably more than less. Howe, with twenty thousand men, had effected his landing by the 26th of August, and on the 11th of September was at Kennett Square, seven miles south of the Brandywine, and thirty south from Philadelphia, of which city it was his aim to possess himself. Washington, on the north side of the river, with his centre at Chad's Ford, on the direct route to the city, had eleven thousand men, poorly armed or recent levies. Maxwell commanded the left, down the river; Sullivan the right, above, having under him, besides his own division, those of Stirling and Stephen, with Hazen's regiment stationed three miles higher up.

Sullivan, in conversation and by letter, had previously expressed his opinion to Washington, that Howe, as a sensible officer, would cross the river above the forks. Knyphausen, with half the British army, early in the morning, marched towards the river, and engaged Washington's attention with his artillery and occasional attacks in force. At the same time, he occupied the right bank of the Brandywine, screening from observation the march of Howe and Cornwallis, who, at daybreak, had started up the Lancaster road. The morning was foggy; and their march, from six to ten miles from the river, lay through thick woods and uneven ground, well guarded on their flanks. Sullivan had but four horsemen, two of whom were needed to keep up communication with headquarters, two miles below, and three-quarters of a mile from Chad's Ford. It was difficult, therefore, to ascertain the movement of the hostile forces; and Washington remained several hours in suspense.

In a foot-note on page 395 of Mr. Bancroft's volume, Sparks's "Washington" (vol. v. p. 109) is cited to prove that the responsibility devolved exclusively on Sullivan to obtain intelligence; and it purports, that the letter cited corrects a misstatement of his on that point. The candid reader, on reference to that authority, will find that the letter, on the contrary, confirms his statement, and that it was alike the constant effort of both Washington and Sullivan, that anxious morning, to obtain intelligence; and what was actually brought to them was as full and frequent as circumstances could have warranted them to expect.

Towards noon came an express from Sullivan to headquarters, that Howe, with a large body of troops and a park of artillery, was pushing up the Lancaster road. Washington ordered Sullivan to cross the Brandywine at Brenton's Ford, near which he was stationed, and to attack the British left. While preparing, in obedience to these orders, to cross the river, Major Spear* came in and informed him, that he had just come down from the Lancaster road, and the country where the British should have been, if coming round by the upper fords, and that they were nowhere to be seen. Sullivan thought Spear must be mistaken, but felt bound to transmit this with all speed to headquarters, as Washington said, in the sequel, he was perfectly right in doing. The movement might well have been a feint to lure us to meet the whole British army. That Washington so reasoned, is plain from the fact, that he did not send back immediate word, as he might have done in twenty minutes, to cross notwithstanding. One hour at least passed on unimproved by Washington, while awaiting more positive information, when Cheyney came in to confirm the earlier intelligence.

It seems reasonable to believe that the information of Colonel Ross and Colonel Bland, that Howe had marched towards the forks, reached Washington soon after eleven. His order to Sullivan to cross was not later than half-past. By twelve, the reports of Major Spear and Sergeant Tucker, that the earlier intelligence was a mistake, were forwarded; and by one, certainly, orders could have been sent to Sullivan still to cross, had Washington deemed it advisable. It was after two when the fact became known to Washington, that the British army was actually coming down the left bank

---

* Most of the authorities write *Spear*; one of the later (Irving) *Spicer*.

of the Brandywine. Ill-natured historians, eager to find fault, overlook completely the fact, that Colonel Hazen, who with his regiment was stationed three miles above Sullivan, up the river, was the person mainly relied upon for knowledge of any movement of the enemy in that direction.

As the proposed movement was based on information previously communicated, in reality correct, but now contradicted on authority equally entitled to respect, Sullivan would have been deservedly blamed if he had hesitated to transmit it, and the army had crossed to encounter the whole British force, double its numbers, with a river but partially fordable in its rear, and, as inevitably would have been the case unless by a miracle, been defeated.

Reasoning from the facts, as in reality they were, if Sullivan had crossed, and with Washington attacked Knyphausen, the force left at Kennett Square was nearly equal to what would have been engaged against it; and the contest could easily have been prolonged until Howe had reached our rear and enveloped us. It is useless to conjecture probabilities, except so far as they bear upon the claim to credit for prudence and military sagacity of those who no doubt took them into account in forming their conclusions. But it would seem that a kind Providence saved us on that day from a terrible blunder, if not the loss of our cause, by keeping us on the left bank of the Brandywine. We fought because public opinion demanded it. It would have been a folly, with such odds, to have expected a victory. The resistance made, although resulting in retreat, was still a step in advance towards independence.

What followed we give in Sullivan's own language, in a letter which we claim to be the best evidence as to the facts related, because proceeding from him who had the best opportunity of knowing the truth; whose character for honor cannot be impeached; and where deception, had he been disposed to deceive, would have been impossible, from the whole army of witnesses to whom the incidents of the battle were perfectly familiar. We feel assured that no candid or competent judge, after reading it, will remain of the opinion, either that Sullivan made too wide a circuit, had any question of etiquette with Stirling or Stephen as to the post of honor, moved his division from half a mile to the left to their right, or that he was otherwise than worthy of all respect for his military capacity, and his natural and acquired qualifications as a general officer and commander, in critical moments requiring coolness and judgment. If we had many better officers than Sullivan, the standard in our Revolutionary struggle was a most unusual one.

The letter to which reference has been made is the following: —

CAMP ON PERKIOMY, Sept. 27, 1777.

MUCH ESTEEMED SIR, — I have long been soliciting for a court of inquiry into my conduct in the expedition against Staten Island. I had applied to the commander-in-chief for one before. I know Congress had ordered it; but such has been the state of our arms, that I have not been able to obtain one, and know not when I shall have it in my power. I however take the freedom to transmit Congress copies of the testimonies I mean to lay before the court, which I beg Congress to peruse; and they can be at no loss what must be the result of an impartial court. I am, however, happy in the assurance, that the evidence will remove every suspicion from the minds of the members of Congress, and from the court, if ever I should be so happy as to obtain one; and I shall take the proper steps to remove the effects from the minds of Americans at large. I was ever at a loss to find what great evil happened from this expedition, unless a spirit of enterprise is deemed a fault; if so, *I think it will need but few resolves of Congress to destroy what remains of it in our army.*

In this expedition, we landed on an island possessed by the enemy; put to rout six regiments; killed, wounded, and made prisoners at least four or five hundred of the enemy;* vanquished every party that col-

---

* There is no more frequent subject of dispute in history than regarding the number of combatants, the dead, wounded, or missing. Returns are rarely exact; and, except in rare instances, where system is unusually thorough, much is left to conjecture. It

lected against us; destroyed them great quantities of stores; took one vessel and destroyed six; took a considerable number of arms, blankets, many cattle, horses, &c.; marched victorious through the island; and, in the whole course of the day, lost not more than one hundred and fifty men, most of which were lost by the imprudence of themselves and officers. Some few, indeed, were lost by cross accidents, which no human foresight could have prevented.

Whether Congress will take any steps against persons who have thus scandalously imposed their falsehoods upon them, I shall not inquire. I find it necessary for me to take the proper steps to do myself justice, which I know the impartial part of mankind will justify. I was still more astonished to find, that, upon the vague report of a single person, who pretends to know all about the late battle of Brandywine, though I am confident he saw but little of it, Congress should suddenly pass a resolve, to suspend me from the service, which resolve was afterwards rescinded. If the reputation of general officers is thus to be sported with, upon every vague and idle report, those who set less by their reputation than myself must continue in the service. Nothing can be more mortifying to a man who is conscious of having done every thing in his power for the good of his country, — has wasted his strength, and often exposed his life, in the service of it, than to find the representatives thereof, instead of bestowing on him the reward of his services, loading him with blame, infamy, and reproach, upon the false representations of a single person, who felt as little of the severity of the engagement, as he knows about the disposition of our troops or that of the enemy.

I enclose Congress the testimony of those brave and experienced officers, who with me endured the hottest of the enemy's fire.

I have never endeavored to establish my reputation by my own pen; nor have I, according to the modern custom, employed others for the purpose; neither have I adopted the still more infamous method, of raising my own reputation by destroying that of others. I have always contented myself with a consciousness of having done my duty

---

was a part of even Washington's policy, full of truth and honor as he was, to mislead the enemy; and the British officers frequently under or over stated, either from design or mistake. If this number seems large, it is quite as likely to be exact as what was stated by the enemy disposed to conceal the extent of their loss, or of persons, from malevolent motives, eager to depreciate the results. Of course in this number are included the prisoners of Ogden, who, if we may judge from his own correspondence, was not in an independent command, as stated by Bancroft, but formed part of that of General Sullivan.

with faithfulness; but, being constrained to say something at this time respecting the late battle and some other matters, I hope Congress will look upon it rather as the effect of necessity, than any desire of making a merit of my services.

I never yet have pretended that my disposition in the late battle was perfect; I knew it was very far from it: but this I will venture to affirm, that it was the best which time would allow me to make. At half-past two, I received orders to march with my division, — to join with, and take command of, that and two others to oppose the enemy, who were coming down on the right flank of our army. I neither knew where the enemy were, nor what route the other two divisions were to take, and of course could not determine where I should form a junction with them. I began my march in a few minutes after I received my orders, and had not marched a mile when I met Colonel Hazen and his regiment, which had been stationed at a ford three miles above me, who informed that the enemy were close upon his heels, and that I might depend that the principal part of the British army were there; although I knew the report sent to headquarters made them but two brigades. As I knew Colonel Hazen to be an old officer and a good judge of numbers, I gave credence to his report, in preference to the intelligence before received. While I was conversing with Colonel Hazen, and our troops still upon the march, the enemy headed us in the road, about forty rods from our advanced guard. I then found it necessary to turn off to the right to form, and so got nearer to the other two divisions, which I at that moment discovered drawn up on an eminence, both in the rear and to the right of the place I then was at. I ordered Colonel Hazen's regiment to pass a hollow way, file off to the right, and face, to cover the artillery. The enemy, seeing this, did not press on, but gave me time to form my division on an advantageous height, in a line with the other divisions, but almost half a mile to the left.

I then rode on to consult the other general officers, who, upon receiving information that the enemy were endeavoring to outflank us on the right, were unanimously of opinion, that my division should be brought on to join the others, and that the whole should incline further to the right, to prevent our being outflanked; but while my division was marching on, and before it was possible for them to form to advantage, the enemy pressed on with rapidity and attacked them, which threw them into some kind of confusion. I had taken post myself in the centre, with the artillery, and ordered it to play briskly to stop the progress of the enemy, and to give the broken troops time to rally and form in the rear of where I was with the artillery. I sent off four aide-de-camps for this purpose, and went myself; but all in vain. No sooner did I form one party, but that which I had before formed ran off, and even at times when I, though on horseback and in front of them, apprehended no danger. I then left them to be rallied by their own officers and my aide-de-camps; I repaired to the hill where our artillery was, which by this time began to feel the effects of the enemy's fire.

This hill commanded both the right and left of our line, and, if carried by the enemy, I knew would instantly bring on a total rout, and make a retreat very difficult. I therefore determined to hold it as long as possible, to give Lord Stirling's and General Stephen's divisions, which yet stood firm, as much assistance from the artillery as possible, and to give Colonel Hazen's, Dayton's, and Ogden's regiments, which still stood firm on our left, the same advantage, and to cover the broken troops of my division, and to give them an opportunity to rally, and come to our assistance, which some of them did, and others could not by their officers be brought to do any thing but fly. The enemy soon began to bend their principal force against the hill, and the fire was close and heavy for a long time, and soon became general. Lord Stirling and General Conway, with their aide-de-camps, were with me on the hill, and exerted themselves beyond description to keep up the troops. Five times did the enemy drive our troops from the hill, and as often was it regained, and the summit often disputed almost muzzle to muzzle. How far I had a hand in this, and whether I endured the hottest of the enemy's fire, I cheerfully submit to the gentlemen who were with me. The general fire of the line lasted an hour and forty minutes; fifty-one minutes of which the hill was disputed almost muzzle to muzzle, in such a manner, that General Conway, who has seen much service, says he never saw so close and severe a fire. On the right where General Stephen was, it was long and severe, and on the left considerable. When we found the right and left oppressed by numbers and giving way on all quarters, we were obliged to abandon the hill we had so long contended for, but not till we had almost covered the ground between that and Birmingham meeting-house, with the dead bodies of the enemy.* When I found that victory was

---

* Rolls of the loss of the enemy at Brandywine were captured at Germantown, and the total is set down as about two thousand. More than half of their loss, no doubt, was during the battle at Birmingham meeting-house.

on the side of the enemy, I thought it my duty to prevent, as much as possible, the injurious consequences of a defeat; for which purpose I rallied my troops on every advantageous piece of ground, to retard their pursuit and give them fresh opposition. How far I exerted myself in this, Congress will readily see by consulting the enclosed testimonies; and that the last parties I assisted to rally and post against them were between sunset and dark. By this means the enemy were so much fatigued, that they suffered our whole army, with their artillery, baggage, &c., to pass off without molestation, and without attempting to pursue us a step.

I wish Congress to consider the many disadvantages I labored under on that day. It is necessary, in every action, that the commanding officer should have a perfect knowledge of the number and situation of the enemy, the route they are pursuing, the ground he is to draw up his troops on, as well as that where the enemy are formed, and that he have sufficient time to view and examine the position of the enemy, and to draw up his troops in such a manner as to counteract their design; all of which were wanting. We had intelligence only of two brigades coming against us, when in fact it was the whole strength of the British army, commanded by General Howe and Lord Cornwallis. They met us unexpectedly, and in order of battle, and attacked us before we had time to form, and upon ground we had never before seen. Under those disadvantages, and against those unequal numbers, we maintained our ground an hour and forty minutes; and, by giving fresh opposition on every ground that would admit, we kept them at bay from three o'clock until after sunset. What more would have been expected from between three and four thousand troops against the chief part of the British army?

. . . .

I now beg Congress to consider whether my services, in political and military life, have deserved so ill as to render me liable, upon vague reports and private opinions, to have my character stigmatized by resolves against me. Though I have never yet wrote, or said any thing in favor of myself, I am compelled at once to alter my conduct. My political character is well known in most parts of America, and the part I have taken in the present dispute. I am exceeding happy, that, in the military line, I have witnesses of all my conduct. Let the commander-in-chief declare who it was that supplied cannon, arms, and ammunition to the army, when they were almost destitute at Cambridge, and who brought the troops to guard the lines, when they were almost deserted; and who, by his influence, prevailed upon them to tarry six weeks after their time was expired. To the officers I had the honor to command on Winter Hill, I appeal whether I was not the means of inducing their men to enlist for the second campaign, and whether, during the whole time I was there, I did not cheerfully brave every danger that could arise from the severe cannonade and bombardment of the enemy. To the officers of the Canada army, let me appeal for the truth of my having found, on my arrival in that quarter, a most miserable army, flying off by hundreds and leaving behind them all their sick, and all the public stores which had been sent into that quarter. Those I speedily collected, and, having joined my other forces, made an effort to penetrate into the country; but the unfortunate arrival of ten thousand British troops put it out of my power. I had then to make a retreat with five thousand sick, and two thousand two hundred and fifty well men, and to secure the public stores scattered throughout the country. This was done in the face of a veteran army, commanded by a brave and experienced officer. The sick and the public stores were not only saved, but the mills, timber, and boards were destroyed, which prevented the enemy from reducing Ticonderoga to the same unhappy situation the last year which they have done this. How far I was active in conducting this retreat, which even our enemies have applauded, let the address of the worthy officers in that army, presented at my departure from them, declare. In the attack upon Trenton, in December last, I appeal to all the officers in the three brigades commanded by Generals St. Clair, Glover, and Commandant Sergeant, whether I did not enter the town, at the head of my troops, and whether my disposition was not the most perfect that could be devised for carrying the town and preventing escapes, and whether, with my division, I did not carry the town before we received any assistance. To the commander-in-chief, and to the same officers, I again appeal, whether I did not by my influence prevail on those troops to tarry six weeks after the first day of January, which in my opinion went far towards saving America;* and whether, at the attack on Princeton, I was not in the front of my line when the enemy began their fire upon us, and whether they ever saw me in the least endeavor to screen myself from the enemy's fire. For the battle of Long Island, I appeal to Major Willis and the other officers who were with me, whether

---

* It was undoubtedly owing, in a great degree, to the exertions of Sullivan and Stark, that a re-enlistment of the troops was effected at this perilous juncture. — See *Collections for* 1822, p. 100.

any person could have exposed himself more, or made a longer resistance with such an handful of men, against so great an army.

It is an observation of one of the wisest of men, that no person can stand before envy; and I am determined not to make the rash attempt. My reputation and my freedom I hold dear. But, if I lose the former, the latter becomes of no importance. I therefore, rather than run the venture to combat against the envy of some malicious officers in the army, when cherished and supported by the influence of their too credulous correspondents in Congress, must, as soon as the court of inquiry have sat, and given their opinion, beg leave to retire from the army, while my reputation is secure. This will afford me an opportunity of doing justice to my reputation, and laying my conduct, with the evidence of it, before the public; and enable me to take the proper steps against those, who, without cause or foundation, have endeavored to ruin one, who has ever shown himself one of the warmest friends to American freedom. I beg Congress will not suppose this to proceed from disaffection, but from necessity; that I may quit a place where I have more to fear, than I could have from the most powerful enemy. If Congress grants me liberty to retire, I shall give in my resignation to the commander-in-chief, when the court of inquiry have sat, and given their judgment, and if it is against me, when a court-martial gives a final judgment, unless that should likewise be against me. But I cannot think that Congress, after examining the evidences, will be at a loss to know what the result of either court must be.

Dear Sir, I have the honor to be, with much respect,

Your Excellency's most obedient servant,

JOHN SULLIVAN.

His Excellency JOHN HANCOCK, Esq.

Stephen exposed himself, that day, to reproach for unofficerlike conduct. De Borre, somewhat ignorant of our language, was obstinate, disobeyed orders, and, shortly afterwarwards, was court-martialled and resigned.

Sullivan, in defending himself from the charges of Burke, — a civilian and member of Congress, who rode out to see the fight, — criminates no one of his subordinates, but is generous to all of them, as he is, afterwards, just and discriminating in describing the battle for the public press. It seems difficult to understand, if any remark ever fell from his lips to which the wildest interpretation could attach the idea of jealousy or etiquette as to position, how any such could have entered his mind. He was commanding the whole right wing, and both Stirling and Stephen were his subordinates; while De Borre commanded the right brigade in his own division. How could it possibly have added to his dignity or responsibility or consequence, that his division should have been posted on the right. His words seem unmistakable, that, in moving to the right and rear, they were closing up to Stephen, when De Borre's brigade broke.

To be held in any degree, however, unjustly responsible for the disasters of the day, was intolerable to one so sensitive as himself; and the following letter to Mr. John Adams expresses his distress under the imputation:—

To John Adams.
        Camp on Perkiomy, Sept. 28, 1777.

Dear Sir,— Far from addressing you in the language of friendship, and desiring your assistance as a friend, I call upon you as a friend to justice and mankind, begging you to acquaint yourself, and make Congress acquainted, with the evidence I have enclosed the President, relative to my conduct. They ought to take time to view, examine, and consider it. They have censured and condemned me without evidence; will they not acquit me upon the clearest testimony? The greatest and the only favor I request from you is, that if, by the evidence, there appears the least fault in my conduct, you will join with the rest against me, to complete that ruin which some members of Congress have long been striving to bring about; but if, on the contrary, you find that it is the person who has silently borne the burthen of the war, has endured the hottest of almost every fire, and braved every danger for his country's good, that Congress has been censuring and resolving against, then, Sir, call upon Congress to do me justice, and restore me that reputation which they have in some degree deprived me of. Should I fail in this, I am determined to quit the service, and employ my tongue, my pen, and every other engine that may be found necessary, to save my reputation. I am now fortifying myself for the purpose. I am well known in America, and exceeding well in the army. The officers who have served with me are worthy, as they are numerous. They will, they must, join with me to exclaim against unjust and ungenerous returns for faithful and laborious service, let them proceed from what quarter they will. No wall can be so sacred as to screen from public censure the persons who, from private views, would ruin the reputation of the faithful patriot and the brave soldier. It is the dignity of America, not the dignity of Congress, we are fighting to support. Treat us justly, reward us for our services, and don't let our characters suffer from every idle report. Pray examine the evidence I have sent to the President, and then determine, with your usual candor, whether the resolves against me were not premature; whether I have not a right to complain; and whether Congress ought not, in justice, to restore me that reputation which they have deprived me of. Why am I singled out as the only person for a court of inquiry, and by a resolve, afterwards rescinded, to be suspended from the service. A fleet was lost on Champlain Lake, the army in Canada ruined, Fort Washington and Fort Lee sacrificed: no courts of inquiry were thought necessary. General Parsons made an attempt on Long Island the same day I went to Staten Island. He had only one regiment to contend with; no re-enforcements could possibly come against him: yet he was repulsed, with loss. I had many regiments to contend with; routed all I came across; did them much mischief. Yet no court of inquiry is ordered upon him. I am the butt against which all the darts are levelled. How does this read? How will it sound when ringing in the public ear? But forgive me for this warmth. I know that, as a friend, you will make the proper allowances for my feeling. I rely upon your exertions to bring Congress to do justice to your much injured friend and humble servant, JOHN SULLIVAN.

Hon. JOHN ADAMS.

Congress, who had for a moment hearkened to Burke, one of its members, who professed to have been an eye-witness of what occurred on the battlefield, immediately rescinded their resolve by an overwhelming vote, one member from Delaware alone siding with Burke. His aspersions, as we hope those of Mr. Bancroft now, if fame be worth the having, will be of service rather than injury to the reputation of General Sullivan, calling attention to what can well stand the test. We select from the numberless letters of his brother officers, including nearly all those who served under him, the following, which are certainly better to be believed than Mr. Bancroft.

OCT. 20, 1777.

Since the battle of Brandywine, I have been sorry to hear illiberal complaints thrown out against the conduct of Major-General Sullivan. As I was present during the whole action, and obliged, from my situation with Lord Stirling, to be near General Sullivan, I had an opportunity of observing such examples of courage as could not escape the attention of any one. I can declare that his uniform bravery, coolness, and intrepidity, both in the heat of battle, and in rallying and forming the troops when broke from their ranks, appeared to me to be truly consistent with, or rather exceeded, any idea I had ever had of the greatest soldier.
ENOS EDWARDS,
Aid to Lord Stirling.

The notes of Lafayette, Hamilton, and Laurens are equally explicit as to his generalship in the battle; and the following from Charles Cotesworth Pinckney, afterwards candidate for the Presidency of the United States, that, in posting Weedon's brigade, and in resisting the enemy till dark, he did quite his part in the preservation of the American army: —

CAMP NEAR POTSGROVE, Sept. 24, 1777.

In compliance with the request of General Sullivan, that I would mention what I saw of his behavior at the action of Brandywine, on the 11th of this month, I declare, when I saw him in the engagement, which was in the evening, about the time that General Weedon's brigade was brought up to the right, he appeared to me to behave with the greatest calmness and bravery; and at that time I had occasion to observe his behavior, as I was then with General Washington, and heard General Sullivan tell him that all the superior officers of his division had behaved exceedingly well, and, after some other conversation with the general, General Sullivan, turning to me, requested I would ride up to General Weedon, and desire him to halt Colonel Spottswood's and Colonel Stephen's regiments in the ploughed field, on our right, and form them there, which I did; and on my return I was informed that General Sullivan, while I was delivering his orders, had his horse shot under him.
CHARLES COTESWORTH PINCKNEY,
Colonel of the First Continental Regiment of South Carolina.

Five days after the battle, Washington again sought an engagement at Goshen; but, a storm of two days' continuance spoiling his ammunition, he was compelled to withdraw for a fresh supply, and Howe entered Philadelphia. There being no suitable accommodation for them within the city, the British general posted his forces at Germantown, six miles out. . Washington determined to attack them on the first opportunity, and submitted the proposition to his generals, who, with few exceptions, advised delay until re-enforcements, that were expected, arrived from the North. When, soon after, intelligence was received that Howe had weakened his army by a strong detachment to Billingsport, Washington concluded upon action. At noon, on the third of October, he issued his orders; and, at nine that evening, the troops had left Matuchen Hills, on the Skippack, for a night-march of fourteen miles. Sullivan says, at nine; Washington, at seven: a discrepancy easily reconciled by the longer route of the left wing, which, having three miles farther to go, no doubt started an hour or two earlier. At daybreak the next morning, the right wing commanded by Sullivan, came into collision with the advanced posts of the British at Chestnut Hill, about two miles north of the village of Germantown.

The following letter to President Weare from Sullivan, dated Oct. 25, 1777, from the camp at Whitemarsh, gives the particulars of the fight: —

General Sullivan's Letter to the President of New Hampshire.

CAMP AT WHITEMARSH, Oct. 25, 1777.

SIR, — I hope the constant movements of our army, since the battle of Germantown, will apologize for my not having before given you a particular account of this unsuccessful affair. Upon receiving intelligence that part of the enemy's force was detached for particular purposes, and that their main army lay encamped, with their left wing on the west side of the road leading through Germantown, flanked by the Hessian forces, who were encamped on the Schuylkill, and their right on the east side of the road extending to a wood about one mile from the town, with their light infantry encamped in a line in their front, within less than a quarter of a mile of their picket at Mount Airy, — upon this intelligence, it was agreed in council that we should march the night of the 3d instant, and attack the enemy in the following manner: —

My own and Wayne's divisions were to compose the right wing, which I had the honor to command. This wing was to be sustained by the corps of reserve, composed of Nash's and Maxwell's brigades, commanded by Major-general Lord Stirling. The right wing was to be flanked by Conway's brigade, which led the column. The whole of these marched down the Skippack road, leading over Chesnut Hill into Germantown. General Armstrong, with about one thousand Pennsylvania militia, was to pass down the road which runs near the Schuylkill, and attack the Hessians, who covered the enemy's left flank. The left wing was composed of Greene's and Stephen's divisions, commanded by Major-general Greene, who were to march down the York road and attack the enemy's right, while the troops I had the honor to command attacked their left. General McDougal's brigade was to attack their right flank, and Smallwood's division and Forman's brigade of militia were to make a larger circuit, and attack the rear of their right wing. The reason of our sending so many troops to attack their right was because it was supposed, that, if this wing of the enemy could be forced, their army must be pushed into the Schuylkill or be compelled to surrender. Therefore two-thirds of the army, at least, were detached to oppose the enemy's right.

The attack was to begin on all quarters at daybreak. Our army left their encampment at Matuchen Hills at nine in the evening, marched all night, and at daybreak the right wing arrived on Chesnut Hill, when one regiment from Conway's brigade, and one from the Second Maryland brigade, were detached to Mount Airy, followed by Conway's brigade, to attack the enemy's picket at Allen's house. My own division followed in the rear of Conway's, and Wayne's division in the rear of mine. The picket was soon attacked, and suddenly re-enforced by all their light infantry. This compelled General Conway to form his brigade to sustain the attacking regiments and to repulse the light infantry. They maintained their ground with great resolution, till my division was formed to support them. The enemy endeavoring to flank us on the left, I ordered Colonel Ford's regiment to the other side of the road to repulse them, till General Wayne's division arrived; and upon finding that our left wing, which had near four miles farther to march than the right, had not arrived, I was obliged to form

General Wayne's division on the east of the road, to attack the enemy's right. I then directed General Conway to draw off such part of his brigade as was formed in the road and in front of our right, and to fall into my rear, and file off to the right to flank my division; but, the morning being too dark to discover the enemy's movements, and no evidence being given of General Armstrong's arrival, I was obliged to send a regiment from Wayne's, and another from my own division, to keep the enemy from turning our right. I also detached Colonel Moylan's regiment of light horse to watch their motions in that quarter.

This being done, my division were ordered to advance; which they did with such resolution, that the enemy's light infantry were soon compelled to leave the field, and with it their encampments. They, however, made a stand at every fence, wall, and ditch they passed, which were numerous. We were compelled to remove every fence as we passed, which delayed us much in the pursuit. We were soon after met by the left wing of the British army, when a severe conflict ensued; but, our men being ordered to march up with shouldered arms, they obeyed without hesitation, and the enemy retired. I then detached my aide-de-camp, Major Morris, to inform his Excellency, who was in the main road, that the enemy's left wing had given way, and to desire him to order General Wayne to advance against their right. His Excellency immediately detached part of the residue on my right and part on the left of the road, and directed Wayne's division to advance, which they did with great bravery and rapidity.

At Chew's house, a mile and a half from where the attack began, Wayne's division came abreast with mine, and passed Chew's house, while mine were advancing on the other side of the main road.

Though the enemy were routed, yet they took advantage of every yard, house, and hedge in their retreat, which caused an incessant fire through the whole pursuit. At this time, which was near an hour and a quarter after the attack began, General Stephen's division fell in with Wayne's on our left, and, soon after, the firing from General Greene's was heard still farther to the left. The left wing of our army was delayed much by General Greene's being obliged to countermarch one of his divisions before he could begin the attack, as he found the enemy were in a situation very different from what we had been before told. The enemy had thrown a large body of troops into Chew's house, which caused Maxwell's brigade to halt there with some artillery to reduce them. This was found very difficult, as the house, being stone, was almost impenetrable by cannon, and sufficient proof against musketry. The enemy defended themselves with great bravery, and annoyed our troops much by their fire. This, unfortunately, caused many of our troops to halt, and brought back General Wayne's division, who had advanced far beyond the house, as they were apprehensive lest the firing proceeded from the enemy's having defeated my division on the right. This totally uncovered the left flank of my division, which was still advancing against the enemy's left. The firing of General Greene's division was very heavy for more than a quarter of an hour, but then decreased, and seemed to draw farther from us. I am not sufficiently acquainted with the facts to determine with precision what was done in that quarter. A regiment commanded by Colonel Matthews advanced with rapidity near the town; but, not being supported by some other regiments, who were stopped by a breastwork near Lucan's mills, the brave colonel, after having performed great feats of bravery, and being dangerously wounded in several places, was obliged, with about a hundred of his men, to surrender.

My division, with a regiment of North Carolinians commanded by Colonel Armstrong, and assisted by part of Conway's brigade, having driven the enemy a mile and a half below Chew's house, and finding themselves unsupported by any other troops, their cartridges all expended, the force of the enemy on the right collecting to the left to oppose them, being alarmed by the firing at Chew's house so far in their rear, and by the cry of a light-horseman on the right, that the enemy had got round us, and at the same time discovering some troops flying on our right, retired with as much precipitation as they had before advanced, against every effort of their officers to rally them. When the retreat took place, they had been engaged near three hours, which with the march of the preceding night, rendered them almost unfit for fighting or retreating. We, however, made a safe retreat, though not a regular one; we brought off all our cannon and all our wounded. Our loss in the action amounts to less than seven hundred, mostly wounded. We lost some valuable officers, among whom were the brave General Nash and my two aides-de-camp, Majors Sherburne and White, whose singular bravery must ever do honor to their memories. Our army rendezvoused at Pawling's mills, and seems very desirous of another action. The misfortunes of this day were principally owing to a thick fog, which, being rendered still more so by the smoke of the cannon and musketry, prevented our troops from discovering the motions of the enemy or acting in concert with each other. I cannot help observing, that, with great concern, I saw our brave commander exposing himself to the hottest fire of the enemy, in such a manner, that regard to my country obliged me to ride to him, and beg him to retire. He, to gratify me and some others, withdrew a small distance; but his anxiety for the fate of the day soon brought him up again, where he remained till our troops had retreated.

I am, &c.,   JOHN SULLIVAN.

To the Hon. the President of New Hampshire.

This relation of what occurred on the right is full and explicit; and little remains to be added, but to correct erroneous impressions from other accounts of the battle. Biographers, in order to illustrate the services that form their especial topic, often convey such impressions without intending it, creating unjust prejudice. It will be observed that Washington accompanied the right wing. Its command and the general direction of its movements devolved upon Sullivan, but in due subordination to the commander-in-chief. The delay of Greene — occasioned by the mistake of his guide, and from being compelled to countermarch his division — exposed the left flank of the right in its advance, and rendered its extension imperative over ground which, as it approached the town, was to have been covered by the division of Stephen. It was with the knowledge and sanction of Washington, that Ford's regiment, and subsequently Wayne's division, were ordered to the east of the road; and, in passing the large stone house of Chief-justice Chew, the latter division and Sullivan's were abreast on either side of it. Washington had halted there half an hour, hoping to compel the six companies of the British Fortieth, under Colonel Musgrave, who had taken possession of the house and fortified it, to surrender; persuaded by Knox of the imprudence of leaving in his rear a post to prove an embarrassment in case of reverse. Maxwell's brigade of Lord Stirling's division was detained, and Wayne's division recalled, to reduce it; but, although artillery was employed, little impression was made on its walls, which were of unusual strength and solidity.

Meanwhile, Sullivan had pressed on with vigor; putting to rout the enemy in his front, who obstinately disputed his progress. When their retreat encouraged an advance on their centre in the town, Sullivan despatched his aid to Washington, to send forward Wayne. This request was immediately complied with; and Washington "detached part of the reserve on the right and part on the left of the road, and directed Wayne's division to advance, which they did with great bravery and rapidity." That no intelligence of this change of disposition reached Greene or Stephen, may be accounted for without imputing blame to any one. No doubt, all suitable precautions to apprise them of it were taken by Washington, through whom alone, as commander of both wings, the communication could with propriety be made; and also by Sullivan, who commanded the right wing, and who had two aids, Sherburne and White, killed in the battle; as well as by Wayne, whose division, from the necessity of the case, found itself, as it approached the centre of the village, where that of Stephen should have been. The latter — who, although generally an able and gallant officer, was not that morning, either from indisposition or imprudence, in condition to command — came up an hour and a quarter after the fight began on the right of the Limekiln Road, which entered the town, near the market-place, at an angle of forty-five degrees with that from the north, along the right and east side of which Wayne had marched from the Chew House. Mistaking, in the obscurity, from mist and smoke, the Americans for the enemy, he opened fire upon them. They returned it, and his division or a part of it fell back — Wayne says, "two miles" (probably less) — to the Chew House, of which the garrison still withstood the efforts of Maxwell, who was beleaguering it. Similar mistakes were made in other portions of the field. As the conflict terminated an hour and three quarters later, more importance seems to have been attached to this, as affecting the ultimate issue, than it deserves; for it was fortunate that, under the circumstances, instead of Stephen as intended, Wayne, who fought well, should have been sent to the front.

No imputation was ever made upon Sullivan for the change or its consequences; and he had enemies ready to do so, had there been ground. His advance, warmly contested, was still onward, extending through the westerly part of the town to the south-west side of it, a mile and a half below the Chew House; and where he commanded proved a complete success. The British left was utterly routed by his division and Conway's, a portion of them crossing the Schuylkill in disordered flight; while Wayne, engaging their right, and "remembering the action of the 20th of September, near the Warren, pushed on with the bayonet, taking ample vengeance for that night's work."

The battle was substantially won, when the Americans, notwithstanding every effort of their officers to rally them, turned away from victory absolutely in their grasp. Their ammunition, forty rounds to a man, after three hours of incessant combat, had become exhausted. Want of efficient organization for the speedy transmission of orders and intelligence, disposition of generals of brigade and division to carry out their plans without communicating them to their superiors, were as fatal elements of weakness and disaster in the armies of the Revolution, as in the Crimea or Spanish peninsula.

The fog — dense with the smoke of artillery and musketry, and of piles of straw and brushwood, kindled by the British to increase the confusion — still farther prevented concert of action. The heavy firing in their rear at the Chew House, and a parley sounded there to summon a surrender, by some misinterpreted as a signal for retreat, has been also suggested in explanation of the event of the day. These causes or some of them, with those mentioned in the foregoing report of the engagement, produced a panic, "which first took possession of Wayne's men, and then of others of the right wing." It spread rapidly. The retreat became general, but, soon reduced to some degree of order, was effected without loss.

Although a defeat, it inflicted a heavy blow on the enemy; their killed and wounded, over eight hundred, being in excess of ours. It raised in public estimation the character of the Americans; ready, so soon after their discomfiture at the Brandywine, to encounter again forces superior in number and equipment. Mr. Dawson, in his account of Germantown, in his "Battles of the United States," very justly remarks, "The plan of General Washington for conducting the enterprise was one of the most carefully elaborated designs which that distinguished man ever issued; and the ultimate failure in its execution, while it did not discourage the Americans, was not productive either of pleasure or profit to the enemy. The ability to design, and the resolution to execute, which were there displayed, commanded their respect; and, notwithstanding the enemy retired to its camp, fourteen miles distant, General Howe sought safety by retiring to Philadelphia."

Washington, in his report to Congress, says, "In justice to General Sullivan and the whole right wing of the army, whose conduct I had an opportunity of observing, as they acted immediately under my eye, I have the pleasure to inform you, that both officers and men behaved with a degree of gallantry that did them the highest honor." Mr. Bancroft, with the same ungenerous prejudice exhibited earlier, ascribes no merit to Sullivan, but cites a letter of General Armstrong to sustain a statement as to his needless waste of powder, which the letter itself fails to confirm. The only ground for such a reflection appears, when investigated, to have been a rumor, rather than an allegation, that the regiment of an inexperienced colonel unseasonably expended their powder. How far the colonel or his men deserved any such reproach, in our ignorance of the circumstances, is not susceptible of proof. It could not have been easy to determine, in an obscurity which, as Washington said, rendered it impossible, at thirty yards' distance, to distinguish friend from foe, what proportion of the bullets accomplished their deadly errand. The loss of the enemy, as indicated by their rolls, bears the usual ratio to the rounds fired, before the introduction of needle-gun and Chassepot disturbed the experiences of modern warfare.

After other unsuccessful efforts to bring the enemy to a conflict, in December, 1777, the American army — a large portion of it barefooted and without blankets — went into winter-quarters at Valley Forge, where Sullivan remained, till March, busily engaged in superintending the construction of bridges and in other duties.

Mr. Bancroft charges him, as a fault, with recommending the appointment of Conway as adjutant-general, and with being on both sides in the cabal which aimed to displace Washington by Gates. Sullivan's own correspondence conclusively proves that he had never faltered in his loyalty to Washington; but it would have been highly prejudicial to the cause for which they were all contending, had he taken sides against Gates, who was then the President of the Board of War. Conway had been under his command; was a brave officer who had seen much service; and, among the Sullivan papers is a virtual denial, under his signature,* of ever hav-

---

* Declaration of Conway: —

I declare that at Whitemarsh Camp, I think one or two days before my departure, I met with General Wilkinson at Colonel Biddle's quarters; that, having called General Wilkinson to an upper room, I asked him if he had knowledge of what I had written to General Gates the preceding month. Upon his answer in the affirmative, I asked him if he remembered to have read in it the following paragraph: —

"Heaven has determined to save this country, or a weak general and bad counsellors would have ruined it."

General Wilkinson assured me that such a paragraph was not in my letter.

3d JANUARY, 1778.   THOMAS CONWAY.

ing written to Gates the offensive passage quoted by Bancroft, which gave displeasure. Opinions differed with regard to his merits. Washington expressed his own, as in duty bound, without reserve, and they were not flattering; and this low estimate wounding his pride, and throwing obstacles in the way of his preferment, provoked resentment: but Conway, later, showed a generous and gentlemanly spirit in acknowledging his mistake. The following letter to John Adams, which was not without influence in inducing Congress to promote him, was evidently prompted by an honest conviction of his merit: —

WHITEMARSH, Nov. 10, 1777.

Nothing has given me more uneasiness than to find General Conway is about leaving the army, on account of some French gentlemen, who were inferior in rank to him while they remained in their own country, being promoted over him. This, he says, was the only thing he guarded against in his agreement with Mr. Dean and with Congress; but is now so unhappy as to find, not only persons, who held inferior rank to him in France, promoted over his head, but some who had no rank at all in the French army.

I have been in two actions with General Conway, and am confident no man could behave better in action. His regulations in his brigade are much better than any in the army, and his knowledge of military matters, in general, far exceeds any officer we have; and I must beg leave to observe, that it is worth the consideration of Congress to retain him.

P.S.— If the office of Inspector-General, with the rank of Major-General, was given him, I think our army would soon cut a different figure from what they now do.

In February, Sullivan requested permission to visit his family. He states that his daily pay of fifteen shillings and eightpence, in the reduced currency, provided for a very inconsiderable part of his expenses. He had depended, throughout the war, on his private resources; and his available means had become exhausted. At Long Island, New York, New Rochelle, and Peekskill, his personal effects had been captured; and it was only by returning to New Hampshire that he could procure what was indispensable for his most pressing wants. In reply to this request, Washington represented to him the necessity of his services in the camp, and urged him to defer his departure, to which he cheerfully submitted. When, later, the presence of other general officers rendered it less important he should remain, he renewed his request, and it was granted. He was, at the same time, recommended by Washington to Congress for the command of the troops at Providence, Rhode Island; the hope being entertained that the British, who were in force at Newport, under Sir Richard Pigott, could be compelled to evacuate it. This recommendation was supported by General Greene, who was himself a native of that State.

At Valley Forge terminates the period embraced in the last volume now published by Mr. Bancroft of the history of the war. This is soon to be followed by another, in which the military services of General Sullivan may possibly be subjected to like ungenerous and disingenuous comment. A brief relation of his campaigns in 1778 and 1779, on Rhode Island and in Western New York, is therefore added, that their history may be understood should they not be fairly presented.

Two years earlier, in March, 1776, immediately after the evacuation of Boston, he had been ordered with his brigade to Providence, to protect Rhode Island from threatened attack; and now, on the 17th of April, 1778, as good tidings of a treaty with France and promised co-operation were reaching America, he was invested by the council of war with the charge of that military department. From the vast amount of correspondence, of extreme interest, that has been preserved amongst his papers, connected with the subsequent campaign, — and all of which, it is much to be wished, may, at some future day, be given to the public, — some few selections are made for our present purpose, either as characteristic of the man or to explain the course of events.

Soon after he took command, Sir Richard Pigott, the commander of the British forces at Newport, endeavored, by order from home, to circulate among the inhabitants of the State, with the design of creating disaffection to the cause of independence, certain bills submitted to Parliament by the Cabinet, but which had never been passed. These bills were sent by Pigott to Sullivan, who returned them with the following letter: —

PROVIDENCE, 27th April, 1778.

SIR, — I received your favor of the 24th instant, requesting me to distribute, among the inhabitants of this State, sundry copies of bills read in the British House of Commons on the 19th February last. Such copies were delivered with your letters.

The inhabitants of this State acknowledge no authority, but that of the civil magistrates and the law of the land; with which authority I have not a wish to interfere, and therefore, while acting in a military capacity, should not be justified in distributing papers of any kind among them. The Legislature of this State is the only power which can regularly take your request into consideration. To that body I have therefore communicated your desire, and with it have lodged the copies you sent.

Had proposals of this kind been properly and sincerely made by the Court of Britain to the supreme authority of America, before the wanton cruelty which has marked the progress of the British arms in this country had taken place, or prior to our own declaring ourselves independent and entering into alliance with foreign powers, they would have been accepted with sentiments of gratitude; but at this time all proposals, except for a peace upon honorable and equal terms, must be ineffectual.

Americans are not now to learn that a bill once read in the House of Commons, without having passed either branch of the Legislature, is itself no authority; and the dispersing, or attempting to disperse, copies of it, discovers a design to amuse and deceive, rather than to bring about reconciliation. Nor are they ignorant of the motives which induce the British Court at this time to mention terms of accommodation, which, at former times, the most humble and dutiful petitions could not produce. Had the proposals for an accommodation, on the part of Britain, been sincere, they would have been properly authenticated and laid before Congress, and not copies of an unauthenticated bill been sent, to be dispersed among the inhabitants, to amuse and disunite them. The design of this procedure is so easily discovered, even by the weakest capacity, that you may assure yourself that it can never answer the purpose which Britain has in view. To convince you, sir, that the American powers wish to hide nothing from a free people, I inclose you a "Providence Gazette," in which those proposed bills are published, though not accompanied by the annexed address, signed by you; which, I apprehend, would be looked upon, by Americans in general, rather as an insult than as a proposal of reconciliation.

In June, he had occasion again to address the British commander upon the unwarranted capture of non-combatants. The strong expressions used had a twofold object; being intended for the public as well as for the person to whom they were addressed: —

PROVIDENCE, June 4, 1778.

SIR, — The repeated applications of the distressed families of persons captured by your troops on the 25th ultimo, induce me to write you upon the subject, as these men were not in actual service or found in arms. I cannot conceive what were the motives for taking them, or guess the terms upon which their release may be obtained.

Had the war, on the part of Britain, been founded in justice; and your troops, in their excursions, completed the destruction of the boats and our military preparations in that quarter, without wantonly destroying defenceless towns, burning houses consecrated to the Deity, plundering and abusing innocent inhabitants, and dragging, from their peaceful habitations, unarmed and unoffending men, — such an expedition might have shone with splendor: it is now darkened with savage cruelty, and stained with indelible disgrace.

In your last letter to me, you gave it as your opinion, that the inhabitants of America, at large, would entertain more favorable sentiments of the views and intentions of Great Britain than I seemed inclined to have. If, sir, the unprecedented cruelty of your troops, displayed upon every petty advantage since the commencement of this contest, the inhuman and unexampled treatment of prisoners, who, by the fortune of war, have fallen into your power, had not sufficiently convinced the inhabitants of the United States that they had nothing to expect from that nation but a continuance of those tyrannical and cruel measures which drove them to a separation, the conduct of your party, in their late expedition, must have stamped it with infallible certainty.

The law of retaliation has not, as yet, been exercised by the Americans: humanity has marked the line of their conduct thus far, even though they knew that their tenderness was attributed to base timidity. But if a departure from the laws of humanity can, in any instance, be justified, it must be when such relentless destroyers are intrapped by the vigilance of the party invaded. Perhaps, at some such period, the Americans, fired with resentment of accumulated injuries, wearied with the long exercise of a humane conduct, which has only been rewarded with barbarity and insult, and despairing to mitigate the horrors of war by persisting in the practice of a virtue which their enemies seem to have banished from their minds, may, by suddenly executing the law of retaliation, convince Britons that they have mistaken the motives of American clemency, and trifled too long with undeserved lenity. Should such an event take place, the unhappy sufferers may charge their misfortunes to the commanding officers of the British army in this country, whose mistaken conduct has weaned the affections of Americans from your nation, driven them to disavow allegiance to your sovereign, and at length roused to acts of retaliation.

I should not have written you so particularly upon the subject, had I not observed, in the "Newport Gazette," that the conduct of your troops, employed in the late expedition, had received your approbation and warmest thanks.

In a letter of the 3d of May, 1778, Sullivan submitted to Congress a statement of the military condition of his department, the strength of the enemy, and their means of annoyance and defence: —

I do myself the honor to inclose Congress a return of the troops at this post. The three last-mentioned regiments leave on this day, so that my force will consist of the residue mentioned in the return. We have not a man from Connecticut, and but part of two companies from Massachusetts Bay. Some few have arrived from New Hampshire, and about half their quota are on the march. With these troops, I have to guard a shore of upwards of sixty miles in extent, from Point Judith to Providence on the west, and from Providence to Seconnet Point on the east, against an enemy who can bring all their strength to any point they choose. I am exceeding happy that they know nothing of our strength, and are fortifying against an attack, which they daily expect. They have, on the island and in the posts adjacent, four regiments of Hessians, and the Twenty-second, Forty-third, and Fifty-sixth British; making, in the whole, 3,600, exclusive of a small regiment, consisting of 127, composed of refugees and deserters, and commanded by one Whiteman. I inclose Congress a plan of their fortifications round the town. They have, besides, a very strong work on Butt's Hill, a small redoubt opposite Bristol ferry, another at the entrance of our common ferry point, and two small works opposite Frog-land Point. They have stopped the course of the water in a small rivulet, to overflow a marsh for security of one part of the town. The water is now five feet deep; but I am informed that the stream dries up in some summers. They have drafted twenty-seven men from the Twenty-second Regiment, and a like number from the Forty-third, to join the light infantry of their Grand Army. These are all the troops taken from Rhode Island. They left it with Lord Howe. There are seven vessels of war, and two galleys, stationed in the following manner, viz.: The "Kingfisher" and two galleys, in the East Passage at Little Compton; in the Main Channel, the "Flora" and "Juno;" in the West Channel, the "Somersett;" at the town, the "Nonesuch," the "Lark," the "Falcon," and a frigate, the name of which I have not learned. This disposition of their shipping was made to entrap Captain Whipple, in the "Providence" frigate; but, on the night of the 30th, he took advantage of a violent north-east storm, passed them under a heavy fire, which he warmly returned, and got safe to sea. Since my arrival at this port, General Pigot favored me with a number of hand-bills, accompanied with a letter, a copy of which I inclose, together with a copy of my answer and of his reply.

As the number of troops destined for this department will be so incompetent to defend it against a sudden attack, I think that the two State galleys, if properly fitted, would be of great advantage. I have applied to the Council of War upon the subject, who seem rather inclined to dispose of them to the Continent, than to fix and man them for service. I beg leave, therefore, to submit to Congress, whether it would not be for the good of the service to purchase them for guarding those places which are most exposed, particularly the rivers of Taunton and Warren. I also beg Congress to order General Stark, who has returned to New Hampshire from Albany, to me at this place, as I shall need two brigadiers when the troops arrive; and the more so, as the extent of country to guard will be so great. Should Congress think that, after the troops arrive here, an attempt upon the island, with them and some militia and volunteers called in, would be practicable, I shall be exceeding happy in executing any order they will please to give.

Count d'Estaing had sailed from Toulon, on the 13th of April, to carry out the plan of joint operations, with twelve ships of the line, six frigates, and a considerable body of land forces. But his voyage being unfortunately protracted to eighty-seven days, the British, by evacuating Philadelphia, and withdrawing their fleet from the Delaware, had, before his arrival, extricated themselves from a position in which they would have been taken at disadvantage. He proceeded to New York; but, unable to cross the bar, it was decided he should assist Sullivan in reducing Newport, then occupied by a garrison, which was immediately strengthened, and soon exceeded six thousand effectives, protected by a naval force.

The main body of the troops lay in the town, which is situated on the west of an isthmus connecting the southern with the northern and principal part of the island, and which was defended by entrenchments and five redoubts, extending nearly across the island, from Tonomi Hill near Coddington's Cove on the west, to Easton's Pond, back of the first beach, towards the south-east. A quarter of a mile within this line extended a second, from the Gibbs farm at the town end of the first or Easton's Beach, where there was a redoubt, to the North Battery, on the shore near the Blue Rocks. Three regiments were stationed on Conanicut, an island in Narragansett Bay, nine miles in length, extending below and above the town: but these troops were withdrawn upon the approach of the French fleet; and three other regiments, which occupied fortified lines at Butt's Hill, at the northerly end of the island, the day before the Americans crossed from the mainland, retired also to Newport.

When, soon after Sullivan assumed command, in April, a predatory attack was made by the enemy on Bristol, he had but five hundred men at his disposal. Even after the Battle of Monmouth, on the 28th of June, although the garrison at Newport had been greatly strengthened, he had but sixteen hundred. But the promised co-operation inspired throughout the country an unusual ardor, and all classes were ready to leave their occupations with alacrity, to take part in an expedition fraught with such brilliant promise. Washington ordered Lafayette, with two brigades, to Providence, when it seemed probable the meditated attack on New York would be abandoned; and early in July, when he learned that D'Estaing had finally decided it was impracticable, he directed also General Greene to join Sullivan, who had now under his command the brigades of Cornell, Greene, Lovell, Titcomb, Glover, and Varnum, light corps under Livingston and West, and militia from Massachusetts, Rhode Island, and Connecticut. This force, amounting to nearly ten thousand men when collected at Tiverton, were for the most part recent levies, without discipline, or knowledge of war. A difficult duty was imposed upon Sullivan to organize and instruct them in season to be of effective service; as also, at a season of almost unprecedented scarcity, to provide them with supplies.

While engaged in these preparations, he received the following letter from Lafayette, between whom and himself existed relations of friendship and esteem, not ending with the war: —

Nothing can give me more pleasure than to go under your orders; and it is with the greatest happiness that I see my wishes, on that point, entirely satisfied. I both love and esteem you; therefore the moment we shall fight together will be extremely pleasant and agreeable to me. Colonel Laurens will explain to you the number of troops, I take with me. The Count d'Estaing, a relation and friend of mine, has offered me the French troops he has on board; so that, in addition to your forces, we shall add a pretty good re-enforcement. Had General Gates or any other gone there, I had already expressed that I did not choose to go; but I confess I feel the greatest happiness to co-operate with you to our glory and the common advantage. For God's sake, my dear friend, don't begin any thing before we arrive.

With the most sincere affection and regard, I have the honor to be your most obedient servant.

P.S. — Laurens is just going, and I have not time to add more.

The French fleet anchored, on the 29th of July, just without Brenton's Ledge, five miles below Newport; and Sullivan, going aboard, concerted, with the admiral, plans for their joint operations. It was agreed, in the expectation their landing would be contested, that the Americans should cross first, and then the French, who were to be commanded by Count d'Estaing in person: the former over the east, or Seconnet passage, under cover of the guns of a frigate; the latter from Conanicut on the west side, a little north of Dyer's Island, thus cutting off the three British regiments at Butt's Hill, which it was expected would thus be easily captured. D'Estaing, subsequently dissatisfied with the arrangement he had made, and tenacious of his superiority of rank as a lieutenant-general, insisted that the landing on both sides of the island should be simultaneous, and that one wing of the Americans should, with the French troops, be commanded by Lafayette. This demand was subsequently modified, and reduced from one wing to one thousand militia. Two frigates were sent on the 5th to either passage, compelling the enemy to burn seven vessels of war that were exposed; and, on the 8th, the fleet sailed up through the harbor to the upper end of Conanicut.

The militia did not arrive as promptly as promised, and this occasioned delay. But on the 9th, Sullivan, discovering the regiments stationed in a strong position at Butt's Hill had been withdrawn, and apprehensive the opportunity might be lost if not improved, should the enemy return, the contingency in view when the arrangement was made being no longer to be considered, crossed over the east passage to the island, informing the admiral at the same time of his movements, and the motives that governed him. D'Estaing was unreasonably offended at not being previously consulted. He was unduly sensitive and punctilious. Although outranking Sullivan, who was only a major-general, he commanded the fleet; and the war was an American war in

America. It was never contemplated, that while co-operating he should direct both the land and naval operations. Nor was it reasonable, that, when a change of circumstances compelled departure from the concerted plan in a point immaterial, he should take umbrage. But an excitable temper was fretted by heavy responsibility; he was unpopular with his officers, who thwarted him whenever occasion offered, and he was more occupied with his own dignity than with the cause. General Sullivan was courteous and forbearing. He expressed himself too sensible of the valuable services rendered by France ever to be unmindful of them; and made every effort, consistent with the main object, to maintain cordiality and a good understanding. This was often difficult without sacrifice of considerations more important.

On the day they crossed, Lord Howe anchored off Point Judith with thirteen ships of the line, seven frigates, and seventeen other vessels; and on the 10th, D'Estaing, eager to engage him, re-embarked the troops he had already landed on Conanicut, and put out to sea with the wind in his favor. For two days the opposing squadrons manœuvred for the weather gage, and were coming into action when dispersed by a violent gale. This storm, described as unprecedented in severity, on shore prostrated tents, destroyed much ammunition, and several volunteers, unaccustomed to exposure, perished. Its fury was hardly spent when Sullivan, whose own divisions had been quartered on the Gibbs place, Greene's being on what was later the farm of Mr. Kidder Randolph, and Lafayette's on what was then called Bower's Garden, advanced his army, on the 15th, to within two miles of the enemy, who were strongly posted in their entrenchments around Newport, where they had been protected from the storm, and suffered little.

One detachment of the Americans occupied Honeyman's Hill. After waiting, from a wish not to offend him, two days for D'Estaing to return, Sullivan, in order not to lose time which was precious, as the enemy were daily strengthening their position, commenced the construction of a four-gun battery on its summit, and on the right of the Green End road. On the 18th, he erected another for five guns. Its fire soon compelled the enemy to remove their encampment farther to the rear, and to construct new lines and batteries to protect themselves. On the 19th, a second line of approach was commenced; on the 22d, two other batteries, for five and seven guns, were constructed, as also a bomb-battery; and on the 25th, a third line of approach. The constant and well-directed fire from these several works was destructive, and Pigott found himself obliged to plant new batteries to silence it. There occasionally occurred skirmishing outside the works, and a point on Honeyman's Hill is mentioned as the scene of some bloodshed and strife, although partial and unimportant.

While the siege was thus being pressed with vigor, the fleet, on the 20th, returned in a crippled condition from the storm. Greene and Lafayette were dispatched by Sullivan on board to confer with D'Estaing, and propose a landing to the south-east of the town, where it was for the most part undefended. But the Admiral, apprehensive he might be shut in by Howe with a superior force to his own, and urging such as his instructions, in the event of his needing to refit, set sail on the 22d for Boston. This unexpected issue to an enterprise, from which so much had been anticipated, and which, if still prosecuted with vigor, seemed certain of success, produced dismay and almost consternation. Sullivan wrote D'Estaing the following letter of remonstrance and protest, signed by all the general officers. Lafayette was sent after him, and, from an idea that prevailed, that the Admiral was disposed to remain, but that his officers, from jealousy, had overruled him, the tone of the communication was warm and earnest:—

CAMP BEFORE NEWPORT, Aug. 22, 1778.

The general officers of the American army now on Rhode Island having, through their commander-in-chief in this department, represented to his excellency the Count d'Estaing the ruinous consequences which would result to this army from his abandoning the harbor of Newport at this time, and proceeding with his fleet to Boston; which representation, with many weighty reasons to induce him to remain at this post, he has been requested to lay before his officers, who seem, in general, to be of opinion that his fleet should proceed immediately to Boston, — esteem it their duty, as officers in the American army, as allies to his Most Christian Majesty, as officers concerned for the interest and honor of the French nation, and interested in the welfare of the United States, to enter their protest against the measures which his Excellency the Count d'Estaing is about to pursue.

First, Because the expedition against Rhode Island was undertaken by agreement with the Count d'Estaing. An army has been collected, and immense stores brought together, for the reduction of the garrison; all of which will be liable to be lost should he depart with his fleet, leave open the harbor for the enemy to receive re-enforcements from New York, and ships of war to cut off communication with the main, and totally prevent the retreat of the army.

Secondly, Because the proceeding of the fleet to Boston can answer no valuable purpose; as the injury it has received can be repaired much sooner here than at Boston, and the vessels secured against a superior naval force much better here than there.

Thirdly, Because there is the most apparent hazard in attempting to carry round Nantucket Shoals those ships which are disabled, and will, in all probability, end in the total loss of two of his Most Christian Majesty's ships of war.

Fourthly, Because the taking of dismasted ships out of port to receive their masts, instead of having their masts brought to them, is unwarranted by precedent, and unsupported by reason.

Fifthly, Because the honor of the French nation must be injured by their fleet abandoning their allies upon an island, in the midst of an expedition agreed to by the Count himself. This must make such an unfavorable impression on the minds of Americans at large, and create such jealousies between them and their hitherto esteemed allies, as will, in a great measure, frustrate the good intentions of his Most Christian Majesty and the American Congress, who have mutually endeavored to promote the greatest harmony and confidence between the French people and the Americans.

Sixthly, Because the apprehension of Admiral Byron's being upon the coast with a superior fleet is not well founded, as it wholly arises from the report of the master of a British merchantman, who says he was told by the " Greyhound" frigate that Admiral Byron was spoken with, the 24th of June, off the Western Islands; and accounts from England, up to the 24th of June, mentioned nothing of his having sailed: and more than eight weeks having elapsed since this fleet was said to be near the Western Islands, and no accounts having been had of their arrival in any part of America, it is evident that this relation must be false. As to the captains of two French ships supposing that they had discovered a three-decker, it is possible that, in the thick weather, they may have been deceived. But, even if they are not, it is by no means evident that this ship belonged to Byron's fleet: and, even if it did, it only proves that his fleet has been separated, and must rendezvous in some place before they can act; of which the French fleet cannot fail to have timely notice, and, before it is probable they can act, the garrison may be easily reduced.

Seventhly, Even if a superior fleet should arrive, the French fleet can be in no greater safety at Boston than at Rhode Island. It can as easily be blocked up in the former as the latter place, and be much easier defended in the latter than in the former.

Eighthly, The order said to be received from the King of France, for his fleet to retire to Boston in case of misfortune, cannot, without doing injustice to that wise and good monarch, be supposed to extend to the removal of his whole fleet, in the midst of an expedition, on account of an injury having happened to two or three of his ships.

Ninthly, Because, even though the facts pretended were fully proved, and it became necessary for the fleet to proceed to Boston, yet no possible reason can be assigned for the Count d'Estaing's taking with him the land forces which he has on board, and which might be of great advantage in the expedition, and of no possible use to him at Boston.

We therefore, for the reasons above assigned, do, in the most solemn manner, protest against the measure, as derogatory to the honor of France, contrary to the intentions of his Most Christian Majesty and the interest of his nation, and destructive in the highest degree to the welfare of the United States of America, and highly injurious to the alliance formed between the two nations.

What occurred has been so often misrepresented, that the following letter from Sullivan to Washington, the 3d of September, is given in explanation: —

PROVIDENCE, Sept. 3, 1778.

DEAR GENERAL, — I had last night the honor of receiving your Excellency's favor of the 1st instant, and impatiently wait your Excellency's sentiments on the steps I have taken since the 29th ultimo, an account of which has been transmitted by Major Morris.

The justice of the observations in your Excellency's letter, respecting the departure of the French fleet, are so obvious, that, if a consciousness of my duty to yield implicit obedience to your Excellency's commands did not even make that obedience a pleasure, the reasoning alone must have pointed out the part I have to act. I have the pleasure to inform your Excellency, that, though the first struggles of passion, on so important a disappointment, were scarcely to be restrained, yet, in a few days, as it subsided, I found means to restore the former harmony between the American and French officers of the army. The Count d'Estaing and myself are in the same friendship as heretofore. The reason of the protest has been explained to him, and he is now perfectly satisfied. He has offered to come on with his land forces, and do every thing which I may request of him and his troops; but the step has become unnecessary.

The reason of drawing the protest was this: The Count himself wished to remain with us, but was, by his captains, overruled in council. To have deviated from the advice of his council would have been attended with ill consequences to him, in case of misfortune. It was supposed that the protest might justify him in taking the part agreeable to his own sentiments and those of the co-operating army. Prudence dictated it as our duty to keep it secret from all but him, your Excellency, and Congress; and no publication of it was even thought of on our part, and your Excellency may rely on my exertions to prevent it. Every thing in my power shall be done for repairing the injury sustained by the French fleet. The fleet off Boston harbor, of which I gave your Excellency an account yesterday, are eight ships of the line, ten frigates, one sloop, and one schooner. There can be no doubt of its being Lord's Howe's fleet watching the motions of the French fleet, to facilitate the relief of Rhode Island, and perhaps cover the retreat of the British army from Rhode Island and New York, to other places where they are more needed. Those ships were out of sight yesterday morning at eight o'clock, but I hear they afterwards hove in sight again. The report here is, that six thousand troops have arrived at Newport I know they are numerous, but cannot, as yet, ascertain the number.

Your Excellency will please to transmit a copy of this letter to Congress; and believe me to be yours, &c.

To counteract, in some measure, the feeling of discouragement in his army from their disappointment, Sullivan, in general orders, expressed a hope, that the event would prove America able to procure, by her own arms, what her allies refused to assist her in obtaining.

He still had some encouragement to persevere; and, though adding little to the efficiency of his army, the militia and volunteers were still present in considerable numbers. It was, however, discovered, by the 26th, that many of them had become disheartened by the defection of the fleet; and, despairing of success, were returning home. Thus the effective force remaining was reduced to only fifty-four hundred men, but fifteen hundred of whom had ever been in action, while the garrison was much more numerous, and their fleet might at any moment return. Sullivan requested the written opinions of his general officers, whether they should prosecute the siege, attempt to take the works by storm at Easton's Beach, or retire. They recommended withdrawing to the end of the island, to await re-enforcements and the aid of the French, should their fleet be refitted in season to render it, or the land forces,* as proposed, march down from Boston.

Sullivan, accordingly, at six in the evening of the 28th, having previously sent off his heavy artillery and baggage, moved his army about eight miles, to Butt's Hill, which they gained before three o'clock in the morning, his right being posted on the west road, his left on the east, with covering parties on the flank, and light corps, under Livingstone, Laurens, Fleury, and Talbot, with Wade's picket, thrown forward about three miles in front.

At daybreak, Saturday morning, their retreat was discov-

---

* An officer of the fleet published, in 1782, an account of the voyage. He states the whole force of the French on board as ten thousand; of whom one-half, at least, could have been available on land.

ered. General Prescott, crossing Easton's Beach, occupied the deserted works, while the British in force started in pursuit; General Lossing, with the Voit and Seabote chasseur regiments, by the west road; General Smith, with the Twenty-second, Forty-third, and a portion of the Thirty-eighth and Fifty-fourth, re-enforced on their way by General Pigott, on the east. At seven, they came up with the American outposts, their left column engaging Major Talbot on the west road. On the east, the Twenty-second, Colonel Campbell, at the head of their right column, when near the Gibbs farm, six miles from Newport, divided, part continuing up the east road, part taking a cross road leading to the west. At this point, in a field bounded by these roads and another running north, lay in ambush a party of Americans awaiting their coming, who, leaping the walls, poured into their bewildered foes two deadly volleys, making great havoc in their ranks, and bringing down one-fourth of the regiment. Before the British could recover from their bewilderment, or receive support, which was immediately sent them, the Americans, according to their instructions, contesting the ground as they went, fell back on the main body. When the firing was heard at Butt's Hill, General Greene advised marching out to meet the British; but as our forces were not so numerous as theirs, had not been long enough together to be well in hand, and defeat would have been disastrous, with the water to cross, while the British, if overpowered, could easily regain Newport, it was thought best not to hazard it.

General Smith, pressing on, soon encountered General Glover, who repulsed him, and the enemy took possession of their works on Quaker Hill, the Hessian columns forming on the high ground which extends from that hill towards the north. By the time these two wings had united in this position, they had been strengthened by nearly all the British reserves. A mile farther north, separated by marshy meadow, interspersed with trees and copse, the main body of the

Americans were drawn up in three lines, the front on Butt's Hill, in advance of their works, the second behind them, and their reserve about half a mile farther back, near a creek.

A heavy cannonade commenced about nine, and lasted throughout the day. There was skirmishing between the advanced parties for the next hour, when two ships of war, and some light-armed vessels, coming up the bay, opened a fire on the American right, under cover of which the enemy endeavored to turn its flank, and storm an advanced redoubt. The action then became general along the line, and for nearly seven hours raged without intermission. The two armies were nearly matched in numbers, equally brave and resolute. The space was limited, and the carnage frightful. Down the slope of Anthony's Hill, the western continuation of Quaker Hill, the Hessian columns and British infantry twice rushed, but were driven back with great slaughter. Sixty were found dead in one spot; at another, thirty Hessians were buried in the same grave.

General Greene commanded on the right. Of the four brigades under his immediate command,— Varnum's, Cornell's, Glover's, and Greene's,—all suffered severely, but General Varnum's, perhaps, the most. A third time, the enemy undaunted, in greater force, attempted to assail the redoubt, and would have carried it, had not some continental battalions, which Sullivan ordered up, seasonably arrived to its relief. It was in repulsing these furious onsets that the newly raised black regiment, under Colonel Greene, distinguished itself by desperate valor. Posted behind a thicket in the valley, they thrice drove back the Hessians, who charged repeatedly down the hill to dislodge them; and so determined were the enemy in these successive charges, that the day after the battle the Hessian colonel, upon whom this duty devolved, applied to exchange his command and go to New York; stating as his reason that he dared not lead his regiment again to battle, lest his men should shoot him for having caused them so much loss.

Lovell's brigade of Massachusetts militia was at the same time engaged with the British right with good success. Two well-served batteries silenced the ships of war, and the British, at last giving way, were driven to their works on Quaker Hill, one of their batteries being captured. Sullivan was disposed to attack them in their lines; but his troops being completely exhausted, — having been thirty-six hours without rest or food, continually on the march, at labor in completing their defences, or in battle, — he was persuaded to defer it. Both armies occupied their camps; but, as the enemy had made the attack and were defeated, the Americans could reasonably claim it as a victory. The artillery kept up a cannonade till night-fall, but the battle was not renewed. The American loss was two hundred and eleven; the British has been stated to have amounted to one thousand and twenty-three, — nearly one-fifth of their force engaged. The contest was in a contracted space, under the immediate direction of Sullivan, and to him certainly belongs the credit accorded to the commander in a successful engagement. On his staff, that day, served two of his brothers, — Colonel Eben Sullivan, his aide-de-camp, and James, then at the age of thirty-four Judge of the Supreme Court of Massachusetts, and subsequently governor of that State, who had laid aside his judicial robes to volunteer on the expedition.

Early the next day, which was Sunday, despatches from Washington apprised Sullivan of Clinton's departure from New York, with re-enforcements for Newport of from four to five thousand men, and advised him to be on his guard. Measures were promptly taken to withdraw his troops from the island. General Glover, who had extricated the American army at Long Island two years before, collected boats and superintended this operation, which was effected without the slightest loss. Lafayette — who had ridden, in the saddle, seventy miles to Boston, in seven hours, to persuade D'Estaing to send down his land forces, and back in six hours and a half

— commanded the rear guard. On Monday, arrived at Newport the British re-enforcements.

"When we consider," says Arnold, the accomplished historian of Rhode Island, from whose account of the engagement — as the battle-field is in his neighborhood, and he has enjoyed peculiar advantages for obtaining, from those who were present, incidents of what took place — we have borrowed largely in the foregoing relation, "that, of the five thousand engaged in this battle, only about fifteen hundred had ever before been in action, and that they were opposed by veteran troops, superior both in number and discipline, with a degree of obstinacy rarely equalled in the annals of warfare, we can understand the remark said to have been made by Lafayette, in speaking of the battle at Rhode Island, that it was the best-fought action of the war."*

The day but one after the battle, — on Monday, the 31st August, — Sullivan wrote Congress the following account of what had taken place. As several particulars of interest, not mentioned in this despatch, have been, from time to time, obtained from other sources of information, the letter has been preceded by a general narrative of the expedition. For students of American history, as well as for the increasing number of intelligent people who, in summer, are attracted to the island by its proximity to the ocean, salubrity of climate, and natural charm, this minuteness of detail, even where involving some repetition, will not be objectionable:—

HEAD-QUARTERS, TIVERTON, Aug. 31, 1778.

ESTEEMED SIR, — Upon the Count d'Estaing's finding himself under a necessity of going to Boston to repair the loss he sustained in the late gale of wind, I thought it best to carry on my approaches with as much vigor as possible against Newport, that no time might be lost in making the attack upon the return of his fleet, or any part of it, to co-operate with us. I had sent expresses to the Count to hasten his return, which, I had no doubt, would at least bring part of his fleet to

---

* 2 Arnold, 437; 1 Charpentier, 418.

us in a few days. Our batteries played upon the enemy's works, for several days, with apparent good success; as the enemy's fire from the outworks visibly grew weaker, and they began to abandon some of those next us: and, on the 27th, we found they had removed their cannon from all the outworks except one. The town of Newport is defended by two lines, supported by several redoubts connected with the lines. The first of these lines extends from a large pond, called Easton Pond, near to Tomminy Hill, and then turns off to the water, on the north side of Windmill Hill. This line was defended by five redoubts in front. The second line is more than a quarter of a mile within this, and extends from the sea to the north side of the island, terminating at the north battery. On the south, at the entrance by Easton's Beach, where this line terminates, is a redoubt which commands the pass, and has another redoubt about twenty rods on the north. There are a number of small works interspersed between the lines, which render an attack extremely hazardous on the land side, without a naval force to co-operate with it. I, however, should have attempted carrying the works by storm, as soon as I found they had withdrawn their cannon from their outworks, had I not found, to my great surprise, that the volunteers, which composed great part of my army, had returned, and reduced my numbers to little more than that of the enemy. Between two and three thousand returned in the course of twenty-four hours, and others were still going off, upon a supposition that nothing could be done before the return of the fleet. Under these circumstances, and the apprehension of the arrival of an English fleet, with a re-enforcement to relieve the garrison, I sent away, to the main, all the heavy articles that could be spared from the army; also, a large party was detached to get the works in repair on the north end of the island, to throw up some additional ones, and put in good repair the batteries at Tiverton and Bristol, to secure a retreat in case of necessity. On the 28th, a council was called, in which it was unanimously determined to remove to the north end of the island, fortify our camp, secure our communication with the main, and hold our ground on the island till we could know whether the French fleet would soon return to our assistance.

On the evening of the 28th, we moved, with our stores and baggage, which had not been previously sent forward, and, about two in the morning, encamped on Butt's Hill, with our right extending to the west road, and left to the east road; the flanking and covering parties still farther towards the water, on right and left. One regiment was

posted in a redoubt advanced off the right of the first line; Colonel
Henry B. Livingston, with a light corps, consisting of Colonel Jackson's
detachment and a detachment from the army, was stationed in the
east road. Another light corps, under command of Colonel Laurens,
Colonel Fleury, and Major Talbot, was posted on the west road.
These corps were posted nearly three miles in front: in the rear of
these was the picket of the army, commanded by Colonel Wade. The
enemy, having received intelligence of our movement, came out, early
in the morning, with nearly their whole force, in two columns, advanced
in the two roads, and attacked our light corps. They made a brave
resistance, and were supported for some time by the picket. I ordered
a regiment to support Colonel Livingston, another to support Colonel
Laurens, and, at the same time, sent them orders to retire to the main
army in the best order they could. They kept up a retreating fire
upon the enemy, and retired, in excellent order, to the main army.
The enemy advanced on our left very near, but were repulsed by General Glover. Then they retired to Quaker Hill. The Hessian column
formed on a chain of hills running northward from Quaker Hill. Our
army was drawn up, the first line in front of the works on Butt's Hill;
the second, in rear of the hill; and the reserve, near a creek, and nearly
half a mile in rear of the first line. The distance between those hills
is about one mile. The ground between the hills is meadow-land, interspersed with trees and small copse of wood. The enemy began a
cannonade upon us about nine in the morning, which was returned with
double force. Skirmishing continued between the advanced parties
until near ten o'clock, when the enemy's two ships of war and some
small armed vessels, having gained our right flank and began a fire, the
enemy bent their whole force that way, and endeavored to turn our
right, under cover of the ship's fire, and to take the advanced redoubt
on the right. They were twice driven back in great confusion; but a
third trial was made with greater numbers and with more resolution,
which, had it not been for the timely aid sent forward, would have
succeeded. A sharp contest of nearly an hour ensued, in which the
cannon from both armies, placed on the hills, played briskly in support
of their own party. The enemy were at length routed, and fled, in
great confusion, to the hill where they first formed, and where they had
artillery and some works to cover them; leaving their dead and
wounded, in considerable numbers, behind them. It was impossible to
ascertain the number of dead on the field, as it could not be approached
by either party without being exposed to the cannon of the other

army. Our party recovered about twenty of their wounded, and took nearly sixty prisoners, according to the best accounts I have been able to collect. Among the prisoners is a lieutenant of grenadiers. The number of their dead I have not been able to ascertain, but know them to be very considerable. An officer informs me, that, in one place, he counted sixty of their dead. Colonel Campbell came out the next day to gain permission to view the field of action, to search for his nephew, who was killed by his side; whose body he could not get off, as they were closely pursued. The firing of artillery continued through the day, the musketry with intermission of six hours. The heat of the action continued near an hour; which must have ended in the ruin of the British army, had not their redoubts on the hill covered them from farther pursuit. We were about to attack them in their lines; but the men having had no rest the night before, and nothing to eat either that night or the day of the action, and having been in constant action through most of the day, it was not thought advisable, especially as their position was exceedingly strong, and their numbers fully equal, if not superior, to ours. Not more than fifteen hundred of my troops had ever been in action before. I should before have taken possession of the hill they occupied, and fortified it; but it is no defence against an enemy coming from the south part of the island, though exceedingly good against one advancing from the north end towards the town, and had been fortified by the enemy for that purpose.

I have the pleasure to inform Congress, that no troops could possibly show more spirit than those of ours which were engaged. Colonel Livingston, and all the officers of the light corps, behaved with remarkable spirit. Colonels Laurens, Fleury, and Major Talbot, with the officers of that corps, behaved with great gallantry. The brigades of the first line — Varnum's, Glover's, Cornell's, and Greene's — behaved with great firmness. Major-General Greene, who commanded in the attack on the right, did himself the highest honor, by the judgment and bravery exhibited in the action. One brigade only of the second line was brought to action, commanded by Brigadier-General Lovell. He, and his brigade of militia, behaved with great resolution. Colonel Crane and the officers of the artillery deserve the highest praise. I inclose Congress a return of the killed, wounded, and missing on our side; and beg leave to assure them, that, from my own observation, the enemy's loss must be much greater. Our army retired to camp after the action; the enemy employed themselves, through the night, in fortifying their camp.

In the morning of the 30th, I received a letter from his Excellency General Washington, giving me notice that Lord Howe had again sailed with the fleet; and receiving intelligence, at the same time, that a fleet was off Block Island, and also a letter from Boston, informing me that the Count d'Estaing could not come round so soon as I expected, a council was called, and, as we could have no prospect of operating against Newport with success without the assistance of a fleet, it was unanimously agreed to quit the island until the return of the French squadron.

To make a retreat in the face of an enemy, equal, if not superior, in number, and cross a river, without loss, I knew was an arduous task, and seldom accomplished if attempted. As our sentries were within two hundred yards of each other, I knew it would require the greatest care and attention. To cover my design from the enemy, I ordered a number of tents to be brought forward, and pitched in sight of the enemy, and almost the whole army to employ themselves in fortifying the camp. The heavy baggage and stores were falling back and crossing through the day; at dark, the tents were struck, and the light baggage and troops passed down; and, before twelve o'clock, the main army had crossed, with the stores and baggage. The Marquis de Lafayette arrived, about eleven in the evening, from Boston; where he had been, by request of the general officers, to solicit the speedy return of the fleet. He was sensibly mortified that he was out of action; and, that he might not be out of the way in case of action, he had ridden hence to Boston in seven hours, and returned in six and a half, — the distance nearly seventy miles. He returned in time enough to bring off the pickets and other parties which covered the retreat of the army, which he did in excellent order: not a man was left behind, nor the smallest article lost.

I hope my conduct through this expedition may merit the approbation of Congress. Major Morris, one of my aids, will have the honor of delivering this to your Excellency. I must beg leave to recommend him to Congress as an officer who, in the last as well as several other actions, has behaved with great spirit and good conduct; and doubt not Congress will take such notice of him as his long service and spirited conduct deserves.

P.S. — The event has proved how timely my retreat took place, as one hundred sail of the enemy's ships arrived in the harbor on the morning after the retreat. I should do the highest injustice if I neglected to mention, that Brigadier-General Cornell's indefatigable industry in preparing for the expedition, and his good conduct through the whole, merit particular notice. Major Talbot, who assisted in preparing the boats, and afterwards served in Colonel Laurens's corps, deserves great praise.

If disappointed, the failure of this expedition was from no fault of Sullivan. In the estimation of the unreflecting, who possess no other criterion of merit but success, he may be censured for not effecting impossibilities. Washington himself, judged by the same standard, came near falling a victim to unreasonable prejudice.

General Greene, always the steadfast friend of Sullivan as of Washington, was ready to acknowledge his good generalship on this as on all other occasions. Emulation in the cause for which they both were gallantly and effectively contending, never degenerated into rivalry, or disturbed their friendly relations. On the 6th of September, he wrote to John Brown: —

SIR, — In all republican governments, every person that acts in a public capacity must naturally expect to have observations and strictures made upon his conduct. This is a tax generally laid, under all free governments, upon their officers, either civil or military, however meritorious. I am not surprised to hear the late unsuccessful expedition against Newport fall under some degree of censure; but I must confess that I am not a little astonished to hear, from such a principal character in society as yourself, illiberal reflections against a gentleman, merely because his measures did not coincide with your opinion.

This expedition was planned upon no other consideration than that of the French fleet co-operating with the American troops. The strength of the garrison was considered, and a force ordered to be levied accordingly, that might be sufficient to complete its reduction. In forming the estimate, the aid of the fleet, and the assistance of 3,500 French forces on board the fleet, were taken into consideration. The loss of this force, and of the aid of the fleet, was a sufficient reason for abandoning the expedition.

You say you think it was ill planned, and worse conducted, and, in the first place, that the forces were drawn together at an improper place. I must beg leave to dissent from you in this opinion. Was there any time lost by the Continental troops coming to Providence?

There was not; for they were all collected there some days before the militia. Would it not have been extremely difficult, if not absolutely impossible, for the forces to act in concert, — one body being at Tiverton, and the other at Boston Neck? Divided, they would have been unequal to the descent. If either party was sufficient of itself, the other was superfluous. Besides the objections to a division and the distance apart, there are two other objections against the measure. One was the difficulty of embarking a body of troops from that rugged shore, the delays that storms and high winds might produce, the accidents that might happen in crossing where there is usually a heavy swell, and the danger that sea-sickness would unfit the men for action. The other, that there were no stores or magazines of any kind at South Kingston to equip and furnish the troops; besides which, it was necessary for the General to have all his troops together, that he might select out the men and officers suitable for the enterprise. If the troops had been collected at South Kingston, it would have too fully explained our intention, and put the enemy upon their guard. Whereas, landing upon the north end of the island led the enemy into a belief that we intended to carry the garrison by regular approaches; which would have given us an opportunity of re-embarking the troops, and landing upon the south part of the island, without being mistrusted. This was the plan of attack; and it might have succeeded, had our strength been sufficient and the disembarkation covered by the fleet.

You cannot suppose that General Sullivan wants spirit or ambition to attempt any thing that reason or common sense can justify. It is the business of every general officer, desirous of distinguishing himself, to court all opportunities to engage with the enemy, when the situation and condition of his own forces and that of theirs will admit of it; but the safety of our country is a greater object, with every man of principle, than present glory.

Before a general officer engages in any hazardous enterprise, he should well consider the consequences of success and failure, — whether the circumstances of the community will not render one infinitely more prejudicial than the other can be beneficial. The strength and quality of the troops to be attacked should be considered; how they can best be approached, and by what means a retreat be secured. He has also to take into consideration the number and quality of his own troops, how they are found, what temper they are of, whether they are regular or irregular, and how they are officered. Even the wind and weather are necessary considerations, and not to be neglected.

I have known people foolish enough to insist that it was only necessary for a general to lead on his forces to ensure success, without regard to the strength or situation of the enemy, or the number or goodness of his own troops. Those that have often been in action only can judge what is to be expected of good, bad, and indifferent troops. Men are often struck with panic; and they are generally subject to that passion, in a greater or less degree, according as discipline has formed the mind, by habit, to meet danger and death. Many a man has gone from home with a determined resolution to meet the enemy, that has shamefully quitted the field from want of habitual fortitude. Men often feel courageous at a distance from danger, that faint through fear when they come to be exposed to it. Pride and sentiment support the officer; habit and enthusiasm, the soldier. Without these, there is no safe reliance upon men.

I remember you recommended an attempt to effect a landing upon the south part of the island, the night we returned from the fleet; but I could not possibly suppose you to be serious, because it was impossible for us to get the boats round seasonably, draw out the men and officers proper for the descent, and effect a landing, before day. It was therefore impracticable, if it had been ever so eligible. But I am far from thinking, under our circumstances, the measure would have been justifiable by reason or common sense, in a common view; much less by military maxims. The day after the fleet sailed, a great change took place in the two armies, but particularly in ours, whose spirits all drooped upon the departure of the fleet, except the few regular troops, and it had its effect upon them. They felt that nothing could be attempted with any hope of success; whereas the garrison in Newport, that before gave themselves up for lost, now collected new courage, and would have defended themselves with double obstinacy.

Suppose General Sullivan had attempted a landing, and actually effected it, and the garrison had defeated his troops, what would have been the consequence? The whole would have been made prisoners; and not only the party that landed, but all those that remained in camp, taken, with all our stores of every kind. Was the object important enough for such a risk? Was the chance equal of our succeeding? Every one that will suffer himself to reflect a moment will readily agree, that neither the importance of the object nor the chance of succeeding would have warranted the attempt. It must be confessed, the loss of such a garrison would have given the British army a deadly wound; but the loss of our army would have put our cause in jeopardy. Remember the effect of the loss of the garrison of Fort Washington. There were men enough there to have defended themselves against all the British army, had they not been struck with panic; but, being most of them irregular troops, they lost all confidence when the danger began to grow pressing, and fell a prey to their fears.

But when you take into consideration the little prospect of our effecting a landing, where there were batteries almost all round the shores, and the enemy had cutters to intercept any attempt, as also guard-boats to discover them, the measure would look more like madness than rational conduct.

There was another objection: our force was wholly inadequate. The party detached to make the landing should have been superior to the whole garrison. That left in camp to cover the stores, and co-operate occasionally with the detachment after they had effected a landing, should have been equally strong. Either might have been so circumstanced as to render it necessary to be able, independent of the other, to resist the whole British garrison. If the party landed had not been superior to the garrison, and been defeated, having no ships to cover their retreat, all would have been lost. Or if, during the embarkation, the garrison had made an attack upon the troops left in the camp, they would have been put to rout, and made prisoners, and all our cannon and stores captured.

These are common and probable events in war, and to be guarded against accordingly. The garrison at Newport was generally thought to be 6,000 strong, including sailors. Our force amounted to almost 9,000; indeed, the field-returns made it but 8,174, and the much greater part of these militia: but I would swell it to the utmost extent, and still you see it will fall far short of the necessary number to warrant the measure, even supposing ours to have been all regular troops. And here I cannot help remarking, that some people seem desirous of deceiving themselves with regard to our strength. They rather incline to credit the votes of Assembly, and the resolves of councils of war, with regard to numbers, than returns actually taken upon the ground. Some assert, that our strength must have been much greater than appears by our returns from the number of rations that were drawn. I remember very well, last winter, at Valley Forge, our army drew 32,000 rations, when the most we could muster for duty was but 7,500 men; and, in all irregular armies, there will be, generally, a third more rations drawn than in a well-appointed one for the same effective strength. No safe conclusion can be drawn from the rations:

their being greater or less is no evidence of the real strength of an army.

I am further informed, that you think this expedition the worst concerted and executed of the war. I differ widely from you in opinion. I think it prudently concerted, and honorably and faithfully executed. If the General had attempted to storm the lines, he would have met with disastrous defeat. It has been urged, that, because the Northern army carried Burgoyne's lines, these might have been attempted with equal success; not adverting to the difference of circumstances. These lines were ten times as strong as those of Burgoyne; besides which, the enemy came out of their lines there, and our people drove them back again, and entered, pell mell, with them. Burgoyne's force was much less than this garrison, his troops much dispirited, the army that surrounded them more than as strong again as ours in regular troops.

Remember the loss of the British army before Ticonderoga, last war, in attempting to storm lines, inconsiderable compared with the fortifications at Newport, and defended with a less number of men in the works than were here; recollect the fate of the British army at Bunker's Hill, attacking slight works, defended by new-levied troops; consider the disgrace and defeat that happened to the Hessians in the attack upon the inconsiderable redoubt at Red Bank, — and then judge what prospect General Sullivan had of success in making an attack, with an army composed, principally, of raw militia, upon a garrison as strong as that at Newport; consisting, almost wholly, of regular troops, and fortified so securely as they were. There was but one possible mode of attack, — by storm, — which was proposed to the General; but the men necessary for the attempt could not be found, and consequently the attack could not be made.

I am told you censure General Sullivan for not bringing on a general action, and urge my opinion as a proof of the propriety. I remember you asked me, when you were at the island, on the evening of the day of the battle, why there had not been a general action. I told you, that I had advised one in the morning; but that I believed the General had taken the more prudent measure. He had fought them by detachment, defeated and disgraced them, without running any great risk.

Our numbers, at the time we left the enemy's lines, were not much superior to the garrison. We knew they expected a re-enforcement hourly. Had any considerable force arrived the night we retreated, landed, and marched out with the old garrison, we should have met with a defeat. The smallness of our numbers, the dispirited state of all troops on a retreat, together with the probability of the enemy's having received a re-enforcement, determined the General not to risk a general action, when he was sure of advantage by keeping on the defensive. By risking a general action, he exposed the whole of the troops to ruin, and he thought the other measure more advisable. Both of us, upon cool reflection, so think now, although I thought otherwise at the time.

I have seen as much service, almost, as any man in the American army, and have been in as many or more actions than any one; I know the character of all our general officers, as well as any one; and, if I am any judge, the expedition has been prudently and well conducted: and I am confident there is not a general officer, from the Commander-in-chief to the youngest in the field, that would have gone greater lengths, to have given success to the expedition, than General Sullivan. He is sensible, active, ambitious, brave, and persevering in his temper; and the object was sufficiently important to make him despise every difficulty opposed to his success, as far as he was at liberty to consult his own reputation: but the public good is of higher importance than personal glory, and the one is not to be gratified at the risk and expense of the other. I recollect your observation when on board the fleet, — that the reputation of the principal officers depended upon the success of the expedition. I have long since learned to despise vulgar prejudices, and to regulate my conduct by maxims more noble than popular sentiment. I have an honest ambition of meriting the approbation of the public; but I will never act contrary to my judgment, or violate my honor or convictions, for temporary repute.

If the Congress, or any particular State which intrusts their troops under my command, thinks proper to give orders to run all risks and hazards to occupy a point, I should cheerfully lead on the men; but, where left discretionary, I must act agreeably to the dictates of my own judgment.

People, from consulting their wishes, rather than their reason, and by forming an estimate of the spirit and firmness of irregular troops more from general orders sounding their praise, than from any particular knowledge of their conduct, are led to expect more from such troops, than is in the power of any person to effect.

I would also remark, that an attack with militia, in an open country where they could retire after defeat, might be very prudent, which would be very rash and unwarrantable upon an island.

I have written this much in justification of one whom I esteem a good officer, and who, I think, is much more deserving your thanks than reproach, as well as that of the public. With regard to myself, it was unnecessary for me tó say any thing in justification of the measure of assembling the troops at Providence. I had no voice in it: neither was I opposed to a storm, providing a proper number of men, of a suitable quality, could be found fit for the attempt. My advice for a general action, I think, was wrong; and the retreat that followed, everybody must allow, was necessary, and that it was well conducted.

I have been told, that your brother Nicholas let fall some very ungenerous insinuations with regard to me, a few days before the action upon the island. These are the rewards and gracious returns I am to expect, for years of hard and dangerous service, when every sacrifice of interest, ease, and domestic pleasure has been made to the service of my country. I flatter myself I am not dependent upon the State of Rhode Island for either my character or consequence in life. Yet I cannot help feeling mortified that those who have been at home making their fortunes, and living in the lap of luxury, and enjoying all the pleasures of domestic life, should be the first to sport with the feelings of officers who have stood as a barrier between them and ruin.

On the 17th of September, on motion of Mr. Marchant, Congress resolved that the retreat was prudent, timely, and well conducted; and that their thanks be given to General Sullivan, and to the officers and troops under his command, for their fortitude and bravery displayed in the action of Aug. 29th, in which they repulsed the British forces, and maintained the field. Complimentary votes of acknowledgment were passed also by the Legislatures of Rhode Island and New Hampshire. Mr. Marchant, in communicating to Sullivan the resolves of Congress, writes as follows: —

Sir, — I have to congratulate you upon the acknowledged generalship which you displayed in the late expedition against Rhode Island. Not to you, sir, or the brave troops under your command, is to be attributed the failing in the full success which appearances at first gave us rational expectations of. I resolve that unto those accidents, or rather counsels of Divine Providence, which are often for good and wise purposes hid from human investigation; and so resolving, I wish we may humbly submit, thankful that it pleased Heaven in the midst of severe disappointment to crown our lives with laurels of honor. I did myself the honor of bringing into Congress such resolutions upon that occasion as I thought wise, due from the public to your zeal and bravery and good conduct, and that display of fortitude and spirit which animates the officers and troops. Those resolutions, with some several alterations, were passed. They are contained in the paper inclosed. I shall not fail to inform the State I have the honor to represent, of the justice you have done to their great exertions and the interest you take in procuring them some relief from their enormous burdens. I assure you, sir, I feel myself interested in whatever affects either your honor or happiness, and it shall ever be my study to promote both while you are thus eminently continuing to merit them; and I doubt not you will find your reward in a grateful country.

General Sullivan continued in command at Rhode Island during the following winter. When he was called to a more active field of service, " a meeting was held in Providence to express the feeling of respect entertained for this favorite general, and addresses were also presented to him from the officers in the state military, medical and staff, and also from the order of Freemasons. A voluntary escort attended his departure as far as Johnston, where a public dinner was given him by his late companions-in-arms."

As but fifteen years had elapsed since Great Britain, by the aid of her colonies, wrested Canada from France, the hope of regaining it naturally mingled in the motives which prompted the alliance. After the capture of Burgoyne, in 1777, measures had been concerted for an expedition in that direction, and in the following year another was proposed from Albany, of which Lafayette was to have taken command. But the resources of the country being completely exhausted by the vigorous exertions of 1777 and 1778, the army reduced to about sixteen thousand men, of whom three thousand were in New England, our financial condition utterly deplorable, the plan was necessarily abandoned, and Lafayette went home. This was, upon the whole, fortunate; for had success attended the co-operation of France, she might have claimed that the province should be restored to herself. For more than a century, she had contended with Great Britain for her American possessions; and some of her statesmen considered the conjuncture propitious to satisfy wounded pride, and regain her lost dominion.

After a conference at Philadelphia with a committee of Congress, as to what should be attempted in the ensuing campaign, Washington, on the 15th January, 1779, stated to them his conclusions in writing. As no reasonable expectation could be entertained of collecting sufficient forces for an attack to advantage on New York or Rhode Island, and the invasion of Canada was too hazardous and expensive, he advised the strictest economy in all branches of public expenditure, that the efficiency of the army should rather be increased by discipline and organization than by numbers, and that, by improving the condition of officers and soldiers, the service should be rendered popular. While prepared to seize any opportunity that might be presented, they should remain on the defensive, except such lesser operations against the Indians as would protect the frontier from their ravages. Should the British troops, as was in contemplation, be withdrawn to the Southern States, whose staples supported the war, the invasion of Canada might become feasible; and he says, that he had already directed preparations to be made against such a contingency. His advice was adopted; and, Schuyler and Gates declining, the command of an expedition against the Five Nations,— Mohawks, Senecas, Oneidas, Cayugas, and Onondagas,— to be pushed, if warranted by events, against Canada, by way of Niagara, a fort whence the Indians drew their supplies, was accepted by Sullivan.

Sullivan immediately proceeded to headquarters to consult with Washington, and the day following their conference addressed him as follows:—

MAY IT PLEASE YOUR EXCELLENCY, — I have examined and compared the several maps with the written accounts of the Indian country, which were laid before me by your Excellency, and have considered the plan of the expedition proposed: and beg leave to make the following observations, viz. : —

That though the number of Indians in that country appears, from information, to be but about 2,000, yet underrating the number of the enemy has been a prevailing error with the Americans since the commencement of the war. This is ever a source of misfortune, and has to some armies proved fatal. As in no instance it could be more dangerous than in the present intended expedition, it will be necessary to consider whether there is not a probability of the enemy being more numerous than General Schuyler's account makes them. It is indeed probable he may have obtained nearly a just account of the number of Indians in each tribe; but it is impossible that he should have gained an accurate account of the number of Tories and fresh volunteers who have joined the parties commanded by Butler and their other leaders. I therefore conclude that his account can only respect the Indians inhabiting the part of the country to be invaded; if so, the number of the enemy which may be expected to oppose our force must far exceed his account.

The enemy are now possessed of an opinion that an expedition is intended against Canada, by way of Lake Ontario. This may probably induce them to send all the force they can possibly spare from Canada to act in conjunction with the armed vessels, to oppose our passing from the Mohawk into the river Iroquois through the Lakes; but, should the demonstrations in the Cohoes country puzzle and perplex them, it can only serve to keep them in Canada, until the real intention is known, which will happen as soon as the main body of the army is found on the Susquehannah. They will then undoubtedly turn their whole force to defeat that party which passes up the Mohawk, that they may be the better enabled to combat the other which advances by the Susquehannah. Should, therefore, the party which advances by the Mohawk be small, they must, if they advance far into the country, be cut off; and, if they do not advance, little or no advantage can be derived from it. I am therefore clearly of opinion, that the main body should advance by that route, and the smaller party by the Susquehannah; though this last party should be at least equal to the estimated force of the Indian nations. If this is the case, they must carry conquest before them, as they can have no other force to engage, but what is derived from the Indians themselves. The force of the other party should be nearly equal to the collective force of the Indians, and that of the Britons and Tories, which may probably be detached from Canada: I say nearly equal, because it cannot be doubted but the advance of the party up the Susquehannah will demand the attention of some of the nations who live nearest Tioga.

It has been objected that the retreat of the main body may be cut off, if they pass up the Mohawk and down to Cayuga Lake; but this objection applies with much greater force and propriety to sending a small party that way. It has been said, that, in case of misfortune, a retreat may be better made by the Susquehannah, than by the Mohawk. This is an argument much in favor of the smaller body passing that way. But the main body should be of sufficient force to command victory wherever they go, and to form a junction with the Susquehannah party at all events. The largeness of the party will much distract the enemy, as they cannot know, until it arrives at the fork of the river, near Lake Ontario, whether the real design is against Canada or the Indian nations.

The party advancing by the Susquehannah may probably be considered as destined to make a feint to keep the Indians at home; but should it be considered intended to destroy the Indian country, it will actually have this effect, give the main body an opportunity to defeat with ease all parties which may be sent against it from Canada, and form a junction with the Susquehannah party between Cayuga Lake and Chemung, which two places are but forty miles distant from each other. There will be an additional advantage in the main body coming this way, as it will come in the rear of the enemy, and prevent their retreat to Niagara. Should the main body advance by the Susquehannah, it will come in front of the enemy, and give them an opportunity to retreat in any direction they think proper; especially as the smaller part of the army, should it advance by the Mohawk, must move with great caution and deliberation lest their retreat should be cut off, and the party subjected to a total defeat. But should the main body advance that way confident of its own superiority, they will move with that necessary firmness which consciousness of superiority seldom fails to inspire; and of course they will be more likely to cut off the retreat of the Indians, and give them a fatal blow. The smaller party, being sure of a retreat, may move without that danger to which it would be exposed on the other route, and much sooner co-operate with the main body.

Besides, let me observe, that, as the party which advances by the Mohawk will have the enemy on all sides, it would be bad policy, as well as contrary to every military rule, to suffer that party to be the smallest. The number of troops to be sent by the Susquehannah should in my opinion be 2,500, which, when the posts for magazines are established at Augusta, Wyoming, Wyalusing, and Tioga, will be reduced to less than 2,000. The party sent by the Mohawk should consist of 4,000, which, by draughts for boatmen, provisions guards, and a detachment to make a feint at Cherry Valley, will be reduced nearly to 3,000. With this force the business may be effectually done, and with such expedition as will prevent the enemy from escaping, and in the end will be attended with much less expense than a smaller party.

As this expedition is intended to cut off these Indian nations, and to convince others that we have it in our power to carry the war into their own country whenever they commence hostilities, it will be necessary that the blow should be sure and fatal; otherwise they will derive confidence from our ineffectual attempts, and become more insolent than before. If, therefore, the circumstances of the army and country will not admit of a proper force, it will be much better not to make the attempt, than to make an ineffectual one. With respect to supplies by way of Albany, it is a great flour country, and a sufficiency of live stock may be procured from Connecticut and other parts, and forage may be had with as little difficulty there, as by way of Susquehannah. Besides this, as the army must embark on the Susquehannah at Augusta, it will not be so long a route from the well-inhabited country on the Mohawk to the centre of the Indian settlements, as from Augusta to Chemung.

In order that the main army may suffer as little as possible from a deduction of force, I would propose, that, in addition to the force already mentioned, Poor's brigade should be taken from Connecticut, where they are not wanted, and Glover's from Providence, the place of which may be supplied by State troops stipulated by the New-England States. And, in addition to these, some militia might be ordered for three months, to complete the number proposed.

The next day he wrote again to Washington: —

DEAR GENERAL, — As your Excellency has honored me with an appointment to command the intended expedition, I must beg leave to lay my sentiments before you in writing; as words used in conver sation may vanish in air, and the remembrance of them be lost, while writing will remain to justify my opinion, or prove it erroneous. The variety of reasons which I urged yesterday, for passing with the main body up the Mohawk River, and down by Wood Creek, to the Cayuga Lake, still have their weight in my mind; but as General Schuyler writes that they cannot be supplied with provisions, the plan must be given up, and that of passing with the main body up the Susquehannah adopted. The force which I have requested for that quarter is 3,000 effective men; after all proper deductions are made for guards at the several posts, for boatmen, hospital guards, tenders.

That these troops should be collected before we enter the Indian country, appears to me essentially necessary, as it is supposed that the principal opposition we shall meet with will be between Wyoming and Tioga. Should this be the case, as seemed to be the general opinion in Council yesterday, we can derive no advantage from the party on the Mohawk, as they are not to join us until we have established a post at Tioga. Should they attempt to join us before, they must be defeated in passing down the Susquehannah; and should our numbers be such as will admit of a defeat before we arrive at Tioga, as we can have no communication with the other party, and they are to regulate themselves by a plan fixed before we march, they will remain ignorant of our defeat, and, proceeding at the time appointed, in all probability fall into the hands of the enemy. If we are to expect the principal opposition before we arrive at Tioga, we cannot reckon, as any part of our force, troops which are not to join us before we have passed the principal danger. Indeed, I have no great dependence upon the advantages to be derived from so small a party in that quarter. It was yesterday said, that we might expect 1,400 Indians to oppose us on our march. Your Excellency will permit me to say, that 1,400 Indians perfectly acquainted with the country, capable of seizing any advantage which the ground can possibly afford, familiar with the use of arms, inured to war from their youth, and from their manner of living capable of enduring every kind of fatigue, are no despicable enemy, when opposed to 3,000 troops, totally unacquainted with the country and the Indian manner of fighting, and who, though excellent in the field, are far from having that exactness with firearms, or that alertness in a woody country, which Indians have.

So many facts have contributed to prove this, it will be unnecessary for me to say more upon the subject. If I was not a party concerned in the expedition, and my opinion was asked of the force necessary to insure success, I should advise, that the force of each party should be equal to the highest estimate of the enemy's force, that they might be able to form a junction at all events, and put the matter beyond the possibility of a doubt; and thus they would be enabled to detach and conquer the country in an eighth part of the time that they would, if obliged for their own security to keep in a body. I know that the force of the Indians is estimated as inconsiderable; but when I consider, that underrating the number of the enemy has been a prevailing error with us since the commencement of the war, that we have had persons from among them, inhabitants and deserters, have had the proceedings, debates, and calculations of Parliament before us, and yet have repeatedly mistaken their numbers more than one half, I cannot suppose but that we are still liable to fall into the same error where we can have no evidence, and every thing told us respecting them is mere matter of opinion.

Let me, moreover, repeat what I observed to you yesterday, that there is some probability of a force being sent from Canada, to prevent our passing into Canada by way of Lake Ontario. When our advance upon the Susquehannah is known, it will probably be conjectured that our intention is against Niagara, which will induce the enemy strongly to re-enforce that post. This they may do in a fortnight, as it is but a hundred and ten miles from Montreal to Oswegatchie, and their vessels can take troops from thence to Niagara in three or four days. When they find our intention is against the Indian settlements, these troops will undoubtedly join them. From these considerations, it must appear that the demand I have made is far from being unreasonable, even exclusive of the party sent on their flanks. I well know that Continental troops cannot be spared for this purpose, but good militia should undoubtedly be called for. This expedition is undertaken to destroy *these* Indian nations, and to convince others that we have it in our power to carry the war into their country whenever they commence hostilities. Should we fail in the attempt, the Indians will derive confidence from it, and grow more insolent than before.

Thus have I submitted my sentiments to your Excellency, and trust that my reasoning upon the subject must prove, that 3,000 good and effective men, at least, will be necessary to march from Tioga; exclusive of those which your Excellency may think proper to direct to operate on the other flank of the enemy.

He wrote two weeks later, on the 29th of April, to Governor Clinton, of New York: —

DEAR SIR, — I take the liberty of communicating to you, in confidence, that I am to have the honor of commanding an expedition against the Indians of the Six Nations.

The main body of our army is to move up the Susquehannah to Tioga; the York troops are to march up to Canojoharie, take batteaux across land into Otsego Lake, pass down the Susquehannah, and form a junction with the main army at Tioga, which is at the mouth of the Cayuga branch of the Susquehannah. As the York regiments are very weak, and as it may be necessary for that party to be of sufficient strength to repel every effort of the Indians, I submit it to your judgment, whether it will not be necessary to have your regiments so far filled up by drafts, or otherwise, as to enable them to force their way at all events, and to destroy on their march such Indian settlements as may be near the river. As it is a matter of the utmost importance to the States in general, and to yours in particular, to have these Indians totally rooted out, I doubt not you will give every assistance in your power towards augmenting the strength of the party; and also towards supplying them with the necessary provisions, as I fear the commissaries may disappoint us in that article. I must intreat every assistance in your Excellency's power, and that you will keep the contents of this letter a profound secret.

Without loss of time, Sullivan proceeded to Easton to expedite preparations. His correspondence with Washington, President Reed, and the Quartermaster's Department, prove that he spared no effort to carry out with despatch and thoroughness the duty assigned him. From the exhausted state of the country, supplies were not very speedily forthcoming, and he occasionally used phrases which were deemed importunate; but the sequel proved that his estimate was correct as to what the exigencies of the service demanded. His movements depended upon others, and there were the usual delays and disappointments attending such enterprises; but, not discouraged, many obstacles in his path were avoided or overcome, and the despatch was certainly beyond all reasonable expectation. Directions for the conduct of the campaign from the commander-in-chief, dated May 31, 1779, reached him after he had promulgated his own orders to the army. These instructions, as received by him, were as follows, the passages in brackets being omitted by Mr. Sparks, in his collection of Washington's Writings, vol. vi., p. 264:—

SIR,— The expedition you are appointed to command is to be directed against the hostile tribes of the Six Nations of Indians, with their associates and adherents. The immediate object is their *total destruction* and devastation, and the capture of as many persons of every age and sex as possible. [It will be essential to ruin their crops now in the ground, and prevent their planting more.]

The troops to be employed are Clinton, Maxwell, Poor, and Hand's brigades, and the independent companies raised in the State of Pennsylvania. In Hand's brigade, I comprehend all the detached corps of Continental troops now on the Susquehannah, and Spencer's regiment. Cortland's I consider as belonging to Clinton's brigade. Alden's may go to Poor's, and Butler's and the rifle corps to Maxwell's or Hand's, according to circumstances. Clinton's brigade, you are informed, has been ordered to rendezvous at Canojoharie, subject to your orders, either to form a junction with the main body on the Susquehannah by way of Otsego, or to proceed up the Mohawk River and co-operate in the best manner circumstances will permit, as you judge most advisable.

So soon as your preparations are in sufficient forwardness, you will assemble your main body at Wyoming, and proceed to Tioga, taking from that place the most direct and practicable route into the heart of the Indian settlements. You will establish such intermediate posts as you think necessary for the security of your communications and convoys; nor need I caution you, while you leave a sufficiency of men for their defence, to take care to diminish your operating forces as little as possible. A fort at Tioga will be particularly necessary,—either a stockade fort or an entrenched camp. If the latter, a blockhouse should be erected in the interior. I would recommend that some fort in the centre of the Indian country should be occupied with all expedition, with a sufficient quantity of provisions; whence parties should be detached to lay waste all the settlements around, with instructions to do it in the most effectual manner, that the country may not be *merely overrun, but* DESTROYED. I beg leave to suggest, as general rules that ought to govern your operations, to make, rather than receive, attacks, attended with as much impetuosity, shouting, and noise as possible; and to make the troops act in as loose and dispersed a way as is consistent with a proper degree of government, concert, and mutual support. It should be previously impressed upon the minds of the men, wherever they have an opportunity, to rush on with the war whoop and fixed bayonet. Nothing will disconcert and terrify the Indians more than this.

[I need not urge the necessity of using every method in your power to gain intelligence of the enemy's strength, motions, and designs; nor need I suggest the extraordinary degree of vigilance and caution which will be necessary to guard against surprises from an adversary so secret, desultory, and rapid as the Indians. If a detachment operates on the Mohawk River, the commanding officer should be instructed to be very watchful that no troops come from Oswegatchie and Niagara to Oswego without his knowledge; and for this purpose he should keep trusty spies at those three places, to advertise him instantly of the movement of any party, and its force. This detachment should also endeavor to keep a constant intercourse with the main body. More than common care will be necessary of your arms and ammunition, from the nature of the service: they should be particularly inspected after a rain, or the passage of any deep water.] After you have very thoroughly completed the destruction of their settlements, if the Indians should show a disposition for peace, I would have you encourage it, on condition that they will give some decisive evidence of their sincerity, by delivering up some of the principal instigators of their past hostilities into our hands,—Butler, Brant, the most mischievous of the Tories that have joined them, or any others they may have in their power, that we are interested to get into ours. They may possibly be engaged, by address, secrecy, and stratagem, to surprise the garrison of Niagara and the shipping on the lakes, and put them into our possession. This may be demanded as a condition of our friendship, and would be a most important point gained. If they can render a service of this kind, you may stipulate to assist them in their distress with supplies of provision, and other articles of which they will stand in need, having regard, in the expectations you give them, to our real abilities to perform.

I have no power at present to authorize you to conclude any treaty of peace with them; but you may agree upon the terms of one, letting them know that it must be finally ratified by Congress, and giving every assurance that it will. [I shall write to Congress on the subject, and endeavor to obtain more ample and definite authority. But you will not by any means listen to overtures of peace before the *total destruction* of their settlements is effected. It is likely enough that fear, if they are unable to oppose us, will compel them to make offers of peace; or policy may lead them to endeavor to amuse us in this way, to gain time and succor for more effectual opposition. Our future security will be in their inability to injure, in the distance to which they are driven, and in the terror with which the severity of the chastisement they will receive will impress them. Peace without this would be fallacious and temporary. New presents, and an addition of force from the enemy, would engage them to break on the first fair opportunity, and all the expense of our extensive preparations would be lost.] When we have effectually chastised them, we may then listen to peace, and endeavor to draw further advantages from their fear. But, even in that case, great caution will be necessary to guard against the snares which their treachery will hold out. They must be explicit in their promises, give substantial pledges for their performance, and execute their engagements with decision and despatch. Hostages are the only kind of security to be depended on.

[Should Niagara fall into your hands in the way I have mentioned, you will do every thing in your power towards preserving and maintaining it, by establishing a chain of posts in such manner as shall appear to you most safe and effectual, and tending as little to reduce our general force as possible. This, however, we shall be better able to decide as the future events of the campaign unfold themselves. I shall be more explicit on the subject hereafter.] When you have completed the objects of your expedition, unless otherwise directed in the mean time, you will return to form a junction with the main army, by the most convenient, expeditious, and secure route, according to circumstances. The Mohawk River, if it can be done without too great risk, will perhaps be most eligible on several accounts. Much should depend on the relative position of the main army at the time, [and it is impossible to foresee what may be the exigencies of the service in that quarter. This, united with other important reasons, makes it essential that your operations should be as rapid, and that the expedition should be performed in as little time, as will be consistent with its success and efficacy.

And here I cannot forbear repeating to you my former caution, that your troops should move as light and as little encumbered as possible, even from their first outset. The state of our magazines demands it, as well as other considerations. If much time should be lost in transporting the troops and stores up the river, the provisions for the expedition will be consumed, and the general scarceness of our supplies will not permit their being replaced; consequently, the whole enterprise may be defeated. I would recommend it to you for the purpose, that the general officers should make an actual inspection of the baggage of their several brigades; and absolutely reject, to be left behind at proper places, every article that can be dispensed with. on the expedition. This is an extraordinary case, and requires extraordinary attention.] Relying perfectly upon your judgment, prudence, and activity, I have the highest expectation of success equal to our wishes; and I beg leave to assure you, that I anticipate with great pleasure the honor which will redound to yourself, and the advantage to the common cause, from a happy termination of this important enterprise.

Despatch and secrecy would have been desirable, if practicable. But time was requisite to collect the army, provide food and transportation, and nothing could be done that was not known to the enemy. Zealous to carry out his orders, and imprudently indifferent to the ill-will he might provoke, by his earnest appeals to the departments for what was indispensable to prevent the expedition becoming a failure, Sullivan displeased Colonel Pickering and his associates, who were probably straining every effort to meet their official obligations. June, and part of July, passed away before the army was in condition to move. Finding his supplies altogether inadequate for the forces collected, Sullivan requested General Clinton to bring with him, from Schenectady, — where they could be had in abundance, — provisions for his own brigade for three months. Washington, fearing these impediments might endanger the march of Clinton through a hostile country, commented in his letter of the first of July, from New Windsor, — where he had recently removed his headquarters from the Clove, — with some dissatisfaction on this order.

But on the fifth, after maturer consideration, — restating his reasons for Clinton proceeding light and unencumbered to effect his junction, — he leaves the matter to Sullivan to determine, not undertaking to interfere with his arrangements. In this letter, the force of Sullivan is estimated at two thousand five hundred; that of Clinton, at one thousand, — together, three thousand five hundred. It communicates intelligence, that seven hundred men had been sent from Canada to reinforce the savages. The event proved, that, but for the supplies brought by Clinton, and which were no impediment to his progress, the expedition must have been abandoned without effecting its object.

If backwardness in forwarding supplies arose mainly from the exhausted condition of the country, other influences may have been also at work, not then politic to discuss. A powerful squadron was sailing from France with re-enforcements. Washington had written, in May, to propose co-operation against New York, or other point to be determined, — promising the concentration of his whole force for the purpose. D'Estaing did not actually leave the West Indies until later; when, proceeding north, he arrived at Savannah early in October. Meanwhile, in alarm for the safety of their West-India possessions, the British embarked troops at New York for their protection. Two thousand men were sent to Halifax and Quebec, as a precaution, — an expedition having been fitted out at Boston, which laid unsuccessful siege to Castine.

How far these movements, anticipated or in progress, induced procrastination, can only be conjectured. The delay could not have been wholly occasioned by actual inability to obtain supplies, since Washington mentions, in his correspondence, that considerable stores, enough for several thousand men, had been privately accumulated near Albany, against the contingency of the British army evacuating New York for the South, and thus opening the door into Canada. The possibility, if not strong probability, of such a step occupied the attention of Washington throughout the summer. And Sir Henry Clinton is known to have had in contemplation a considerable reduction of the garrison, to strengthen other points that were menaced. The result was a vacillating policy, — troops being sent away, to be again recalled; and no change of consequence took place in the disposition of the British forces before October, when they evacuated Rhode Island.

There was another reason, and all potential, for not being precipitate. One principal object was effectually to destroy the crops in the country of the Six Nations, so that they should be destitute of means the following winter to trouble the frontier. By dint of continued importunity, Sullivan succeeded in obtaining what was necessary for the expedition — though with nothing to spare — in season to move at the right moment, when the corn could be destroyed as it ripened, and no more could be planted that year. In the mean time, he had opportunity, which was diligently improved, to organize and discipline his troops, — rendering them efficient for service.

As the time drew near, however, beyond which it was not prudent to defer action, he felt disappointed and perplexed at the backwardness to meet his requirements. He was, besides, naturally sensitive under the sting of unfriendly criticism, which had been, without reason, visited upon him in his former campaigns, and now, in consequence of these delays, was again assuming form. On the 21st of July, he wrote as follows to Congress, from Wyoming, to which place — sixty-five miles from Easton — he had advanced: —

I have hitherto delayed troubling Congress, in the hope that I should have been able before this to have given them more favorable accounts from this quarter. My duty to the public, and regard to my own reputation, compel me to state the reasons why this army has been so long delayed here, without advancing into the enemy's country. In April last, it was agreed that the army should be put in motion the 15th of May, and rendezvous at Easton on the 20th, to proceed immediately on the expedition. The necessary preparations were to be made in the quartermaster and commissary departments, that no delay might take place; success in a great measure depending on secrecy and despatch. I immediately detached parties to clear a road from Easton to Wyoming, which was done in season, and might have been done sooner, had not the backwardness of affairs in other quarters obliged me to hold a great part of the army at Easton, to prevent the unnecessary consumption of stores destined for the expedition.

The plan for carrying on the expedition was not agreeable to my mind; nor was the number of men destined for it sufficient, in my opinion, to insure success. This Congress will see by the inclosed copies of my letters to General Washington, Nos. 1 and 2, which eventually had no other effect than to alter the route of General Clinton's detachment from the Mohawk to the Susquehannah. I had, early in April, received, from the heads of the quartermaster and commissary departments, assurances that every thing should be in a perfect state of readiness upon my arrival at this post. But, on my arrival at Easton, I was informed by General Hand, who then commanded here, that there was not the least prospect of the boats or stores being in readiness in season; upon which I halted the army at Easton, sending forward only such corps as were necessary to defend this post and assist in forwarding the stores.

When I felt encouraged by the flattering accounts that were sent me, I came to this place, and here have remained without its being in my power to advance toward the enemy. To prove this clearly to Congress, I inclose a return of provisions, made me in April, which were said to be deposited on the Susquehannah, and would be at Kelso's Ferry so as to be transported here by the time specified. The notes at the bottom of the return will show what we now have on hand, and of what quality. Nearly one-half the flour, and more than two-thirds of the live stock mentioned, I have caused to be procured from Easton, fearing to meet with those disappointments I have too often experienced. The inspector is now on the ground, by order of the Board of War, inspecting the provisions; and his regard to truth must oblige him, on his return, to report that, of the salted meat on hand, there is not a single pound fit to be eaten, even at this day, though every measure has been taken to preserve it that possibly could be devised. I also inclose a list of articles in the quartermaster's department which were to have been procured, with notes thereon of what have been received. Upon examining these returns, Congress will be at no loss to account for the delay of this army. I requested Commissary Blaine to forward a thousand head of cattle; some few more than two hundred arrived; and about one hundred and fifty more sent to Sunbury were left there, being too poor to walk, and many of them unable to stand. Three hundred of our horses came in with Colonel Copperthwait on the 20th inst.; but there is not a sufficiency of them, and no pack-saddles for one-half we have.

I inclose a letter from Major Clayburn, of the 19th of May, to show that the boats were then unbuilt which were to have brought the provisions to this post by the 20th; and to show that the first boats, upon presumption that others would be procured, were ordered not to return; but the small number procured has occasioned them to be sent down the river four times since. The other copies of letters, numbered from 5 to 10 inclusively, will show the steps which have been taken to procure provisions, point out the deficiencies, and explain the mortifying necessity I have been under of remaining in a state of inactivity at this post. They will show that we are now bringing on pack-horses, from Carlisle, flour destined for the use of this army, which ought to have been here the 20th of May last. I beg leave to assure Congress that these deficiencies did not arise from want of proper and repeated application, nor has a single step been left untried, which was possible for me, or the army under my command, to take, for procuring and forwarding supplies. Having been taught by repeated disappointments to be cautious, I early gave orders to General Clinton to supply his troops with three months' provisions, and wrote to Governor Clinton for his assistance in April last. This has been done, and they are supplied. I have procured provision from Easton and other places, which, with what is now on its way from Sunbury, to be here on Sunday, will enable us to move the beginning of next week.

To avoid censure in case of misfortune, I beg Congress to recur to the reasonings in my letters to General Washington, respecting the numbers necessary to insure success, and then to examine the inclosed return of the forces here. They now stand at two thousand three hundred and twelve, rank and file. General Washington, in consequence of my letters, wrote the Executive Council of Pennsylvania for rangers and riflemen. They engaged seven hundred and twenty, and the President frequently wrote me that they would be ready in season. Not a man of them has joined us, nor are any about to do it. The reason assigned by them is, that the quartermaster gave such extravagant prices to boatmen, that they all enlisted into the boat service; but this is evidently a mistake, for we have not a hundred boatmen engaged for the army, and but forty-two pack-horsemen, so that I must draft near nine hundred for boatmen and pack-horsemen. This will reduce my numbers to fourteen hundred and twelve; then I must deduct for drivers of cattle and for the artillery one hundred and fifty, for the garrison one hundred, which leaves me eleven hundred and sixty-two; from these, I deduct the officers' waiters and managers of battery-horses, two hundred and twenty-four; this reduces me to nine hundred and thirty-eight, and more than a third of them without a shirt to their backs.

This is the force with which I am to advance against an enemy allowed to be two thousand strong, and who have certainly been lately reinforced with seven hundred British troops from Canada. I need not mention, that it is easy for the enemy to act with their whole force against either part of our army before the junction is formed, and that common prudence will prompt to this. I have therefore nothing to rely on, but the ardor and well-known bravery of my troops, which I trust will surmount all opposition. But should a defeat take place, and the ruin of the army be the consequence, whether I do or do not perish in the action, I call upon the members of Congress to witness to the world, that I early foresaw and foretold the danger, and used every means in my power to procure a force sufficient to insure success, but failed to obtain it.

It was not without reason that he considered his forces insufficient, either to insure success or prevent disaster. General Schuyler, on the 7th, wrote from Albany, " that an Indian, Colonel Louis, had returned from Canada by the way of Oneida. He left the neighborhood of Caughnawaga in the beginning of June. As a reward was offered for apprehending him, he did not dare to venture among the inhabitants. His Caughnawaga friends assured him, that no troops had been sent up the River St. Lawrence this spring, and that no preparations were making for any force to come through Lake Champlain. Brant had not been able to prevail on any of the Caughnawagas to go westward, but a few of the Conodesagas would accompany him. A thousand Ottawas and Chippeways, from Lake Huron, were to join the Senecas, as Brant gives out, to desolate the frontiers." As the efficient force of the Six Nations for service was estimated at two thousand, and the British auxiliaries at seven hundred, if these Western tribes should have sent their promised contingent, Sullivan might expect to encounter four thousand men, with every advantage on their side of superior knowledge of the country and skill in forest warfare. The whole aggregate which he had to oppose to them would have been inferior, even in numbers. His army, after Clinton joined him, has been sometimes stated at five thousand, which, as the correspondence shows, is greatly exaggerated, and at least one-third more than his actual force, effective and non-effective.

That his complaints as to the character and quantities of provision for the army were well grounded, is abundantly evident from the disorganized condition of the commissariat at the time. Large amounts of public property were wasted, from negligence and incompetency, or misappropriated by the dishonesty, of inferior officials. In a letter of Colonel Pickering, from the War Office, bearing date the same day as the foregoing letter of Sullivan to Congress, he frankly admits there was cause for remonstrance. He says: —

We have received your favor of the 18th instant. We cannot but regret exceedingly the delay of an expedition whose success greatly depended upon secrecy and despatch. Your remarks on the Staff Department have undoubtedly but too much foundation: at the same time, we must observe, that there are, in many cases, almost insuperable difficulties in the way. Among these may be received the want of men and proper materials. Of the former, the country is much drained; and, of the latter, the old stocks are generally worked up or used, and no provision made for future wants. Hence, in particular, they have been obliged to use green stuff for casks, which, in summer, is ruinous to whatever is put in them. To this cause may be imputed the badness of some of the salted provisions destined for your army; for we have, upon inquiry, received satisfactory evidence that no care was wanting in the salting and repacking of the far greater part of them.

If, in his wish to prevent misconception, alike injurious to himself and the cause, Sullivan expressed too candidly to Congress his vexation at the dilatoriness of the departments, there is hardly a word in his letter that could fairly be construed into a reflection upon the commander-in-chief. Washington, to whom it was communicated, equally sensitive under the unjust and ungenerous spirit of detraction abroad, that spared neither himself nor his subordinates, felt called upon to shield from reproach his own reputation, which, for a moment, he deemed to be implicated. His response restates the course of events and considerations which had determined the plan of the campaign as presented in the foregoing correspondence, but neither leaves, nor seems, if closely analyzed, to have intended to leave, any censure upon Sullivan. He substantially admits the justice of every one of his complaints, excepting that, in the article of shirts, the main army was no better off. His letter is too long for insertion in full; but the following extracts indicate some of the embarrassments with which they had to contend, as well as the inducements, nevertheless, to persevere: —

"On that part of General Sullivan's letter which relates to the quartermaster's and commissary's departments, I shall only observe that there have, no doubt, been very great delays. Whether these have proceeded in part from a want of exertion, or wholly from the unavoidable impediments which the unhappy state of our currency opposes at every step, I have not sufficient information to determine; but from the approved capacity, attention, and assiduity with which the operations of these departments are conducted, I am inclined to make every allowance, and to impute our disappointments to the embarrassments of the times, and not to neglect. General Sullivan's well-known activity will not permit me to think he has not done every thing in his power to forward the preparations. But, however the delays may have happened, I flatter myself no part of the blame can fall upon me."

"General Sullivan says: 'Having been taught by repeated disappointments to be cautious, I early gave orders to General Clinton to supply his troops with three months' provisions, and wrote Governor Clinton for his assistance in April last. This has been done, and they are supplied.' The idea here held up is really extraordinary. My letter to General Schuyler, No. 1, will show, that, so early as the beginning of December, magazines were ordered to be formed in that quarter for ten thousand men, with a view to an expedition to Niagara. By the subsequent letters to him, Nos. 2 and 3, these were partly discontinued, and limited to the plan of an Indian expedition, the extent of which was to be governed by his judgment of the force necessary. This being three thousand men, the preparations were, of course, for that number. Schenectady was afterwards made the depositary by General Clinton, as appears by his letter, No. 5, in answer to mine, No. 4."

"General Sullivan states his force at two thousand three hundred and twelve rank and file, which, by a variety of deductions, he afterwards reduces to nine hundred and thirty-eight, which he holds up as his combating force. I should be unwilling to overrate the means of any officer, or to create a greater responsibility than is just; but, at the same time, I think it a duty I owe to the public and myself to place a matter of this kind in a true point of light. If almost the whole of the two thousand three hundred men are not effectually serviceable in action, it must be General Sullivan's own fault. Nearly all the men he speaks of as pack-horsemen, bat-horsemen, &c., may be to the full as useful as any others. The number he mentions is only necessary for the sake of despatch on a march; in time of action, the horses and cattle may be committed to the care of a very few, and the rest may be at liberty to act as occasion requires. Should he even be attacked on a march, those animals may be made a shelter, rather than an incumbrance. If the operations he is to be concerned in were the regular ones of the field, his calculation would be better founded; but, in the loose, irregular war he is to carry on, it will naturally lead to error and misconception. General Sullivan makes no account of his drummers and fifers, and other appendages of an army who do not compose the fighting part of it. I have too good an opinion of his judgment, not to believe he would find very useful employment for them. These, and the few drivers and pack-horsemen whom he acknowledges to have, will be nearly, if not quite, sufficient, with a small guard, to take care of his horses and cattle in time of action.

"As before observed, his *real force* will be less than it ought to be, to put him out of the reach of contingencies; but I hope, with prudent management, it will still suffice. The estimate made by General Schuyler, of the enemy's force, from every subsequent information, was not too low; and it is to be hoped the want of provisions will prevent its being exerted in a vigorous and formidable opposition. My chief solicitude is for General Clinton; if he effects the meditated junction, there will, in my opinion, be nothing to fear afterwards. Notwithstanding what may be said of the expertness of Indians in the woods, I am strongly persuaded our troops will always be an overmatch for them, with equal numbers, except in case of surprise or ambuscade, which it is at our own option to avoid. I hope the event may answer our wishes; but, if not, my anxiety to stand justified in the opinion of Congress has induced me to give them the trouble of this lengthy communication."

"I beg leave to conclude with one observation. It may possibly hereafter be said that the expedition ought not to have been undertaken unless the means were fully adequate, or that the consequences of a defeat ought not to have been hazarded when they were found to be otherwise. The motives to the undertaking, besides the real importance of rescuing the frontier from the alarms, ravages, and distresses to which it was exposed, — and which, in all probability, would have redoubled this year, — were the increasing clamors of the country and the repeated applications of the States immediately concerned, supported by frequent references and indications of the pleasure of Congress. The combined force of these motives appeared to me to leave no alternative. The means proposed to be employed were fully sufficient; the disappointments met with, such as could not have been foreseen, and we had no right to expect. So far as the business did not depend on me, I had the strongest assurances from those who were concerned, and who were to be supposed the proper judges, that my expectations would be fulfilled.

"After such extensive preparations have been made, so much expense incurred, the attention and hopes of the public [aroused], the apprehensions of the enemy excit[ed, their] force augmented, their resentment inflam[ed], — to recede, and leave the frontier a prey to their depredations, would be, in every view, impolitic, when there is still a good prospect of success. To avoid possible misfortunes, we must, in this case, submit to many certain evils, — of the most serious nature, too obvious to require enumeration."

The force collected at Wyoming on the 23d of July consisted of the First, Second, Third, and Fourth New Jersey; First, Second, and Third New Hampshire; the Eleventh and a German regiment from Pennsylvania; Shott's free corps, Spaulding's company, besides Colonel Proctor's regiment of artillery, with two five and a half inch howitzers, two six, and four three-pounders. On the following day arrived one hundred and thirty-four vessels, laden with provisions; and, on the 31st, the army took up its line of march, encamping the first night at Lackawana. Penetrating a wilderness of lakes and mountains, their progress was slow; but amidst their toils, some of those who attended the expedition have recorded their impressions of the grandeur and beauty of the scenery that surrounded them. On the 5th, they passed through Tuscarora; on the 11th, reached Tioga; and the 13th, after a long night's march of twelve miles, the town of Chemung, which they found the enemy had just abandoned in great confusion, after flinging away their baggage in their flight. It was a place of about fifty houses, surrounded by cornfields, which they destroyed. A portion of the army, sent in pursuit of the enemy, were fired upon by a party in ambush, of whom they killed several; sustaining themselves a loss of seven killed and nine wounded. The Indians fled with a yell, and disappeared into retreats where it would have been useless to follow them.

Sullivan returned to Tioga, to meet General Clinton, who had been delayed by the rains, which, indeed, greatly impeded, throughout the month, the march of the army. From that place he writes Washington on the 15th of August: —

DEAR GENERAL, — I have the honor to inform your Excellency that I arrived at this place with the army on the 11th inst., without any loss, and without having received the least opposition from the enemy. All the accounts received from your Excellency, as well as from every other quarter, seemed to agree that they were collecting their whole force at Chemung, in order to give us battle. I thought, if these accounts were true, it would not be prudent to detach a large part of my force to meet General Clinton, and expose the residue to their collective force. I therefore detached Captain Cummins, of Colonel Shreeve's regiment, with eight active men, to reconnoitre Chemung. He arrived there on the morning of the 12th, and took post on a mountain which overlooked the town, where he remained till twelve o'clock. He returned into camp late in the afternoon of the same day, and reported that he saw both white people and Indians busily employed; but he could not ascertain whether they were preparing for action, or for evacuating the place.

Immediately upon receiving this intelligence, an attack was agreed on, and the troops moved at nine o'clock the same evening. General Hand, with the light corps, moved in front to attack on the north of the town; General Poor was to attack on the east side. Two regiments were detached across the Cayuga to prevent the enemy escaping across the river. I moved on in the main road towards the lower end of the town for the purpose of supporting the attacking parties, and to prevent escape in that quarter, having with me the Jersey troops, some volunteers, and some of the artillery corps, with a cohorn carried by hand, a machine invented by Colonel Proctor. The attack was to begin on all sides at daybreak. Though the morning was exceedingly foggy, our troops all arrived at their respective posts not long after daybreak, and moved on so as nearly to meet at the same time in the town; but we found the town had been evacuated the evening before. General Hand, with the light troops, moved up on the east side of the Cayuga branch about a mile beyond the town, where he found the place of the enemy's encampment the night of the 13th. He followed them up the road about half a mile, when a party of about thirty rose and fired upon his advanced party; the General, with his troops, immediately moved up to charge them, upon which they fled with precipitation. They were pursued a little further up; but, there appearing no prospect of overtaking them, the troops returned, and destroyed the town, together with all their fields of corn, and whatever else was found to destroy. A small party fired upon our people when destroying their corn, but was soon forced to fly. We had, in the course of the day, seven men killed and thirteen wounded, among whom were Captain Carbury and Lieutenant Huston, of Colonel Hubley's regiment. Captain Carbury is dangerously wounded, I hope not mortally. Mr. Huston's arm was broken by a ball; all the others are wounded very slightly, except Mr. Franklin, one of our guides, who is badly wounded, though said not to be dangerously. Most of the injury was sustained by General Hand's advanced guard, and from one fire only, as our troops did not give them opportunity to make a second. One was killed and four wounded of General Poor's, and two were wounded of the Jersey brigade.

I cannot say what loss the enemy sustained; but it must have been inconsiderable, as their flight was too sudden to admit of their receiving much injury. Some of their hats were found, and one with a ball through the crown; but no dead body, which induces me to believe that none of them were killed outright. I am much surprised that they did not make a greater opposition in defence of their town. It was most beautifully situated, contained a chapel, with between thirty and forty other houses, many of them very large, and some of them tolerably well finished. There were extensive fields of corn, with great quantities of potatoes, pumpkins, squashes, and, in short, most other things which farms produce. The whole was destroyed.

Our troops having completed the business, returned the same evening to camp; having performed a march of at least forty miles in less than twenty-four hours, besides going through the fatigue of destroying these extensive fields. Their conduct was exceedingly praiseworthy: if there was any fault, it was their too great eagerness to rush upon the enemy at first sight. I am happy in assuring your Excellency, that I am well convinced, no force that this country can produce, can stand before troops so determined as this army. I forgot to mention to your Excellency in my last letter, that the enemy had erected a new town near Scheshequeening, containing twenty-two houses, which they abandoned on our approach. Colonel Proctor, who had charge of the fleet, sent on shore and burnt it. I am now sending off a strong body to meet General Clinton. When he joins, will proceed, without loss of time, to execute the residue of my orders.

Clinton, who had opened a road from Canojoharie to Lake Otsego, a sheet of water of romantic beauty, effected his junction with Sullivan on the 22d of August. He brought with him two hundred and twenty-eight batteaux, which he floated into the Susquehannah by constructing a dam, and raising the lake several feet above its usual level. The rush of waters, that bore his fleet safely into the river, devastated Oghwaga and other plantations, to the astonishment and dismay of the Indians, unaccustomed to any such flood at that season.

A few days were allowed for rest, and necessary arrangements for their future movements. The post consisted of four block-houses, near the forks of the Tioga and Susquehannah, called "Fort Sullivan." This was to be left in charge of Colonel Shreeve, with two hundred and fifty men, and two six-pounders; and with him were left their sick, women, heavy baggage, and all but what was absolutely indispensable. The united forces broke camp on the 26th, and proceeded on their way. Part of their supplies were on pack-horses, part in a fleet of one hundred and fifty vessels, which accompanied them up the river.

It must be remembered, that, in so wild a country, it was quite easy for the Indians to avoid them; and, with their large force, it would have been futile to attempt concealment. The object was to destroy the villages, to discourage, by showing our power to retaliate, depredations, and to overawe. Some military critics have censured the morning and evening guns of the camp; but the Indians were ever peculiarly sensitive to the sound of heavy artillery, and, as one main object of the expedition was to intimidate, there was no reason why this usage of a camp should have been omitted. It may not be out of place to quote the opinion of a good judge in military matters, who says, that the instructions given by General Sullivan to his officers, the order of march he prescribed to his troops, and the discipline he had the ability to maintain, would have done honor to the most experienced ancient or modern general.

Having reason to believe the enemy not far distant, they moved with caution. The disposition of the troops which had been transmitted was determined by the character of the country they were traversing, and well adapted, for facility of formation, to guard against surprise or resist attack. On the third day, they fortunately discovered, in good season, that a large force was before them, prepared to dispute their further progress; and they fought the battle of Newtown, the only engagement of the campaign. Its incidents are described, with fulness of detail, in Sullivan's official report to Congress, written the next day from that place; being substantially a duplicate of one to Washington.

I have the pleasure to inform your Excellency, that, having formed the junction with General Clinton without loss, we marched from Tioga the 26th, in the afternoon. The rains had swelled the Cayuga, so as to render our march to Chemung very difficult, as we had to ford the river twice in our route. We arrived there in the evening of the 28th, and marched for the place early in the morning of the 29th. About eleven o'clock, a messenger from Major Par, who commanded the rifle corps, the advance of the light troops of the army under General Hand, informed me the enemy had, about a mile in front of the town, a very extensive breastwork erected on a rising ground which commanded the road, in which we were to pass with our artillery, and which would enable them to fire upon our flank and front at the same time. This breastwork they had endeavored to mask in a very artful manner, and had concealed themselves behind it in large numbers.

I had before been apprised of the enemy's having a very large encampment at that place. I found that the work was in a bend of the river, which, by turning northward, formed a semicircle. There was a deep brook in front of this work, over which the road passed, and then turned off to the right, parallel to the course of the rising ground, upon which their works were constructed. This would have enabled them to flank the line of march of one column of our troops, had it advanced without discovering the work. They had also posted on a hill about a hundred and fifty rods in their rear, and considerably on their left, a strong party, in order, as I suppose, to fall on our right flank when we were engaged with the works in front, and to cover the retreat of the troops which occupied the works in case they should be carried, and to take advantage of any disorder which might appear among our troops in the pursuit. This hill was very advantageously formed for their purpose, as it terminated in a bold bluff about a mile in the rear of their works, and about two hundred yards from the river ; leaving a hollow way between the hill and the river of about one hundred and fifty yards, and ending on the north in a very narrow defile. This hollow way was clear of trees and bushes, and was occupied by them as a place of encampment for part of their army.

General Hand formed the light corps of the army in the wood within four hundred yards of their works. The riflemen in his front kept skirmishing with the enemy, who frequently sallied out and suddenly retired, apparently with a view of drawing our men into the works, which they supposed had not been discovered. The growth upon the hill being pine, interspersed with very low shrub oaks, they had cut off shrubs and stuck them in the ground in front of their works, and had some reason to suppose that we should not distinguish them from those growing on the eminence. General Hand remained at his post until I arrived with the main army. General Poor's brigade, which formed the right wing of the main army, deployed in the rear of General Hand's ; General Maxwell's brigade, which formed the left wing, came abreast with General Poor, and remained in column ready to act as occasion might require. It was observed, that there was another chain of hills terminating in a point rather in rear of our right, and about one mile distant from the right of our line. It was conjectured, that the enemy had taken post upon one or both the hills, in order to fall on our right and rear, when we attempted to attack their works. General Poor was therefore detached to gain the hill first described, and fall into the enemy's rear. Small reconnoitring parties were likewise detached to make discoveries at the other hill, and to give notice of any appearance of the enemy there, and still to guard more effectually against any attempt from that quarter. General Clinton's brigade, which forms the second line of the army, was ordered to turn off, and follow in the rear of General Poor, to sustain him in case of necessity, or to form a line to oppose any force which might fall in his rear, or attempt to gain the flank or rear of the army. When sufficient space of time had been given to General Poor to gain the hill in their rear, our artillery was to announce our attack in front, which was to be made by General Hand's corps, supported by General Maxwell's brigade if necessary. Maxwell's brigade was therefore held in a closed column in order to give the necessary support to the attacking party, or to form a line to oppose any force which might attempt to attack us either in our front or rear.

Colonel Dubois, with the right flanking division of the army, consisting of two hundred and fifty men, was advanced on the right of General Poor; and Colonel Ogden, with the left flanking division, of two hundred and fifty more, was posted near the river, with directions, as soon as the attack began, to advance along its bank, and gain the enemy's right, to prevent any escape across. General Poor moved on to gain the hill, and General Clinton followed as directed, but both of them were for some time delayed by a morass. General Poor had already arrived near the foot of the hill when the cannonading began in front of their works, but, upon attempting to ascend it, he found a large body of the enemy posted there, who began to fire upon him. His troops charged with bayonets, and sometimes fired as they advanced. The enemy retreated from tree to tree, keeping up an incessant fire, until his troops had gained the summit of the hill. General Clinton detached two regiments to re-inforce General Poor, and then followed himself with the residue of his brigade, as directed. The two regiments arrived just before the summit of the hill was gained, and prevented the enemy from turning his right, which they were then attempting. Our cannonade in front, and, I doubt not, the unexpected fire from General Poor on the enemy's left, occasioned them instantly to abandon their works in the utmost confusion. They fled in the greatest disorder, leaving eleven of their Indian warriors and one female dead on the ground, with a great number of packs, blankets, arms, camp equipage, and a variety of their jewels, some of which are of considerable value.

We took two prisoners,—one a Tory, the other an enlisted negro in one of the Tory companies. They both agree that there were five companies of whites, and their main strength consisting of the Indian warriors of seven nations, and that this was the place where they meant to make their principal opposition, and that they had been waiting here eight days. Both the Butlers, Brant, and Captain McDonald were here, each having a separate command. Brant had some time since [been] slightly wounded in the foot, but had recovered. They further say they sent off their wounded on horseback. Some of them no doubt were carried off in canoes. Many of their dead must have been carried off or concealed, as we found many bloody packs, coats, shirts, and blankets, and, in short, every appearance, not only of havoc, but of fright and confusion, was left behind them. The main army pursued them about a mile, and the light corps about three; but fear had given them too great speed to be overtaken.

Our loss was three killed and thirty-nine wounded, principally of General Poor's brigade. Among the latter were Major Titcomb, Captain Cloyse, and Lieutenant McAuley, all badly; the latter is since dead; the other two, it is hoped, will survive: the residue are principally slightly wounded. General Poor, his officers and men, deserve the highest praise for their intrepidity and soldierly conduct, as do Colonel Proctor and the whole artillery corps. Major Par and the rifle corps also distinguished themselves by their great vigilance and spirited conduct. In short, every officer and soldier conducted in a most soldierly manner, and those who were not immediately in the engagement, manifested their eagerness for the combat in every action. Indeed, the conduct of the whole army was truly pleasing, and gave the most striking evidence that no equal number of troops can oppose their progress. I cannot help saying, that the disposition of the enemy's troops, and the construction of their works, would have done honor to much greater officers than the unprincipled wretches who commanded them. The numbers of the enemy cannot be ascertained; but from the extent of their works, and the posts they occupied, they must have been numerous.

This place, in English called Newtown, was a large, scattered settlement, abounding with extensive fields of the best corn and beans; so extensive and numerous as to keep the whole army this day industriously employed in destroying, and the business yet unfinished. From the vast quantity of corn planted at this place and its vicinities, I conclude it to have been designed as their principal magazine. The town, which contained about twenty houses, was burnt; and Generals Clinton and Poor, on their yesterday's route, fell in with another of thirty buildings, about two miles to the east of this, which is also destroyed. The number of Indian towns destroyed since the commencement of the expedition, including those burnt by General Clinton previous to the junction, is, I think, fourteen; some of them considerable, others inconsiderable.

The journals of the expedition that have been preserved abound in interesting incident, and fully confirm the record presented by himself as to the towns and dwellings of the Indians. It had been urged, that he described them as more substantial and well-built than they actually were. They were destroyed, and with them all proof that he added any colors of his own; but the diary of an officer in the expedition fully confirms his relation. If charged that he demanded more supplies than were needed, already a scarcity began to be felt. His request to his army, on the 30th of August, the day following the battle of Newtown, to be contented with half-rations, to which they cheerfully submitted for many weeks, proved their insufficiency. If circumstances had warranted an attack on Niagara, it would, on this account, have been quite impracticable. Fault was also found, at the War Office, with an unguarded expression in the orders, reflecting on the commissary department; but it is doubtful if the army, as human nature is constituted, would have acquiesced as readily in the sacrifices proposed, had not some reasonable cause been assigned for the deficiency. The request he made to them reads as follows:—

The commander-in-chief informs the troops that he used every effort to procure proper supplies for the army, and to obtain a sufficient number of horses to transport them; but, owing to the inattention of those whose business it was to make the necessary provision, he failed of obtaining such an ample supply as he wished, and greatly fears the supplies on hand will not, without the greatest prudence, enable him to complete the business of the expedition. He therefore requests the several brigadiers and officers commanding corps, to take the minds of the troops under their respective commands, whether, while in this country, which abounds in corn and every kind of vegetable, they will be content to draw half a pound of flour, and half a pound of meat, and half allowance of salt per day; and he desires the troops to give their opinion upon the proposal with freedom, and as soon as possible. Should they generally fall in with the proposal, he promises that they shall be paid for that part of the rations which is held back, at the full value in money. He flatters himself that troops who have discovered so much bravery and firmness will freely consent to a measure so essentially necessary to accomplish the important purposes of this expedition, and to enable them to add to those laurels they have already gained. The enemy have subsisted a number of days on corn, without either salt, bread, meat, or flour; and the General cannot persuade himself, that troops who so far surpass them in valor and true bravery will suffer themselves to be outdone in that fortitude and perseverance which not only distinguishes, but dignifies, the soldier. He does not mean to continue this through the campaign, but only wishes it to be adopted in those places where vegetables may supply the place of part of the common rations of meat and flour; and he thinks, with a plenty of vegetables, half a common ration of meat and flour will be much better than the whole without any.

The troops will please to consider the matter, and give their opinion as soon as possible.

These orders offended the Board of War, of which Timothy Pickering was an influential member; and, on the first of September, they brought them to the notice of Congress, complaining "that their characters had been made very free with in the army, who, being under a deception, censured them with great bitterness." They prayed investigation; but the committee, of which Mr. Matthew, of South Carolina, was chairman, never reported. That dissatisfaction with the Board extensively prevailed, in some measure occasioned by causes not within their control, cannot be disputed. William Barber, on the thirtieth of July, writes from Wyoming, that the delay from insufficient supplies was a mortification to every officer on the ground. Intelligence was, at that time, constantly arriving of massacres and depredations, of the affair at Minnisinks, and the capture of Fort Freeland, by a party said to be under Butler, — movements and operations unaccountable, unless designed to divide our force by alarming the different frontiers. If fretted then, there was the more reason now that they were entering upon a long, and probably perilous, incursion into the wilderness, with insufficient supplies. In the temper that prevailed, to have subjected the army to short rations, without reference to what occasioned its necessity, would have prejudiced the cause. It would have been to exhibit a culpable indifference to the just claims of soldiers, who were already patiently enduring many privations, and as much entitled to be considered and protected as the Board.

Sending back, on the night of the 30th, all his heavy artillery, and retaining only four brass three-pounders and a small howitzer, and loading their necessary ammunition on packhorses, they proceeded, on the 31st, for Catherine's-town, near the southern extremity of Lake Seneca; destroying, on their way, Konowahola, a town of twenty houses, at the confluence of the Cayuga and Tioga branches. From some unexpected detention, the rear guard, under Clinton, were forced to pass the night of the 1st of September in a swamp. While at Catherine's-town, Sullivan sent a friendly Indian with the following address to the Oneidas:—

TO THE WARRIORS OF THE ONEIDA NATION: BROTHERS,— The enemies of the United States, and of your nation, have often threatened to destroy you, and you have called upon us for assistance. You have said that our arm was long and strong, and therefore called upon us for that protection which we ever wish to afford to our brethren, friends, and allies; and you have promised to join us in our operations. The grand American Congress have thought proper to send a powerful army into this country, for the purpose of totally destroying the enemies to your peace, and have thought proper to intrust me with the command of the army, and the execution of their orders. It is with no small degree of surprise that I find, though I have far advanced into the enemy's country, that only four of your warriors have joined me, and they totally unacquainted with every part of the country through which I have yet passed. I would not wish to suspect your declarations of friendship to the American States, nor am I under the least necessity to ask your aid as warriors; but, as your immediately joining my force is the best evidence you can give of the sincerity of your professions, I shall expect shortly to be joined by those of your people who are friendly to the American cause, and particularly by such as have a perfect knowledge of the country through which I am to pass. Unless this is complied with, I shall be compelled to think that the chiefs of your warriors, if not really unfriendly to us, are very inattentive to their own interest and safety, as well as indifferent with respect to the interest of the United States.

Should you, by joining with me, furnishing me the necessary information, and affording me every assistance in your power, give evidence of that attachment to the American cause, which I ever have and now do believe you to possess, the army which I have the honor to command will be able totally to extirpate our common enemy, and leave you in a perfect state of tranquillity, enable you to enjoy your possessions, and carry on with the Americans a commerce which will tend to the mutual advantage of both. The bearer of this letter, Oneiga, will inform you particularly of my progress thus far.

It was some time afterwards — indeed, on his return march — that the response of the Oneidas reached him, with the report of his messenger. They will be more intelligible if presented in connection with the address. Their purport, as interpreted, was as follows: —

BROTHER CHIEF WARRIOR OF THE WESTERN ARMY, — Some time ago, you sent me to Oneida with a message to the warriors of that tribe, and directed me to give them an account of the battle you had with Butler's party, near Newtown. Brother, I have faithfully executed your orders, as will appear from what took place on my arrival at Oneida. A council was immediately called, and your written speech publicly delivered; the warriors expressed great joy, both on account of your success and the opportunity now given them to testify their friendship to the American cause. Seventy of the Oneida warriors set out with me to join your army, agreeable to your desire; thirty more were to have followed the next day; near Onondaga we met our brother Conowago, on his return from your army, which he said he left at Kanasadagia. This brother informed us that you said they were too late; they should have met you at Kanadasega; that you had men enough, and did not want them, unless some good guides; the party then returned, though with reluctance. Our chief warriors then delivered the following speech, to which I beg your attention: —

BROTHER, — We have been informed by our brother, of Conowaga, that you were disposed to show clemency to the Cayugas, and had desired him to direct them to repair to Oneida, should he meet with any of that tribe on his way from your army. We are glad you manifest such a disposition, and are willing to make peace with them. We will assist you, and the rather that we know there is a party, of the Cayuga tribe, who have ever wished to be at peace with their

American brethren. We will endeavor to find them, as we are confident they are not fled to the enemy, but suppose them to be somewhere concealed in the country. We therefore request that you would not for the present destroy their cornfields, as we cannot furnish them with provisions, should we be able to find them, and bring them to our town, — having, already, so many of the Onondagas to support. Tegatteronwane, who is at the head of the party, is disposed for peace, and has delivered up four prisoners, on General Schuyler's proposal of exchange; three more, who are sick, he will give up as soon as they recover their health. He has declared that he never would set his face towards Niagara, but, on the approach of the American army, would take himself to the woods, where they might find him if he did not make his way down to the Oneidas. Brother, this is all we have to say.

Catherine's-town being destroyed on the 3d of September, the march was continued up the east side of Seneca Lake; burning, as they went, the town of Kendaia. The 6th, they crossed the outlet of Seneca, and, moving in three divisions, reached Kanadasega, the capital of the Seneca tribe, which they found deserted. Two days later, they arrived at Canandaigua; which, with Honayaga, a village near by, they destroyed. Here Boyd started to make a reconnoissance, with twenty-six men, — a larger force than was intended. Their numbers exposed them to observation; they were not sufficiently prudent, were surrounded, and destroyed. On the 16th, the army reached the beautiful valley of the Genesee, spreading for many miles with ripening harvests; all of which, with the town of one hundred and twenty-eight dwellings, unusually large and commodious, they gave to the flames. The grain was gathered and burnt in the houses, or in kilns constructed for the purpose.

Finding his supplies would not admit of farther progress, and having utterly laid waste the country, Sullivan commenced his homeward march. On the 20th, he recrossed the outlet of Lake Seneca. The army reached Chemung on the 28th. From that place Sullivan wrote Washington; and at Tioga, on the 30th, addressed Congress the continuation of his narrative of the expedition. These letters embrace, substantially, the same incidents, with slight variations in the description. The last and more brief we select, which is as follows: —

Sir, — In mine of the 30th ult. to His Excellency General Washington, and by him transmitted to Congress, I gave an account of the victory obtained by this army over the enemy at Newtown, on the 29th August. I now do myself the honor to inform Congress of the progress of this army, and the most material occurrences which have since taken place.

The time taken up in destroying the corn in the neighborhood of Newtown, employing the army near two days, and there appearing a probability that the destruction of all the crops might take a much greater length of time than was first apprehended, and being likewise convinced, by an accurate calculation, that it would not be possible to effect the destruction of the Indian country with the provision on hand, which was all I had in store, and, indeed, all I had pack-horses to transport from Tioga, — in this situation, I could think of but one expedient to answer the purpose of the expedition, which was to prevail, if possible, on the soldiers to content themselves with half a pound of flour and the same quantity of fresh beef per day, rather than leave the important business unfinished. I therefore drew up an address to them, — a copy of which I have the honor to inclose you, — which, being read, was answered by three cheers from the whole army. Not one dissenting voice was heard, from either officer or soldier.

I had then on hand, from the best calculation I could make, twenty-two pounds of flour and sixteen pounds of beef per man, — the former liable to many deductions by rains, crossing rivers, and defiles; the latter much more so, from the almost unavoidable loss of cattle, when suffered to range the woods at night for their support. I was, however, encouraged in the belief that I should be enabled to effect the destruction and total ruin of the Indian territories by this truly noble resolution of the army, for which I know not whether the public stand more indebted to the persuasive arguments which the officers began to use, or to the virtuous disposition of the soldiers, whose prudent and cheerful compliance with the requisition anticipated all their wishes, and rendered persuasion unnecessary.

I sent back all my heavy artillery on the night of the 30th, retaining only four brass three-pounders and a small howitzer; loaded the necessary ammunition on horseback, and marched early on the 31st for

Catherine's-town. On our way, we destroyed a small settlement of eight houses, and town, called Konowahola, of about twenty houses, situated on a peninsula at the conflux of the Tioga and Cayuga branches. We also destroyed several fields of corn. From this point Colonel Dayton was detached with his regiment and the rifle corps up the Tioga about six miles, who destroyed several large fields of corn. The army resumed their march, and encamped within thirteen miles and a half of Catherine's-town, where we arrived the next day, although we had a road to open for the artillery through a swamp nine miles in extent, and almost impervious. We arrived near Catherine's-town in the night, and moved on in hopes to surprise it, but found it forsaken.

On the next morning, an old woman belonging to the Cayuga nation was found in the woods. She informed me, that, on the night after the battle of Newtown, the enemy, having fled the whole night, arrived there in great confusion early the next day; that she heard the warriors tell their women they were conquered, and must fly; that they had a great many killed and vast numbers wounded. She, likewise, heard the lamentations of many at the loss of their connections. In addition to this, she assured us that some other warriors had met Butler at this place, and desired him to return and fight again. But to this request they could obtain no satisfactory answer, for, as they observed, "Butler's mouth was closed." The warriors who had been in the action were equally averse to the proposal, and would think of nothing but flight and removal of their families; that they kept runners on every mountain to observe the movements of our army, who reported, early in the day on which we arrived, that our advance was very rapid, upon which all those that had been before sent off fled with precipitation, leaving her without any possible means of escape. She said that Brant had taken most of the wounded up the Tioga in canoes. I was, from many circumstances, fully convinced of the truth and sincerity of her declaration, and the more so, as we had, the day we left Newtown, discovered a great number of bloody packs, arms, and accoutrements thrown away in the road, and in the woods each side of it. Besides which we discovered a number of recent graves, — one of which has been since opened, containing the bodies of two persons who had died by wounds.

These circumstances, when added to that of so many warriors being left dead on the field, a circumstance not common with Indians, were sufficient to corroborate the woman's declaration, and to prove, what I before conjectured, that the loss of the enemy was much greater than was at first apprehended. I have never been able to ascertain, with any degree of certainty, what force the enemy opposed to us at Newtown, but from the best accounts I have been able to collect, and from the opinion of General Poor and others, who had the best opportunity of viewing their numbers, as well from the extent of their lines, I suppose them to have been fifteen hundred; though the two prisoners, whom I believe totally ignorant of the number at any post but their own, as well of the enemy's disposition, estimates them only at eight hundred, while they allow that five companies of rangers — all the warriors of Seneca and six other nations — were collected at this place. In order to determine their force with as much accuracy as in my power, I examined their breastworks, and found its extent more than half a mile. Several bastions ran out in its front to flank the lines in every part. A small block-house, formerly a dwelling, was also manned in the front. The breastwork appeared to have been fully manned, though I suppose with only one rank. Some part of their works being low, they were obliged to dig holes in the ground to cover themselves in part. This circumstance enabled me to judge the distance between their men in the works. A very thin, scattering line — designed, as I suppose, for communicating signals — was continued from those works to that part of the mountain which General Poor ascended, where they had a very large body, which was designed, I imagine, to fall on our flank. The distance from the breastwork to this was at least one mile and a half. From thence to the hill, in the rear of our right, was another scattering line of about one mile, and on the hill a breastwork with a strong party destined, as it is supposed, to fall on our rear. But General Clinton being ordered so far to the right occasioned his flank to pass the mountain, which obliged them to abandon their post. From these circumstances, as well as from the opinion of others, I cannot conceive their number to be less than what I have before mentioned.

The army spent a day at Catherine's, destroying corn and fruit-trees. We burnt the town, consisting of thirty houses. The next day we encamped near a small scattering settlement of about eight houses, and two days after reached Kendaia, which we also found deserted. Here one of the inhabitants of Wyoming, who had been last year captured by the enemy, escaped from them, and joined us. He informed us that the enemy had left the town, in the greatest confusion, three days before our arrival. He said he had conversed with some of the Tories on their return from the action of Newtown, who assured him they had great numbers killed and wounded, and there was no safety but in flight. He heard Butler tell them he must try to make a stand at Kanadasega; but they declared they would not throw away their lives in vain attempt to oppose such an army. He also heard many of the Indian women lamenting the loss of their connections; and added, that Brant had taken most of the wounded up the Tioga in water-craft, which had been provided for that purpose in case of necessity. It was his opinion the King of Kanadasega was killed, as he saw him go down, but not return, and gave a description of his person and dress, corresponding with those of one found on the field of action. Kendaia consisted of about twenty houses, which were reduced to ashes; the houses were neatly built and finished.

The army spent a day at this place, in destroying corn and fruit-trees, of which there was great abundance. Many of the trees appeared to be of great age. On the next day, we crossed the outlet of the Seneca Lake, and moved in three divisions through the woods, to encircle Kanadasega, but found it, likewise, abandoned. A white child, of about three years old,—doubtless the offspring of some unhappy captive,—was found here, and carried with the army. A detachment of four hundred men was sent down on the west side of the lake to destroy Gothseunga, and the plantations in that quarter; at the same time a number of volunteers, under Colonel Harper, made a forced march towards Cayuga Lake, and destroyed Schuyero, while the residue of the army were employed in destroying the corn at Kanadasega, of which there was a large quantity. This town consisted of fifty houses, and was pleasantly situated. In it we found a great number of fruit-trees, which were destroyed with the town.

The army then moved on, and in two days arrived at Canandaigua, having been joined on the march by the detachment sent along the Seneca Lake, which had been almost two days employed in destroying the crops and settlement in that quarter. At Canandaigua we found twenty-three very elegant houses mostly finished, and, in general, large. Here we also destroyed very extensive fields of corn, which having been destroyed, we marched for Honayaga, a small town of ten houses, which we also destroyed. At this place we established a post, leaving a strong garrison, our heavy stores, and one field-piece, and proceeded to Geneseo, which the prisoners informed us was the grand capital of the Indian country; that Indians of all nations had been planting there this spring; that all the rangers and some British had been employed in assisting them, in order to raise sufficient supplies to support them while destroying our frontiers; and that they themselves had worked three weeks for the Indians when planting.

This information determined me, at all events, to reach that settlement, though the state of my provisions, much reduced by unavoidable accidents, almost forbade the attempt. My flour had been much reduced by the failure of pack-horses and in the passage of creeks and defiles, and twenty-seven of the cattle had been unavoidably lost. We, however, marched on for the Genesee town, and on the second day reached a town of twenty-five houses, called Kanoghsauga. Here we found some large cornfields, which part of the army destroyed, while the other part were employed in building a bridge over an unfordable creek between this and Geneseo. I had, the preceding evening, ordered out an officer, with three or four riflemen, one of our guides, and an Oneida chief, to reconnoitre the Genesee town, that we might, if possible, surprise it.

Lieutenant Boyd was the officer intrusted with this service, who took with him twenty-three men, volunteers from the same corps, and a few from Colonel Butler's regiment, making in all twenty-six; a much larger number than I had thought of sending, and by no means so likely to answer the purpose as that which had been directed. The guides were by no means acquainted with the country, mistook the road in the night, and, at daybreak, fell in with a castle six miles higher up than Geneseo, inhabited by a tribe called Squatchegas. Here they saw a few Indians, — killed and scalped two: the rest fled. Two runners were immediately despatched to me with the account, and informed me that the party were on their return. When the bridge was almost completed, some of them came in and told us that Lieutenant Boyd and men of his party were almost surrounded by the enemy; that the enemy had been discovering themselves before him for some miles; that his men had killed two, and were eagerly pursuing the rest, but soon found themselves almost surrounded by three or four hundred Indians and rangers. Those of Mr. Boyd's men who were sent to secure his flanks, fortunately made their escape; but he, with fourteen of his party and the Oneida chief, being in the centre, were completely encircled. The light troops of the army, and the flanking division, were immediately detached to their relief, but arrived too late; the enemy having destroyed the party, and escaped.

It appears that our men had taken to a small grove, the ground around it being clear on every side for several rods, and there fought till Mr. Boyd was shot through the body, and his men all killed except one, who, with his wounded commander, was made prisoner. The firing was so close before this brave party was destroyed, that the powder of the enemy's muskets was driven into their flesh. In this conflict, the enemy must have suffered greatly, as they had no cover, and our men were possessed of a very advantageous one. This advantage of ground, the obstinate bravery of the party, with some other circumstances, induced me to believe their loss must have been very considerable. They were so long employed in removing and secreting their dead, that the advance of General Hand's party obliged them to leave one alongside the riflemen, and at least a wagon-load of packs, blankets, boots, and provision, which they had thrown off to enable them to act with more agility in the field. Most of these appeared to have appertained to the rangers. Another reason which induces me to suppose they suffered much, was the unparalleled tortures they inflicted upon the brave and unfortunate Boyd, whose body, with that of the equally unfortunate companion, we found at Geneseo. It appeared they had whipped them in the most cruel manner, pulled out Mr. Boyd's nails, cut off his nose, plucked out one of his eyes, cut out his tongue, stabbed him with spears in sundry places, and inflicted other tortures which decency will not permit me to mention; lastly, cut off his head, and left his body on the ground, with that of his unfortunate companion, who appeared to have experienced nearly the same savage barbarity. The party Mr. Boyd fell in with was commanded by Butler, posted on an advantageous piece of ground, in order to fire upon our army when advancing; but they found their design frustrated by the appearance of this party in their rear.

The army moved on that day to the castle last mentioned, which consisted of twenty-five houses, surrounded by very extensive fields of corn, which being destroyed, we moved on the next day to Geneseo, crossing, in our route, a deep creek, and the Little Genesee River; and, after marching six miles, we reached the castle, which consisted of one hundred and twenty-eight houses, mostly large and elegant. The town was beautifully situated, almost encircled with a clear flat for a number of miles, covered by the most extensive fields of corn, and every kind of vegetable that can be conceived. The whole army was immediately engaged in destroying the crops. The corn was collected, and burnt in houses and kilns, so the enemy might not reap the least advantage from it, which method we have pursued in every other place.

Here a woman came to us, who had been captured at Wyoming. She told us the enemy evacuated the town two days before; that Butler at the same time went off with three or four hundred Indians and rangers, as he said, to get a shot at our army. This was, undoubtedly, the party which cut off Lieutenant Boyd. She mentioned they kept runners constantly out, and that, when our army was in motion, the intelligence was communicated by a yell, immediately on which the greatest terror and confusion apparently took place among them. The women were constantly begging the warriors to sue for peace, and that one of the Indians had attempted to shoot Colonel Johnson, for the falsehood by which he had deceived and ruined them; that she overheard Butler telling Johnson it was impossible to keep the Indians together after the battle of Newtown; that he thought they must soon be in a miserable situation, as all their crops would be destroyed, and that Canada could not supply them with provisions at Niagara; that he would endeavor to collect the warriors to assist in the defence of that fort,—which he was of an opinion this army would lay siege to,—and the women and children he would send into Canada.

After having destroyed this town,—beyond which, I was informed, there was no settlement,— and destroyed all their houses and crops in that quarter, the army having been advancing seventeen days, with the supply of provisions before mentioned, and that much reduced on the march by accidents, and the Cayuga country being as yet unpenetrated, I thought it necessary to return as soon as possible, in order to effect the destruction of the settlements in that quarter. The army, therefore, began its march to Kanadasega. I was met on the way by a sachem from Oneida, and three warriors, one of whom I had sent from Catherine's with a letter, a copy of which I have the honor to inclose Congress. They delivered me a message from the warriors of that nation respecting the Cayugas: copies of that and my answer I also inclose from this place. I detached Colonel Smith with a party down the west side of the lake, to destroy the corn which had been cut down, and to destroy any thing further which might be discovered there. I then detached Colonel Gransvoort, with one hundred and five men, to Albany, to forward the baggage of the York regiments to the main army, and to take with him such soldiers as were at that place. I directed him to destroy the lower Mohawk castle in his route, and capture the inhabitants, — consisting only of six or seven families, — who are constantly employed in giving intelligence to the enemy, and in supporting their scouting parties when making incursions on our frontier. When the Mohawks joined the enemy, these few families were, undoubtedly, left to answer such a purpose, and to keep possession of their lands. The upper castle, now inhabited by Orkeskes, our friends, he was directed not to disturb. With him I sent Mr. Deane, who bore my answer to the Oneidas.

I then detached Colonel Butler, with six hundred men, to destroy the Cayuga country, and with him sent all the Indian warriors, who said, if they could find the Cayugas, they would endeavor to persuade them to deliver themselves up as prisoners, — the chief of them, called Teguttelawana, being a near relation of the sachem. I then crossed the Seneca River, and detached Colonel Dearborn to the west side of the Cayuga Lake, to destroy all the settlements which might be found there, and to intercept the Cayugas, if they attempted to escape Colonel Butler. The residue of the army passed on between the lakes towards Catherine's. Colonel Dearborn burnt, in his route, six towns, including one which had been before partly destroyed by a small party, — destroying, at the same time, quantities of corn. He took an Indian lad and three women prisoners, — one of the women being very old, and the lad a cripple; he left them, and brought on the other two, and joined the army on the evening of the 26th.

Colonel Cortland was then detached, with three hundred men, up the Tioga branch, to search for settlements in that quarter, and, in the space of two days, destroyed several fields of corn, and burnt several houses. Colonel Butler joined the army on the 28th, whereby a complete junction was formed, at Conowalahala, on the twenty-ninth day after our leaving Newtown. Here we were met by plenty of provisions from Tioga, which I had previously directed to be sent on. Colonel Butler destroyed, in the Cayuga country, five principal towns and a number of scattering houses, — the whole making about one hundred in number, exceedingly large and well built. He also destroyed a hundred acres of excellent corn, with a number of orchards, — one of which had in it fifteen hundred fruit-trees. Another Indian settlement was discovered near Newtown, by a party, consisting of thirty-nine houses, which were also destroyed. The number of towns destroyed by this army amounted to forty, besides scattering houses. The quantity of corn destroyed, at a moderate computation, must amount to one hundred and sixty thousand bushels, with a vast quantity of vegetables of every kind. Every creek and river has been traced, and the whole country explored, in search of Indian settlements, and I am well persuaded that, except one town situated near the Alleghany, about fifty miles from Geneseo, there is not a single town left in the country of the Five Nations. It is with pleasure I inform Congress that this army has not suffered the loss of forty men in action, or otherwise, since my taking the command; though, perhaps, few troops have experienced a more fatiguing campaign.

Besides, the difficulties which naturally attend marching through an enemy's country abounding in woods, creeks, rivers, mountains, morasses, and defiles, we found no small inconvenience from the want of proper guides; and the maps of the country are so exceedingly erroneous, that they serve, not to enlighten, but to perplex. We had not a single person who was sufficiently acquainted with the country to conduct a party out of the Indian path by day, or scarcely in it by night: though they were the best I could possibly procure. Their ignorance, doubtless, arose from the Indians having ever taken the best measures in their power to prevent their country's being explored. We had much labor in clearing our roads for the artillery, notwithstanding which the army moved from twelve to sixteen miles every day, when not detained by rains or employed in destroying settlements. I feel myself much indebted to the officers of every rank, for their unparalleled exertions, and to the soldiers, for the unshaken firmness with which they endured the toils and difficulties attending the expedition. Though I had it not in command, I should have ventured to have paid Niagara a visit, had I been supplied with a fifteen-days' provisions in addition to what I had, which, I am persuaded, from the bravery and ardor of our troops, would have fallen into our hands.

I forgot to mention that the Oneida sachem requested me to grant his people liberty to hunt in the country of the Five Nations, as they would never think of settling again in a country once subdued, and where their settlements must ever be in our power. I informed him, in answer, that I had no authority to grant such a license; that I could not at present see reason to object to it; but advised them to make application to Congress, who, I believed, would, in consideration of their friendly conduct, grant them every advantage of this kind that would not interfere with our settlement of the country, which, I believed, would soon take place. The Oneidas say, that, as no Indians were discovered by Colonel Butler at Cayuga, they are of opinion they are gone to their castle, and that their chiefs will persuade them to come in and surrender themselves on the terms I have proposed. The army began its march from Conowalohala yesterday, and arrived here this evening. After leaving the necessary force for securing the frontiers in this quarter, I shall move on to join the main army.

It would have been very pleasing to this army to have drawn the enemy to a second engagement; but such a panic seized them after the first action, that it was impossible, as they never ventured themselves within reach of the army, nor have they fired a single gun as it was on its march or in its quarters, though in a country exceeding well calculated for ambuscades. This circumstance alone would sufficiently prove that they suffered severely in the first effort.

Congress will please to pardon the length of this narrative, as I thought a particular and circumstantial detail of facts would not be disagreeable, especially as I have transmitted no accounts of the progress of this army since the action of the 29th August. I flatter myself that the orders with which I was intrusted are fully executed, as we have not left a single settlement or field of corn in the country of the Five Nations, nor is there even the appearance of an Indian on this side Niagara. Messengers and small parties have been constantly passing, and some imprudent soldiers, who straggled from the army, mistook the route, and went back almost to Genesee without discovering even the track of an Indian. I trust the steps I have taken with respect to the Oneidas, Cayugas, and Mohawks will prove satisfactory; and here I beg leave to mention, that, in searching the houses of these pretended neutral Cayugas, a number of scalps were found, which appeared to have been lately taken, which Colonel Butler showed to the Oneidas, who said that they were then convinced of the justice of the steps I had taken. The promise made to the soldiers, in my address at Newtown, I hope will be thought reasonable by Congress, and flatter myself that the performance of it will be ordered. Colonel Bruin will have the honor of delivering these despatches to your Excellency. I beg leave to recommend him to the particular notice of Congress, as an officer, who, on this as well as several other campaigns, has proved himself an active, brave, and truly deserving officer.

On the 1st of October, as the expedition was at Tioga, approaching the point from which it started two months before, General Sullivan addressed the friendly Oneidas gathered in his camp, in the following language, which was interpreted to them by Rev. Samuel Kirkland, long a devoted missionary among the Massachusetts and New-York tribes, and who, by his good sense and nobleness of character, ever possessed their friendship and confidence. He accompanied the Western army as chaplain and interpreter; and, on various occasions,—then, as before and after,—from his familiarity with the Indian dialects, did good service.

BROTHER WARRIORS,—It is with the highest sense of gratitude I now return you my thanks for your zealous and very faithful services with this army. As part of these troops will soon return to assist the grand army in subduing and totally extirpating our common enemy, I must beg you to bear the following message to the chief sachems and warriors of the Oneida nation:—

BROTHERS, SACHEMS, AND WARRIORS OF THE ONEIDA NATION,— It is the interest of the United States to use every means in their power to render your nation so respectable as to become the terror of all its enemies, and so numerous as to be able to furnish a respectable body of warriors when called upon by your allies to assist in extirpating a common enemy. It was with this view I advised those Cayugas who now profess friendship for us, to come in and obtain liberty to incorporate themselves with you; and it is, in my opinion, your highest interest to bring about this event, which must be even more advantageous for them.

I am well persuaded that Congress will totally extirpate the other five nations, except those who have joined you and continued friends to the United States, and such others as may think proper to come in and enter into a firm league to join our friends, the Oneidas.

Your own eyes have convinced you of the justice of the measures I pursued against the pretended friendly Cayugas, as the witnesses of their hostile, barbarous conduct were found in their houses. Notwithstanding which, should they or any other, who are sensible of the error they have been led into, come in upon the terms I have held out, they may depend on being well treated. Brothers, I am now returning with a part of the army, leaving a sufficient number to chastise such as may be hardy enough again to molest our frontiers. And I call upon you as friends and allies, that, if you know of any towns on the east side of the lake which belong to the unfriendly nations, and are not destroyed, you will send your warriors to demolish them. I have heard of a small, forsaken town, called Connasawactine, laying about thirty or forty miles from Onaguaga. This, in particular, I must request you to destroy.

Brothers, this is all I have to say.

The answer of Aghsarigowa, a young sachem of the Tuscaroras, and Teheaniyoghiwat, warrior of the Oneida nation, to Major-General Sullivan, interpreted by Rev. Mr. Kirkland, was as follows: —

BROTHER CHIEF WARRIOR, TEGEAGHTOGEA, — Open a candid ear! We are but children, compared with our wise men, and only three in number: we shall, therefore, speak our sentiments as individuals. Brother! You have expressed great satisfaction with our services since we joined your army: we are very happy to meet your approbation in any thing we have done, but are more pleased with your conduct and generous sentiments as a chief warrior.

Brother, you have intrusted us with an important message to our nation. Any answer to this, otherwise than as individuals, would be improper; we say, therefore, we wish we had been so fully possessed of your real sentiments at Kanadasega as we now are, respecting those of the Cayuga nation who have not taken an active part against the States: we think they might have been found, and, with great ease, prevailed upon to resign themselves as prisoners of war. Since their towns and fields are destroyed, they may not so readily admit this declaration of yours to be sincere: however, we believe it; as individuals, we say there is a propriety and justice in your laying waste their settlements and burning their cornfields, that not an ear of their corn should be left, lest it might fall into the hands of the enemy. Your clemency toward them, and friendship to the Oneidas, are equally conspicuous in proposing to spare any of them.

We are now convinced that your suspicions of the Cayugas, expressed at Kanadasega, were not without foundation: you see far into things, and judge well. Brother, you have assured us, upon the word of honor of a chief warrior, that such of the Cayugas as may come in and join themselves to our nation, first repairing to headquarters, shall be spared and well treated. This is all we can wish; this will animate our warriors to exert themselves, — both from friendship to some of the Cayugas and policy to their own nation, — that their strength and numbers may be increased, which you have so much at heart. Brother, we comply with the proposal, and shall faithfully execute the trust. As to the village called Kanaghsavaghtayen, you may depend on its being deserted last spring. Two of the chief warriors came to Oneida; the others went off to the Indian Butler. In consequence of Joseph Brant's advice to the one party, and threats to the other, some of the Tory party that went from Kanaghsavaghtayen built two houses and cleared some small cornfields betwixt that place and Ojeningo, as we have been credibly informed; and, as to any other settlements on this side the lakes, we declare upon honor we know nothing. As to the above-mentioned houses, betwixt Kanaghsavaghtayen and Ojeningo, be assured they shall be laid in ashes.

Brother, we hope to succeed in bringing in some of the Cayugas, and shall forward them immediately to the chief warrior of America, where we hope to see you. Brother, this is all we shall say.

AGHSARIGOWA.
TEHEANIYOGHIWAT.

This address, and the answer, Sullivan communicated to Congress from Tioga, on the 2d of October, with the following letter to Mr. Jay, the President: —

SIR, — I have the honor to inclose your Excellency copy of a speech made by me to the Oneidas yesterday, with a copy of their answer. I hope Congress will approve of the measures I have adopted with a view of raising the ambition of the Oneidas, and bringing in the repenting savages. The warriors assure me that numbers will come in upon the terms I have proposed, and that they will send them to headquarters or to Congress. Should Congress apprehend that I have pursued measures not founded on good policy, I flatter myself that proper allowances will be made for the situation I was in. I was too remote from Congress and from the commander-in-chief to receive the necessary instructions, and therefore was obliged to follow those steps which my own judgment dictated; and, though I may have erred in judgment, I can, with great truth, declare that I have been influenced by no motive but that of rendering service to my country; and nothing will be more pleasing to me than to hear that my conduct is approved by the wisdom of that body.

On two several occasions after their defeat at Newtown, the Six Nations, as ascertained subsequently, came to the determination to oppose the invading army. The first ground selected was at what is now known as Henderson's Flats, between Honeoye Creek and Lake Connissius. Placing themselves in ambush, they made a sudden attack on the advanced guard, who, after a severe skirmish, fell back on the main body. The Indians recognized the folly of assailing forces greatly superior to their own, who were prepared to receive them; and, disheartened, withdrew. Again, on the 13th of September, with a strong body of rangers to aid them, they showed a disposition to make a stand and provoke an engagement. The army was brought into order of battle; and Clinton moved, with his brigade, to gain their rear: upon which they fled with precipitation. They became utterly discouraged; and, if his orders had justified his proceeding to Niagara, Sullivan might have reduced it. But his provisions, carefully husbanded, were barely sufficient for the homeward march.

It has been suggested, that the crops destroyed might have fed the army. But Indian corn or maize dries slowly for the mill, and could not have been ground into meal, on a march, in sufficient quantities. It might have served for forage, but not for rations. Moreover, the post at Niagara was easily defended. It was well fortified; and its garrison, with open water communications, could have been indefinitely strengthened. Without artillery or supplies, had its investment been protracted at this late period of the season, the result would probably have been disaster. Four hundred miles from their base of operations, their retreat through an almost unbroken wilderness, the combined forces of British and Indians would have had them at advantage, and greatly distressed, if not annihilated, them. It was prudence, part of that policy which — in praise or blame, termed Fabian — achieved independence, not to make an attempt which, if unfortunate, might have endangered the success of the cause.

Washington wrote Lafayette from West Point, 12th September, that "the expedition must convince the Indians that their cruelties could not pass with impunity; and that they had been instigated to arms and acts of barbarism by a nation unable to protect them, and which had left them to that correction due to their villany." On the 28th, he writes Colonel John Laurens, "By this time I expect General Sullivan will have completed the entire destruction of the whole settlements of the Six Nations, excepting those of the Oneidas and such other friendly towns as have merited a different treatment. He had, by my last advices of the 9th, penetrated beyond their middle settlements, had burned between fifteen and twenty towns, destroyed all their crops, and was advancing to their exterior villages. Men, women, and children were flying before him to Niagara, distant more than one hundred miles, in the utmost consternation, distress, and confusion, with the Butlers, Brant, and others at their head." In another letter to Lafayette, Oct. 20, he says, "General Sullivan, having completed the entire destruction of the country of the Six Nations, is at Easton, on his return to join the army with the troops under his command. While the Six Nations were under the rod of correction, the Mingo and Muncey tribes, on the Alleghany, French Creek, and other waters of the Ohio above Fort Pitt, met with similar chastisement from Colonel Brodhead, who, with six hundred men, advanced upon them at the same instant, and laid waste their country."

After what has been said, it seems superfluous to vindicate further either the policy or propriety of these acts of reprisal. But should a like disposition be exhibited in the forthcoming volume of the work which has led to this publication, or any future writer detract or asperse, a calm consideration of all the circumstances may serve to protect the memory of Sullivan from misconstruction. Much has been said in censure of the expedition, on the score of humanity. Retaliation, prompt and decisive, has ever proved a stern necessity in dealing with savage tribes,—the only method of staying their brutalities. In carrying out that policy in this campaign, the aim was to strike a salutary terror, without unnecessary destruction of life. Few Indians were slain, except at the battle of Newtown. Unreasoning sensitiveness may be shocked at the approach, in a Christian nation, to savage warfare, even with a savage foe. But what the best men of the country, who knew well the Indian character, deemed justifiable and expedient, needs little apology.

Even in these days, practices are tolerated, in hostilities between civilized nations, when temper has gained the ascendant, that are repugnant to all dictates of humanity. In the Revolution, warfare as unsparing and relentless was waged by British officers, with the sanction of their government, against non-combatants, incapable of resistance. The Jersey prison-ships; employment of Hessians, instructed to give no quarter; use of the tomahawk and scalping-knife, as at Wyoming and Cherry Valley; the perpetration, in their forays into Jersey, of barbarities not to be surpassed; the brutalities of Mowatt and Arnold; and the inroad into Connecticut, this very summer, when Fairfield, Norwalk, and New Haven were reduced to ashes,—equalled in atrocity the most flagitious enormities of any people, ancient or modern, Christian or Pagan. However reluctant Washington and Sullivan, both more than ordinarily generous and humane, may have been to inflict such wide-spread devastation, public duty demanded it; and Sullivan had no alternative but to carry out his instructions, and obey the orders of Congress.

Without undue digression, some particulars relating to

the Six Nations may render our narrative of the events of the campaign more intelligible, and be acceptable to readers not familiar with their history. According to tradition, a confederacy subsisted, from periods anterior to the earliest European exploration, composed of the Mohawks, Oneidas, Onondagas, Cayugas, and Senecas. They dwelt along the St. Lawrence and the Great Lakes; wresting, in 1603, from the Adirondacks, a branch of the Algonquins, the valley of the Mohawk. In 1712, the Tuscaroras, — a cognate tribe, if a common dialect be any indication, — driven from North Carolina, joined them; and they were afterwards known as the Six Nations. The French gave them the generic term of "Iroquois:" their most usual designation among themselves was "Aquanuscioni," or the "United People." Their territory they termed "The Long House:" the Mohawks guarding the east door, — Skënektäde, — at Albany; the Senecas, the west. The former, as most warlike, furnished the military chieftain; the Onondagas, the principal sachem, and kept alive the national council fire.

Surrounded by tribes as restless as themselves, — the Chippewas, Hurons, Miamis, to the north and west; the Lenni Lenape, or Delawares, to the south; Adirondacks to the north; and the Mohegans along the Mohickannittuck, or Hudson, — much of their time was spent in war or diplomacy. For both they displayed natural taste and aptitude; surpassing most other Indian tribes in sagacity and shrewdness as in courage. They had sense to perceive their inability to resist the rapid encroachments of our settlers on their hunting-grounds, and that their annihilation or expulsion from the land of their fathers was but a question of time. This discouraging prospect naturally deepened their characteristic gravity into sadness, and also greatly envenomed their hatred against the intruders. Before the introduction of fire-arms, their warfare amongst themselves consisted chiefly of stealthy approaches, hand-to-hand encounters, implacable resentments, fierce delight in inflicting pain and subjecting to indignity. With more reasonable ground to dislike those of another race who were taking possession of their territories, they were little inclined to substitute, for their ancient methods of warfare, refinements of their adversaries which placed themselves at disadvantage. In contending for the mastery with hostile tribes, they were no doubt wily and treacherous: but, with a civilized foe, they employed the more craft on account of their comparative weakness; were more cruel and merciless, when opportunity presented temptation, from the feeling that they had been wronged, and were still exposed to aggression. Their longing for fire-water, which the whites furnished them, made them dependent, and far less formidable. Under its influence, they became uncontrollable, and glutted their fiendish taste for torture, at the cost of those who supplied the poison. Excess debased and degraded the red man as much, if not more, than it ever has the white. Could they have been spared this scourge, the impression left of them would have much more nearly approached the ideal standard of fiction. Few Indian races anywhere have presented a higher natural type than that of the Iroquois.

Their laws and customs, of immemorial sanction, were well defined, and, if simple, suited to their condition. Their conception of God — of a Great Spirit, who had created and still governed the universe, so far as it was known to them — was rational and elevated. Their moral sense was discriminating, and they expiated sin by vicarious sacrifice. Living in a region of extraordinary grandeur and beauty, — amidst mountains and cataracts and lakes of exceeding loveliness, — they were, as is found often the case with people similarly placed, imaginative and emotional. They were affectionate and loyal, attaching sacred regard to the rites of hospitality; and forming friendships, life-long and intimate, by exchange of names, — a practice not unknown among the Germans. Self-respect, a dignity of character that brooked no superiority, that flinched from no pain or peril, were distinguishing traits, not of the chiefs alone, but of their warriors generally. If taciturn, as they are commonly described, this was probably less from pride than ignorance of our language. Their own vocabulary was ample, and abounded in euphonious polysyllables, requiring practice to use with facility.

The Six Nations had borrowed largely from the civilization along their borders. Missionaries and traders frequented their villages, and instructed them in its virtues and vices, inventions and arts. Many of the chieftains were well informed and intelligent; some few among them possessed of education. If characters like that of Uncas are creations of romance, the wisdom and eloquence they occasionally displayed in intercourse with their conquerors, claimed admiration and inspired respect. They were bold and fearless, excellent marksmen, and, in their peculiar warfare, formidable antagonists. Their houses were convenient, their fields well tilled, their orchards thrifty, the forests abounded in game, the lakes and rivers with fish. But where now nearly two millions of people crowd, with opulent cities or marts of trade, a continuous garden teeming with plentiful harvests, ninety years ago were sparsely scattered, not many more than one hundredth part that number gathering a precarious subsistence.

With pioneers, like Sir William Johnson, whose castle still stands on the Mohawk, or with the garrisons on the frontier, they had constant traffic and intercourse; and, deriving from Canada powder and ball, and articles of luxury which they prized, they were easily persuaded to take part in any scheme of rapine or hostility. Efforts were early made in the war, by the Congress, to secure their neutrality; but, their supplies depending upon their siding with the Crown, these were of little avail. The influence which Sir William Johnson, who died in 1774, possessed over them, descended to his son, Sir John, who, with Guy Johnson, Colonel John Butler, and his son Walter, and other British officers, incessantly instigated them to join in incursions upon defenceless settlements, — to massacres and atrocities, in which both races showed themselves equally savage. Joseph Brant, or Thayendanegea, a half-breed, the brother of the last Lady Johnson, known as Molly Brant, had been sent in 1761, at the age of nineteen, to a seminary at Lebanon in Connecticut, where he passed, it is said, three years. Upon his return, he soon gained an ascendancy throughout the confederacy, which he retained during the Revolution, and long afterwards, till his death, in 1807. He was brave, and often led in the war-path; but the imputation of cruelty, often made against him, appears to be without foundation, and anecdotes are numerous of his generosity and kindness.

At the massacre with which his name was associated by the poet Campbell, in his "Gertrude of Wyoming," he was not present. Indeed, this was rather a contest between Tories who had been driven away from their possessions, and the friends of independence. The valley of Wyoming had for many years been an object of contention between the Iroquois and Delawares, the latter being finally compelled to yield. Embraced in the patents of Connecticut, and also in Penn's, rival claimants from either colony had later striven in arms for its possession. Compromise had been partially effected; and, at the beginning of the war, five thousand people, in its several settlements, pursued the arts of peace and industry. The larger number favoring the American cause, the Tories were ejected; but they returned, with Indian auxiliaries, when the young men were, for the most part, away in the Federal army, to wreak their resentment.

But Wyoming in 1778, Cherry Valley in 1779, formed a small portion of the bloody raids along the border. They inspired the greater dread, that they came without warning and when least expected, and seemed only to be distinguished by their increasing atrocities. Tidings that the British were fomenting hostilities throughout the West, and that combinations had been actually formed for a general attack upon our frontier settlements, produced alarm, and demanded vigorous measures. Washington, who had been much among the Indians, shared with them in the chase, tarried in their villages, and well knew their character, had proposed retaliation, from a conviction that an offensive war was the only mode to deter them from repetition of their enormities. He could not have supposed that any measures, however vigorous or successful, would change their nature or stop their ravages; but he hoped, by destroying their resources, to check them, and this he effectually accomplished.

The army resumed its march, and arrived at its starting-point, at Easton, the 15th of October. It had traversed, going and returning, from six to seven hundred miles of a most difficult country, intersected by numberless watercourses, without roads, where the Indian trails were often rather a perplexity than an aid. If the expedition was not particularly eventful in startling incidents, the journals and diaries of several of the officers, as also numerous private letters that have been preserved, mention occurrences of much interest to the inhabitants of the country, as well as to the descendants of those who took part in the campaign. Many of the local names that occur in them, as also in the foregoing correspondence, still designate the waters, or towns that occupy the sites of Indian villages; and their musical cadence causes regret that more have not been retained. With this exception, few vestiges remain, over all the twenty to twenty-five thousand square miles which constituted their domain, of these once-powerful tribes.

Shortly after Great Britain acknowledged the independence of her revolted colonies, measures were taken to determine the title to the territory. This was disputed; both New York and Massachusetts claiming it. The latter, under its patent from the Plymouth Company, bounded on the Western Ocean. The Dutch colony of New York, surrendered to

Charles II., had been by him given to his brother, the Duke of York, afterwards James II. This grant only covered what the Dutch had reduced to possession; and, though their settlements had extended along the Hudson, they had not spread far beyond its western bank. The charge of the claim, on the part of Massachusetts, was left to a committee of its legislature, of which James Sullivan — a brother of General Sullivan, who had recently resigned his seat on the Supreme Bench, and afterwards Governor of the State — was the chairman. He was chosen, at the same time, to the Continental Congress; and the title was submitted for adjudication to a tribunal, constituted as provided under the articles of confederation. It was agreed between the litigants, in 1786, to divide equally the territory between them. Unfortunately for Massachusetts, her legislature resolved to dispose of her share prematurely, and far less was obtained for it than might have been realized had she waited a few years longer. But her debt was large, her taxes burthensome, and the charge of such a territory, outside her borders, was an embarrassment. Precautions were taken, in her agreement with New York and with her own grantees, to protect the Indians; and, nearly forty years later, agents were appointed by her executive to attend negotiations with the remaining Indian proprietors, and see that their rights were respected.

When the letter of General Sullivan of the 28th of September, transmitted by Washington on the 9th of October, reached Philadelphia on the 14th, on motion of Mr. Gerry, seconded by Mr. Morris, "the thanks of Congress were voted to his Excellency General Washington for directing, and to Major-General Sullivan and the brave officers and soldiers under his command for effectually executing, an important expedition against such of the Indian nations as, encouraged by the councils and conducted by the officers of his Brittanic majesty, had perfidiously waged an unprovoked and cruel war against these United States, laid waste many of their defenceless towns, and, with savage barbarity, slaughtered the inhabitants thereof;" and it was ordered, that the second Thursday in December should be set apart as a general day of thanksgiving.

As the campaign was now ended, and the army to be broken up, the usual testimonials of respect and kindly feeling were tendered General Sullivan by those who had served under him. The following, dated the 16th of October, is signed by General Maxwell, Colonels Shreeve and Spencer, and the other officers of the Jersey Brigade. The expression of approbation of his services may seem out of place, unless interpreted by the disposition, manifested in preceding campaigns, to hold him responsible for not succeeding where success was not to be expected.

We, the Generals and Field-officers of the Jersey Brigade, in their behalf beg leave to offer to your Honor the just tribute of our grateful applause for your polite attention to your officers, your unwearied and indefatigable endeavors to serve your country and your army, during your command on the Western expedition. We are filled with the most agreeable sensations when we reflect on the important success of this part of the American army, and the harmony and universal satisfaction that subsisted in it, which, we are convinced, was owing in a great degree to your impartiality and superior abilities. We have the pleasure to assure you, that not only the officers, but the soldiers, unanimously approve of your conduct during your present command; and they trust it will be the same in future, whenever they shall have the honor of serving under you. We are, with the greatest respect and esteem.

In his letter to Washington occurred the following passage, alluding to his health: "I should have acknowledged the receipt of your Excellency's favors of the 15th and 24th of August, and those of the 3d and 15th instant, had not my ill state of health, which has continued through the campaign, the constant fatigue, and the difficulty of forwarding expresses, prevented. That of the 15th reached me the 26th. I am happy to find that your wishes therein expressed were anticipated; as there is not, at this time, even the appearance of an Indian on this side of the Genesee, and I believe there is not one on this side Niagara, nor is there any kind of sustenance left for them in this country."

For five years Sullivan had been in active service, winter and summer. His incessant duties and limited resources prevented much attention to his health; and his physicians now advised him, that, in its present condition, further exposures in the field would be fatal. He accordingly concluded to resign. Perhaps the nature of his last campaign, and the injustice to which he had had to submit, may have strengthened this determination. On the 6th of November, he wrote Washington as follows, from Sovereign's tavern: —

DEAR GENERAL, — I am sorry to inform your Excellency, that I am under the painful necessity of leaving a service to which I am, by principle and interest, attached. And among the variety of mortifications which I must suffer in quitting it, that of being deprived of the pleasure of serving under your Excellency stands among the foremost. My health is too much impaired to be recovered, but by a total release from business. And, though the physicians give me encouragement that this will restore me, I am myself convinced of the contrary; and fear that I must content myself with enjoying the reflection of having used my utmost to serve my country, as the only thing I shall receive in exchange for a constitution sacrificed in endeavoring to promote its interests. Should there be a probability of the Count d'Estaing's arrival, I would willingly wait to give the little assistance in my power to extirpate the enemies of the country. But should this not be likely to happen, and the season be too far advanced, I must beg your Excellency's leave to retire as soon as possible, that I may take every measure in my power to restore my health in some degree; or, at least, to live in such a measure as will not tend to put it beyond a possibility of being restored, which a longer continuance in the service undoubtedly will.

Three days later, he sent a communication to Congress, requesting leave, on account of ill health, to retire from the army. It was moved that his resignation should not be accepted, but that he should have leave to retire from the service as long as he should judge it expedient for the recovery of his health. This was left to a committee, who reported, on the 30th, that Congress had a just sense of the services and abilities of Major-General Sullivan, and greatly regret the indisposition which deprives them of so gallant an officer; but that, as his health would not permit him to remain in the American army, his resignation be accepted. It being then moved by Mr. Gerry, seconded by Mr. Peabody, that General Sullivan should have leave to retire so long as he should judge necessary for the recovery of his health, four States — Massachusetts, New Hampshire, Rhode Island, and North Carolina — voted in favor, and New York, New Jersey, Pennsylvania, Maryland, and one member from Virginia, were opposed. The report of the committee was accepted, and the usual thanks voted for his past services.

These votes have been cited by the ill-natured, who take pleasure in disparagement, as proving a low estimate of Sullivan as a general officer. Some of the Congress may have been biassed. The Board of War was all influential; and he had offended them. The secret history of the Cabal reveals the unscrupulous expedients to which they at times resorted to promote their favorites, in the place of Washington, Sullivan, and Greene. But continuance on the army rolls was wholly incompatible with his health, resources, or obligations to his wife and children; and he was sincere in his request to be relieved. Many who opposed the amendment, proposed to be substituted in part for the report of the committee, were doubtless his friends, and voted as he wished.

Other generals retired from the army, but none with any more flattering testimonials. Popular favor for military men is sufficiently capricious; but that of politicians, swayed by selfish or party interests, is no test whatever of merit. This was especially true of Congress in 1779, which had degenerated since 1775. Many would have gladly seen Washington supplanted by Gates, who had received the surrender of Burgoyne at Saratoga, — the great success of the war. Prejudices and animosities, rife at that period, still taint the pens of the superficial and malignant. But an impartial study of the materials that remain for forming an exact estimate of the military characters of the Revolution dispels such delusions. The foregoing correspondence cannot fail to convince the candid that Sullivan possessed unusual aptitudes for military service, which experience and criticism had served to improve. However vexatious to encounter cavil and detraction in the path of duty, there is no more effective spur to excellence. Sullivan had his share of them, and knew how to profit by what was disagreeable.

In taking leave of Washington, in a letter not printed in full, but which is probably still in existence, he thus cautions him to be on his guard against those who were seeking to undermine him in public confidence: " Permit me to inform your Excellency, that the faction raised against you, in 1777, into which General Conway was unfortunately and imprudently drawn, is not yet destroyed. The members are waiting to collect strength, and seize some favorable moment to appear in force. I speak not from conjecture, but from certain knowledge. Their plan is to take every method of proving the danger arising from a commander who enjoys the full and unlimited confidence of his army, and alarm the people with the prospect of imaginary evils; nay, they will endeavor to convert your virtues into arrows, with which they will seek to wound you.

" The next stage is to persuade Congress that the military power of America should be placed in three or four different hands, each having a separate quarter of the continent assigned to him, and each commander to answer to Congress only for his conduct. This, they say, will prevent an aspiring commander from enslaving his country, and put it in the power of Congress, with the assistance of the other commanders, to punish the attempt. This is a refinement in politics, an improvement on public virtue, which Greece and Rome could never boast. The present time is unfavorable to their designs. They well know that the voice of citizens and soldiers would be unanimously against them; but they wait a more favorable opportunity, which they will certainly improve. I am well convinced that they cannot succeed; yet I thought it my duty, on the moment of my departure, to give you this notice, that you may not only be on your guard, but avoid intrusting those persons in matters where your interest and honor are nearly concerned. I persuade myself that your steady and prudent conduct will baffle every attempt."

To this letter Washington writes, in reply, from Morristown, Dec. 15: —

"I had the pleasure of receiving, a few days since, by Captain Bruin, your letter of the 1st inst. I assure you, I am sensibly touched by so striking an instance of your friendship, at a time and in a manner, that demonstrates its own sincerity, and confirms the opinion I have always entertained of your sentiments towards me. I wish you to believe that your uneasiness, on the score you mention, had never the least foundation. A slender acquaintance with the world must convince every man, that deeds, not words, are the true criterion of the attachment of his friends, and that the most liberal professions of good-will are far from being the surest marks of it.

"I should be happy, if my own experience had afforded fewer examples of the little dependence to be placed upon them. I am particularly indebted to you for the interesting information you give me of the views of a certain party. Against intrigues of this kind, incident to every man in a public station, his best support will be a faithful discharge of his duty, and he must rely on the justice of his country for the event.

"I flatter myself it is unnecessary for me to repeat to you how high a place you hold in my esteem. The confidence you have experienced, and the manner in which you have been employed on several important occasions, testify the value I set upon your military qualifications, and the regret I must feel, that circumstances have deprived the army of your services. The pleasure I shall always take in an interchange of good offices, in whatever station you may hereafter be placed, will be the best confirmation of the personal regard with which I have been, and am,

"Very sincerely, dear sir," &c.

In his expressions of regret, from Morristown, that Sullivan was leaving the army, Greene gives this gloomy picture of the condition of affairs: "Our military exertions, however great, leave us but a dull prospect, while administration is torn to pieces by faction, and the business of finance is in distress. False pride and secret enmity poison our counsels, and distract our measures; indeed, the States are so local in their policy, that we are more like individuals than a united body." But it was not in consequence of these discouraging circumstances that Sullivan resigned. Had his health and obligations permitted his retaining his post, he would have accepted the situation as did others, and persevered, submitting in patience to that injustice and caprice which are apt to sway when deliberative bodies control military movements. But he had done his duty; and, justified in his own mind in quitting the service, must have gladly welcomed emancipation from a thraldom fretting his sensitive nature to the quick.

Here closes his connection with the army. Readers can form, from this review of his campaigns, their own estimate of his military character. Neither his civil nor military claims, to be remembered, would have been probably recalled to public notice, had not the latter been impugned. It is, upon the whole, fortunate, as so much of interest remained in manuscript, not likely otherwise to reach the light, that the subject has been disturbed. After impartial examination, the conviction seems irresistible, that he displayed, in the field, abilities of the same high order that distinguished him at the bar, as a member of Congress, in his administration as executive of his State. It cannot be reasonably disputed, that, after Washington and Greene, he ranked among the ablest generals of the Revolution.

In coming to this conclusion, no allowance is made for want of preparatory training, limited means or opportunities. Other good generals had no better, and all alike must be judged by what they were and did. Any extraordinary embarrassments, common to them all, should be taken into view. There were many exceedingly discouraging. Throughout the early period of the war, the soldiers were to be instructed in their duties in the intervals of toilsome marches, or in the presence of the enemy. Freedom from restraint in their previous pursuits made discipline irksome, and no less motive than the object at stake and consequences of defeat could have reconciled them to its necessity. Officers often knew less than their men, and had few advantages over them to command obedience or inspire respect. There was little uniformity of drill; the guns were of different sizes and descriptions; and, from short enlistments, soldiers, by the time they became effective, left the ranks, and were replaced by raw recruits.

Out of such material to form an army able to cope with veterans well organized, armed, and officered, demanded strenuous effort, patience not easily perturbed, a vigilance never relaxed. The best of tact and temper were requisite to insure subordination, render attractive midnight marches, or work upon the lines. Sullivan possessed these, and many other natural and acquired qualifications, for his share of this task. He had the happy faculty, invaluable in a civil war, of winning affection from officers and men, testified on occasions proving its sincerity. His dignity of character and bearing conciliated their confidence, yet repelled undue familiarity; and a buoyant temperament and kindly nature made him easy of approach, and his intercourse agreeable. He was generous and sympathetic, never sparing time or means to do a service. His consideration for the sick and wounded, his attention to the comfort and enjoyment of all, his justice and impartiality, have been specially recorded.

Coolness in critical moments; equanimity never perplexed

or disconcerted; intuitive perception of all possible contingencies and probabilities; sagacity to anticipate the designs of his adversaries, and wisdom, by rapid combinations, to baffle and circumvent them; confidence in his own resources, which awaits events without anxiety, encounters unexpected conjunctures with composure, improves occasion promptly and with vigor; moral courage and loyalty to obligation, which assumes responsibilities, regardless of selfish considerations,—are essential elements in the character of a good commander, and there is evidence to show that Sullivan possessed them. If by nature of a fiery and impetuous temper, and indifferent to personal danger, he was mindful of the lives intrusted to his keeping, and cautious how he needlessly exposed them.

Active and indefatigable, he shared with the men in their toils and hardships, was ever at the post of danger to lead the attack or cover the retreat, when there was hesitation or panic. Emergencies were frequently occurring in which the example of their commander was needed to embolden the brave as well as the timid. The popularity which he gained by these traits, he improved by timely words, to keep aglow their ardor, and attach them to the cause.

As the war proceeded, this was a more difficult task. The country, in time, became exhausted. The soldiers were famishing, without shoes or garments. If paid at all, it was in a depreciating currency, which lost what little it had of value before expended. Hope of success, however remote, appeared irrational. To keep an army in the field, under circumstances so deplorable, demanded ability, the noblest traits, in the general officers. Had they not possessed them, their forces would have melted away, and resistance ceased for lack of combatants. All credit is due to the indomitable spirit that animated the patriots; but, if they had not reposed implicit faith in their leaders, they would not have served under them. They were fighting in a rebel cause; realizing that defeat would expose both themselves and their officers to ignominious punishment, reduce all ranks to the same level. Not their own safety alone, but the cause for which they were incurring risk and sacrifice, depended upon the competency of their generals. Not one of them, unless Washington, received from their soldiers more genuine and unqualified marks of their confidence than Sullivan. If this resulted, in some instances, from his having been traduced, as by Mr. Burke after Brandywine, they generally were the spontaneous recognition of his considerate care, and prompted by affection. He did not court their favor by any sedulous arts, but by deserving it. But he understood human nature, had tact to perceive when severity should be tempered by lenity, and continued a favorite though maintaining authority.

In an army so constituted, very rigid discipline would have thinned the ranks, and circumspection was to be used. Sullivan was exacting, and occasionally gave offence, as in June, 1777, by insisting upon conformity to the rules. But he kept within the limits of moderation, aiming rather at what would be judicious under the circumstances, than best under more favorable conditions. That his division was considered effective, may be inferred from Washington confronting it so often with the enemy. It consisted chiefly of good materials, — New-Hampshire and Maryland regiments forming part of it.

Sullivan was said to have always the best intelligence of any in the army. His instructions for special or partisan service are minute and sensible. His marches were well arranged and expeditious, and, on several occasions, at night; and, although through a strange country, they were without the least confusion. He was ever on the alert for opportunity; willing, with a fair chance of inflicting a blow upon the enemy, to brave the possible mortification of defeat. The several occasions on which he held independent commands afforded little opportunity for the display of strategy on any extended scale. But his correspondence indicates that grasp of mind and acquaintance with principles which plans campaigns and constitutes generalship. The best evidence of his abilities on the battle-field has been already spread before the reader, and needs no repetition. Lafayette said that the engagement at Butt's Hill was the best-fought battle of the war. From the outset of the Revolution, Sullivan took pains to fit himself for its exigencies. He purchased a valuable collection of military works, and studied them, until they, unfortunately, were captured.

Whatever the post assigned him, he accepted it cheerfully, and discharged its duties with all his energies. After withdrawing the troops from Canada in 1776, eliciting the admiration of the whole army, he was superseded by Gates; and again, a month later, he was placed at Long Island, under Putnam. If ambitious for positions of greater responsibility, what general of that war or any other has not exhibited a sentiment universal among soldiers? But throughout his military life — at the siege of Boston; in Canada, at Long Island, in West Chester, at Trenton, in 1776; at Princeton, in the Jerseys, in front of Morristown, in the descent on Staten Island, at Brandywine and Germantown, at Valley Forge, in 1777; in the campaigns on Rhode Island, in 1778; in Western New York, in 1779 — he did his full part towards bringing about American independence. As is ever the case with subordinates in war, the prudence and bravery that won the victory, or prevented disaster in defeat, did not always get the credit.

Among his brother officers, there were few, of any note, who were not warmly attached to him. Arthur St. Clair — a very good officer, but unfortunate then, as a dozen years later, when defeated on the Indian frontier — he had censured for his retreat from Ticonderoga. Parsons felt offended at some strictures upon an expedition to Long Island, that should have been attended with better success. De Borre, his brigadier, who took advantage of his long European service to dictate, when he did not understand our language or the character of our people, was a block of stumbling. But these were exceptional; and numerous letters exist, to show that he was highly esteemed and tenderly beloved, not only by those who served under him, by Poor, Varnum, Stark, Maxwell, Cornell, Glover, Hazen, Wayne, Laurens, and Scammell, all honored names, and none more gallant than the last; but by Washington, Greene, Lafayette, Knox, Sterling, Schuyler, Steuben, Hamilton, Heath, Putnam, Stephen, McDougall, Lincoln, and every other officer of rank and character whose respect or friendship was worth having.

As the war went on, members of the Congress who had served with him withdrew to other posts of duty. The success of Gates at Saratoga had covered him with glory, to be as speedily lost in the Southern campaign. But, while he continued in the ascendant, the intrigues of his friends, to supplant Washington, worked to the prejudice of all who stood in the way. Sullivan, who was associated with the great expectations of the Rhode-Island expedition and with its disappointments, may have fallen somewhat in the estimation of Congress. But recent experience shows how little reliance can be placed upon popularity as a test of merit.

Allusion has already been made to the bias evident in Gordon. His book was published in England. He had had a bitter controversy with James Sullivan, of Massachusetts, upon the impropriety of Sir John Temple — a loyalist and alien enemy — being permitted to remain in the country. Gordon was a friend of Bowdoin, father-in-law of Temple; and a letter of General Sullivan to Hancock, congratulating him on his triumph over Bowdoin, in the contest for the chief magistracy, intercepted, and printed at New York in Rivington's Gazette, still further imbittered his dislike. Any one who compares Gordon's statements with historical documents, will discover gross carelessness, if not deliberate misrepresentation.

The character and conduct of all historical personages are fair subjects for scrutiny. Neither the descendants nor the friends of General Sullivan can desire that his should be exempt from that ordeal which whoever engages in public affairs accepts. They have no reason to apprehend, that a thorough study of his life and correspondence, of his civil and military career, will otherwise than redound to his glory and honor.

From early manhood, for thirty years, he was incessantly in the public service. He shared the friendship and esteem of Dr. Franklin, Jefferson, Jay, John and Samuel Adams, the Morrises, Lees, Livingstons, and others of the best men of his day. He was repeatedly elevated by his own State to the highest places of trust and confidence. During the war, whenever censured from temporary misapprehension, he was invariably applauded when the truth was ascertained. He risked life, lost health, sacrificed a considerable portion of his estate, in establishing the liberty of his country. He considered neither hardships nor privations of any consequence, in her service. If he had little experience of military movements, this was true also of Washington, and of nearly all our Revolutionary commanders. He ever acted under a deep sense of responsibility to promote the cause for which, if unsuccessful, in common with other more conspicuous personages, he was likely to be selected for the pains and penalties of treason.

Lights and shades may add to the interest of a narrative, but are dearly purchased at the sacrifice of truth. Character, and the susceptibilities of descendants, are too sacred to be sported with for the entertainment or instruction of readers. What wealth or personal endowment, what social distinction or laurels, literary or political, are more precious to possess than the privilege of having sprung from such a character as General Greene, or from Washington, had he left posterity? Not for any vainglory or consequence in the sight of other men, but from a natural pride implanted in every generous breast. Honorable public service, self-sacrifice for national objects, transmit, to those that come after, a share in their rewards, and shed a lustre on succeeding generations. Under monarchical forms, this, carried to excess, may foster hereditary exclusiveness, or build up a privileged class; but there is no such tendency under free institutions. There is little danger anywhere, that the grand qualities and noble traits which history delights to honor can be too highly estimated, too much extolled or respected, either in their original brightness or their reflected splendors.

An humble wish to vindicate the memory of General Sullivan from reflections upon his military character, proceeding obviously from prejudice, led to this publication. The evidence offered proves those reflections undeserved. It is for the public, now and hereafter, to decide if this judgment be correct. It is our duty, who cherish his memory, — descendants, kindred, friends of free institutions, the State he so long and faithfully served, the American people, — to take heed that every fact, circumstance, motive, be considered, before his fair fame, as an efficient leader in the achievement of our national independence, is unjustly tarnished.

The specific allegations that have been brought against him, and which it has been our aim to refute, are: First, Want of discretion in submitting to Congress propositions of reconciliation from Lord Howe. Second, An injudicious descent on Staten Island, in August, 1777. Third, Transmitting intelligence to Washington which was subsequently found to be incorrect; disobedience of orders; and marching his troops to the right of Stirling, at Brandywine, Sept. 11, 1777. Fourth, Wasting powder at Germantown, Oct. 4, 1777. Fifth, Recommending Conway as inspector-general. Sixth, Keeping on terms of courtesy with Gates.

From these charges, the following condensed summary presents what seems a conclusive vindication: —

I. That General Sullivan should have gladly embraced the proposal of Howe, to go to Philadelphia, where he could best effect his exchange for Prescott, was far from being an indiscretion. It certainly would have been the height of indiscretion to have refused to communicate Howe's friendly dispositions, in such form as he inclined to make them,—not certainly again in writing, as they had already been so received; and it was for Congress to determine what notice to take of them.

After such a defeat as that of Long Island, to gain time by negotiation, to recover strength for more effectual resistance, was the part of prudence; and prejudice must travel far to find, in the course pursued by Sullivan, any ground for censure.

II. Marshall says, the descent on Staten Island was well planned and conducted, although boats enough were not secured to warrant the attempt. Gordon shows there were boats enough; but the persons in charge were frightened off from the landing, by seeing the eighty prisoners captured by Ogden, in their red uniforms, on a vessel he had seized.

Smallwood was to have placed a regiment at the Cross roads, to have intercepted, at the Neck, fugitives from the Provincial regiments routed by Ogden, while on their way to give the alarm to the regulars; but, as Marshall tells us, he was misconducted, by his guides, to the front, instead of to the rear, of the enemy. Accidents are apt to attend such attacks by night, and should not be attributed, *as faults*, to any one.

Ogden says, if Congress had not been imposed upon by misrepresentations, no court of inquiry would have been ordered, and its decree exonerated Sullivan from all reproach. If the public are not also imposed upon by misrepresentations, they will confirm this decree. In the eagerness to censure, no notice is taken of the reasons why the expedition proved less successful than anticipated. As to any consequent delay in joining Washington, this is absurd. The British fleet was reported in the Chesapeake on the 21st, and Sullivan had returned from the island on the 22d.

III. The transmission, at Brandywine, of the intelligence of Major Spear, Washington said was the duty of Sullivan.

As to disobedience of orders, had Washington seen fit to persist in his plan, orders to cross the Brandywine would have reached the right wing in fifteen minutes; yet from one to two hours elapsed before Cornwallis was heard of, on the left bank.

As to marching too far to the left, instead of going to the right of Lord Stirling, any person familiar with the localities and relative position of the armies, — any tyro in military science, — knows, that, instead of marching too far to the left, he was actually marching *from the left;* that, when headed off by the British, he was not far enough to the right to connect with the divisions of Stephen and Stirling; and there is no evidence his division ever endeavored to march to their right.

Muhlenberg (p. 92), which has often been quoted, goes to show that *De Borre* raised some question as to his position on the right, but not *Sullivan;* and neither De Chastellux nor any other authority, certainly not any one that is cited, sustains the statement, that " Sullivan undertook to march his division from half a mile beyond the left, to his proper place on the right."

Sullivan's own letter is full and extremely clear as to what he did. It is the best evidence; and the natural impression left by it on any mind unprejudiced is, that we were fortunate in possessing generals as efficient as himself, in our Revolutionary armies. It certainly is unnecessary to disparage them, — to find a reason why twelve thousand British veterans triumphed, after nearly two hours' hard fighting, over four thousand American continentals and militiamen.

IV. As to powder wasted at Germantown, this is stated,

without any authority or justification, as a reflection on Sullivan. The only ground on which the statement is made, is, that an inexperienced colonel in his wing of the army, in the obscurity of the morning, did not check his men when firing oftener than was worth while, as it chanced. This is matter of opinion. It was not certainly the fault of Sullivan, who had no means of knowing, in the darkness, what any particular regiment had in its front.

The loss of the battle is generally ascribed to the waste of time at the Chew House, from Washington preferring the advice of Knox, not to leave a castle in his rear, to that of Pulaski, who cited the case of an Italian army returning from victory to capture a similar post. Washington no more than Sullivan was infallible: both were liable to mistake; both in their day were, and have been since, bitterly censured. Mr. Adams said Washington was no general; but this does not lessen our own faith that he was first as well in war as in peace, and in the hearts of his countrymen.

V. No one who studies the career of Conway, and realizes how sensitively he must have felt the low estimate that Washington formed of his military qualifications, as communicated to Congress, can be surprised at his favoring Gates, whose army at Saratoga had achieved the great success of the war, rather than Washington, who, with the exception of Trenton and Princeton, had met only with disaster. Sullivan had had occasion to think well of him; and Congress, by giving the appointment, appear to have agreed with him.

VI. As to Sullivan siding with Gates to supplant Washington, this is sufficiently disproved by other correspondence, as well as the last letter quoted.

This brief narrative of his military career has appeared to us the best mode of refuting these charges. A more extended biography would require time for preparation. But abundant evidence has been adduced to satisfy intelligent minds, that they are without foundation, either in fact or reasonable inference. It also compels the conviction, that any writer, who makes such unscrupulous statements on the testimony, betrays a prejudice and want of fidelity to historic truth, proving him to be far less qualified for his task, as an historian of the Revolution, than he would have us believe some of its most honored generals were for the command of its armies.

Success is a low criterion of merit or character. To struggle with adversity, to contend against odds, to be persevering notwithstanding discouragement, to have one's good evil spoken of, to be maligned and misrepresented, and yet preserve an amiable temper, an imperturbable spirit, a steadfast determination in the discharge of duty, characterized Washington, Sullivan, and many other of the patriots. Their difficulties, disappointments, or reverses afford more valuable lessons for example and emulation, and far better deserve our respect, than glory or triumph. The times that tried men's souls on the banks of the Delaware in 1776, and at Valley Forge in the winter of 1778, exhibited courage and fortitude more worthy of admiration, than Saratoga, Monmouth, or Yorktown. He is neither generous nor patriotic who describes our great heroic epoch in a spirit of detraction or cynicism. Nor is it truth or honor to stigmatize or applaud for the sake of lights or shades which may attract or amuse. A writer of history has no peculiar privilege to dishonor the dead, nor can he with impunity wound the sensibilities of the living.

It seems difficult to credit the sincerity of any one who thus wantonly trifles with a just sensitiveness. If the actuating motive be to gain a reputation for candor, it is quite sure to result in a signal failure. Heath, Putnam, Wayne, Schuyler, Greene, as Sullivan, did enough good service in the cause of American independence to save their memories from sacrilegious sneers, or reflections upon their sense or courage. Reed had committed no act, expressed no opinion, that could warrant a charge little short of treachery. If untiring and steadfast devotion to the noblest cause ever contended for is no shield against cavil and reproach; if sacrifice of home, health, and fortune must only expose those who come after to harsh epithets and cruel aspersions upon memories they hold sacred,— there probably will be still the same noble self-immolation on national altars: but what a discouragement, what a sorry requital!

It is unfortunate for the cause of truth, that writers, whose works circulate where no vindication can follow them, and who are in a measure beyond the reach of responsibility, should make such unworthy use of their position, to tarnish reputations, amongst the most precious heir-looms of the American people. Our generals may not have been accomplished officers, they had few opportunities of learning the profession of arms, and made occasional mistakes; so did Cæsar and Wellington: but they patiently sacrificed fortune, health, life, in the cause of our national independence; and it seems a sacrilege, in these degenerate days, to pass harsh judgment upon their services, or deprive them of their well-earned laurels.

Our immediate task has ended with the retirement of Sullivan from the army. A brief narrative of the events of his subsequent career will help to indicate the estimation in which his services were held in New Hampshire, and generally throughout the country. It will abundantly prove that the opinion entertained of them by the communities and generations that knew him best, essentially differed from the stinted praise of Gordon, or the perversions of later writers. In the animosities engendered by competition for popular favor in contested elections, in which for several years he was the candidate generally successful for the chief magistracy or other official honors, and consequently the frequent subject of comment in the press, not a word of censure or disparagement is found to detract from the high reputation which he was universally conceded to have won as a general in the war.

He left the camp in December, and, by the fifth of February, 1780, was under his own roof at Durham. After nearly six years of separation, excepting for a few days at long intervals, he had the happiness of being once more with his wife, to whom he was tenderly attached; and with his children, already old enough to need his guidance. His health had been greatly impaired, if not undermined, by hardship and exposure; and even its partial restoration depended on rest and medical care. But his nature was too energetic for repose, and his affairs, from prolonged absence, claimed attention. His expenses during his campaigns, not reimbursed by Congress as in the case of Washington, had made a serious inroad on his previous accumulations. Depreciated values, from the prostration of trade, rendered it imperative for him to resume his profession, if he would meet his engagements, or supply the wants of those dependent upon him, without sacrifice of property.

The eminent position he had taken before the war as an able advocate, derived fresh lustre from his public services; and, with his frank and generous disposition and prepossessing manners, he was not compelled to wait for clients. He engaged in practice with his wonted ardor, and every prospect of distinguished success. But he was not long permitted to pursue his professional labors. It was believed that he could render valuable assistance at Philadelphia, in settlement of a controversy then raging with extreme virulence, and which disturbed the tranquillity of the State. The point in dispute was as to whom belonged the property and jurisdiction of the country west of the Connecticut, and lying between that river and Lake Champlain. From the more verdant tint of the mountains that in ranges or clusters extended over it, when compared with the grayer hue of the granite hills east of the river, it had received the name of Vermont.

The title of this territory embracing an area of over ten thousand square miles had been earlier disputed by France, and also by Massachusetts, which province had built a fort within its limits. After the French ceded Canada, in 1760, New York claimed it, as having been included in the grant, a century before, from Charles II. to his brother, the Duke of York. It was also supposed to be covered by some of the early patents of New Hampshire; and that State had conveyed to her own people a portion of the tract in litigation, known as the Hampshire Grants. The fifty or sixty thousand inhabitants, acknowledging no right in either claimant, asserted their independence, and insisted upon recognition as a separate State. Some of the settlements between the Mason Grant and east bank of the river were disposed to transfer to it their allegiance.

The Assembly, in June, elected Sullivan as a delegate to the Continental Congress, and agent to establish their claim. He was not in the State at the time of his election; and when, apprised of it, upon his return, the legislature had already adjourned. He declined to accept the appointment, and stated his reasons to the Committee of Safety; but they urging the great injury the State would sustain should New York prevail in the controversy, and the inconvenience and expense of calling the Assembly together to fill his place, he reluctantly consented. Neither his health nor affairs rendered it prudent to undertake a journey of four hundred miles, — substantially at his own charge, since the compensation allowed would not defray the expenses of the road. Few, if any, public conveyances were on the route, and he would have to depend upon his own horses. There was no alternative, however, and he felt constrained to go.

George Atkinson was his colleague, and their election was for one year from the first of November, but they were authorized to supply the place of either of the actual delegates wishing to return home before the expiration of their term of service. On the 29th of August, the Committee of Safety, convened at Exeter, informed Sullivan "that General Folsom wished to retire, and requested him forthwith to proceed to Congress, and act as agent for the State in the dispute between New Hampshire, New York, Vermont, and Massachusetts Bay." He accordingly repaired to Philadelphia, and, on the 11th of September, producing his credentials, took his seat.

On the Thursday after his arrival, Congress gave a hearing to the parties in the Vermont controversy, and this was followed up by many more; but no definite result was arrived at till the 20th of August, 1781, as Sullivan was about returning home. New York had sent special agents to argue her claim, — able men, and among the most eminent lawyers of the continent. The questions involved were complicated; and Sullivan was obliged to acquaint himself with all the various grants, discoveries, possessions, and claims, of the earliest grantees and proprietors, especially of those north of the Hudson. Most of the titles asserted were by implication, or by virtue of authority delegated by proclamations to royal governors, who, having general powers to grant crown lands, had conveyed to the settlers. These settlers had improved and erected habitations, and, being in actual possession, had rights to be respected.

Sullivan was left alone to oppose the pretensions of New York, urged with all the zeal and eloquence of its able counsel. He argued the case in its several stages nearly twenty times; and the result, if not all that New Hampshire claimed as to jurisdiction, was more than she was entitled to, if restricted by her patents. New York, to the prejudice of her cause, insisted that the grants by New Hampshire were invalid. The Green-Mountain Boys, as they were called, a bold and warlike people, were not inclined to be peaceably dispossessed, and some among them had opened negotiations with the British authorities in Canada. The easiest solution for the difficulty was to recognize Vermont as an independent State. To this New Hampshire was willing to consent, if claim were waived to fifty-four of her townships on the east bank of the Connecticut and outside her limits of sixty miles from the sea, the wish of some of whom to be consolidated with the new State caused her alarm.

Congress applied to the several legislatures for authority to adjust the dispute, and, when this was granted, after conference with commissioners from Vermont, made a proposition sufficiently reasonable. A resolution was passed, that, as a preliminary to recognition as a State, Vermont must explicitly relinquish all pretensions to land or jurisdiction east of the Connecticut, and west of a line drawn twenty miles east of the Hudson, extended to Lake Champlain. This was not at once received with favor. Contention and strife and a war of legal process — on frequent occasions flaming into barn-burning and personal violence — continued a few years longer. But finally, in 1789, Vermont acquiesced in the settlement proposed, and in 1791 was received as one of the United States.

When Sullivan resumed his seat in Congress, after an interval of five years, with the exception of Sam Adams and Roger Sherman, very few remained of his former associates. Franklin was in France; John Adams, in Holland; Hancock, Governor of Massachusetts; Jefferson, of Virginia. In their stead were many men of distinguished ability and character, among whom may be mentioned James Madison, Oliver Wolcott, James Duane, Chancellor Livingston, Theodoric Bland, Dr. Witherspoon, Dr. Boudinot; and of his late brethren in arms, Generals Ward, Cornell, Varnum, and MacDougal. Mr. Huntington, of Connecticut, was President. The spirit of party is said to have raged unusually high, — souring the temper of the members towards each other, and essentially obstructing the adoption of efficient measures for the public service. A committee, who had been since April at headquarters, had become unpopular, and been recalled. From their strenuous endeavors to increase and render more permanent the military force, they were considered too strongly tinctured with "army principles" imbibed in camp.

The prospect of a speedy termination of the war, in independence, was sufficiently gloomy. On the 12th of September, the day after Sullivan took his seat, Washington wrote the Count de Guichen, "The situation of America at this time is critical. The Government is without finances. Its paper credit is sunk, and no expedients can be adopted capable of retrieving it. The resources of the country are much diminished by a five years' war, in which it has made efforts beyond its ability. Clinton, with an army of ten thousand regular troops, aided by a considerable body of militia, — whom, from motives of fear and attachment, he has engaged to take arms, — is in possession of one of our capital towns, and a large part of the State to which it belongs. The savages are desolating the frontier. A fleet superior to that of our allies not only protects the enemy against any attempts of ours, but facilitates those which they may project against us. Lord Cornwallis, with seven or eight thousand men, is in complete possession of two States, — Georgia and South Carolina, — and, by recent misfortunes, North Carolina is at his mercy. His force is daily increasing, by an accession of adherents whom his successes naturally procure in a country inhabited by emigrants from England and Scotland, who have not been long enough transplanted to exchange their ancient habits and attachments to their new residence."

Gates had been defeated at Camden on the 16th of August, losing an army of four thousand men, composed largely of militia utterly inexperienced, and for the first time in battle, but opposed to a force inferior in number. The Northern army was much reduced, poorly clad, insufficiently fed, and disaffected from arrearages of pay. What was also disheartening, baseness — ever eager to desert in season a cause becoming desperate — assumed, in this very month of September, its worst shape, in the treachery of Arnold. The alliance with France had as yet proved only a source of disappointed expectation, — inducing exhausting efforts without result, and tending to delude and demoralize the native energies of the people. Her fleet was blockaded in Newport. Sullivan had, previous to the blockade, advised Washington that it should repair to Boston, where it would have been sheltered and safe; and the large land force disembarked, and employed to menace New York, and deter Clinton from reinforcing the British army at the South. Washington replied, that he had himself advised the same course; and says, later, that, if it had been adopted, two thousand men sent Cornwallis would have been detained.

Without ascribing to any one individual the magical changes produced in the financial and military departments of the government during this second period of Sullivan's connection with Congress, he certainly was an active and influential member of the committees which shaped and organized the reforms in administration that brought them about. He was ardent and indefatigable, and, from having long held responsible positions in the army, was able fully to apprehend what were the mistakes and abuses most prejudicial to the cause, quick to discern and devise the best methods to correct them.

The journals are exceedingly meagre, and afford no direct intimation of what part he took in the debates. But this can in some measure be inferred from his frequent election on committees. He appears to have had imposed upon him his full share of responsibility and labor. His appointment on standing committees does not appear. He probably succeeded to the places vacated by General Folsom, his predecessor. His name is found upon many appointed for special purposes, especially where the matter referred was connected with the army. Such matters, when simply administrative, went to the Board of War; but most of Washington's communications, proposing modifications and reforms in the service, were sent to a committee of which he was a member. This committee recommended the appointment of Greene to the Southern army, in the place of Gates; projected an entire re-organization of the army; fixed the period of enlistment for the war; revised the rules of promotion; advised that half-pay for life should be promised to all officers who served to the close of the war; proposed restriction of furloughs, better modes of exchanging prisoners, the transfer to Congress of all purchases and supplies of clothing. They reported, besides, regulations for clothing the men in a neat, uniform, and comfortable manner. These and many other similar recommendations were adopted and carried out.

From his position on this committee, and long intimacy with Washington, their correspondence was naturally renewed; and, on the 20th of November, 1780, Washington wrote him as follows: —

You have obliged me very much by your friendly letter, and I can assure you that I shall be very happy in your correspondence. You are too well acquainted with my course of business, to expect frequent or long letters from me; but I can truly say, that I shall write to no one with more pleasure, when it is in my power to write at all, than to you.

The determination of Congress to raise an army for the war, and the honorable establishment on which the officers are placed, will, I am persuaded, be productive of much good. Had the first method been adopted four, or even three years ago, I have not the smallest doubt in my mind but we should at this day have been sitting under our own vines and fig-trees, in the full enjoyment of peace and independence; and I have as little doubt, that the value which I trust officers will now set upon their commissions will prove the surest basis of public economy. It was idle to expect, that men who were suffering every species of present distress, with the prospect of inevitable ruin before them, could bear to have the cord of discipline strained to its proper tone; and, where that is not the case, it is no difficult matter to form an idea of the want of order, or to convince military men of its consequent evils.

It is to be lamented, that the call upon the States for specific supplies should come at this late hour; because it is much to be feared that, before those at a distance can be furnished with the resolves and make their arrangements, the season for salting provision will be irretrievably lost. And this leads me to a remark which I could wish never to make, and which is, that the multiplicity of business in which Congress are engaged will not let them extend that seasonable and provident care to many matters which private convenience and public economy indispensably call for. It proves, in my opinion, the evident necessity of committing more of the executive business to small boards or responsible characters, than is practised at present; for I am well convinced, that for want of system in the execution of business, and a proper timing of things, our public expenditures are inconceivably greater than they ought to be.

. . . .

I will take the liberty to give it as my opinion, that a foreign loan is indispensably necessary to the continuance of the war. Congress will deceive themselves if they imagine that the army, or a State that is the theatre of war, can rub through another campaign like the last. It would be as unreasonable as to suppose that, because a man had rolled a snow-ball till it had acquired the size of a horse, he might do so till it was as large as a house. Matters may be pushed to a certain point, beyond which we cannot move them. Ten months' pay is now due to the army. Every department of it is so much indebted, that we have not credit for a single express; and some of the States are harassed and oppressed to a degree beyond bearing. To depend, under these circumstances, upon the resources of the country, unassisted by foreign loans, will, I am confident, be to lean upon a broken reed.

The situation of the Southern States is very embarrassing, and I wish it were in my power to afford them relief in the way you have mentioned; but it is not.

The very measure which you suggest I urged, as far as decency and policy would permit me to do, at the interview at Hartford; but to no effect. I cannot be more particular on this subject, and what I now say is in confidence. The report of Sir Henry Clinton's going to the southward was groundless, and I believe few troops have left New York since those under Leslie.

A few days later, on the 25th of November, he wrote introducing the Baron de Chastellux, whose interesting memoirs afford much light as to the events and characters of the Revolution: —

DEAR SIR, — This letter will be presented to you by the Chevalier de Chastellux, a major-general in the French service, a gentleman of polite and easy manners, and of literary as well as military abilities. I intended in my last, but, having spun my letter to an enormous length, deferred it, to observe, that as Congress had made one or two late promotions from brigadiers to major-generals, apparently on the principle of a State proportion (which, by the way, if made a general rule, I am persuaded will be found hurtful), an idea has occurred to me, that possibly from the same principle, on a future occasion, one might take place which would be particularly injurious. I mean with respect to General Knox.

Generals Parsons and Clinton have been superseded by Smallwood. Parsons is since restored to his rank. Knox now stands, after Clinton, first on the list. If from the consideration I have mentioned, or from his being at the head of the artillery, he should be overlooked, and a younger officer preferred, he will undoubtedly quit the service; and you know his usefulness too well not to be convinced, that this would be an injury difficult to be repaired. I do not know, all things considered, who could replace him in his department. I am sure, if a question of this kind should be agitated when you are present, this intimation would be unnecessary to induce you to interpose; but, lest you should be absent at the time, I think it would be advisable to apprise some other members, in whom you have confidence, to guard against it.*

The month following his joining Congress, on motion of Mr. Matthews, of South Carolina, seconded by himself, he was chosen on a committee "to draft a letter to the States, representing fully the present situation of our affairs, and urging in the strongest terms the necessity of their con-

---

* In a letter to the President of Congress, dated the 25th of November, General Washington said: "The death of that useful and valuable officer, Mr. Erskine, geographer to the army, makes it requisite that a successor should be appointed. I beg leave to recommend Mr. Simeon Dewitt. His being in the department gives him a pretension, and his abilities are still better. From the character Mr. Erskine always gave of him, and from what I have seen of his performances, he seems to be extremely well qualified." In compliance with this recommendation, Mr. Dewitt was appointed geographer to the army.

tributing effectual aid and support in order to extricate these United States from impending danger, baffle the designs of the enemy, and conduct the war to a happy issue." Mr. Scott, Henry, and Ingersoll were also on the committee. It was reported, recommitted, and adopted the 9th of November, which date it bears.

Of the tributes paid Rochambeau, Sumpter, Major Tallmadge, Paul Jones for his capture of the "Serapis," and to the memory of General Poor, of New Hampshire, recently deceased, several were of his suggestion and probable drafting. On his nomination, General Cornell was elected a commissioner of the Board of War; MacDougal, Secretary of Marine. When Henry Laurens, of South Carolina, formerly President of Congress, was taken at sea, and imprisoned in the Tower of London, on a charge of high treason, Sullivan proposed that the "Alliance," at Boston, should be fitted out to take to Europe Colonel John Laurens, — who had been with him in Rhode Island, — on a private mission to the court of Versailles, that he might be near, and render his father any aid that was possible. Congress, in June, empowered Dr. Franklin to offer General Burgoyne in exchange for Laurens; and when this was effected, the following year, Laurens proceeded to Paris, and signed the preliminaries of peace, as one of the commissioners, — the others being Dr. Franklin, John Adams, and John Jay. Colonel Laurens succeeded in obtaining a loan of four millions of dollars.

Before proceeding to glean more particularly from the journals of Congress what is to be gathered of his services in helping to re-organize the army and finances, allusion should be made to the mutiny in the Pennsylvania line, then commanded by Wayne, which broke out on the 1st of January, 1781. They had become discontented from their scanty subsistence and arrearages of pay, and aggrieved that they were not discharged at the close of their three years' service, according to what they insisted was the condition of their enlistment. When the intelligence reached Congress, Sullivan, Dr. Witherspoon, and Mr. Matthews were appointed a committee to confer thereon with President Reed, the supreme executive of Pennsylvania. They immediately proceeded to Trenton; and, on the 9th, Lafayette wrote Sullivan as follows from Morristown: —

DEAR SIR, — Agreeable to the desire of the Committee of Congress, I delivered their message to General St. Clair, who had also seen your President and that of the State, so that you will receive from him long public letters which relate to the unhappy disturbances in the Pennsylvania line. I shall only write you this private letter, and let you know that the affair appears to be of a most serious nature.

The establishment of a committee, and the organization of this body of men, renders it impossible for us to address the bulk of the soldiers; and, a negotiation being set on foot by General Wayne, it was thought better for us to take the advice of their leaders, who, dreading either our number or our influence, determined that we should not stay two hours more in the town. I think it is necessary for the States of Pennsylvania and Jersey to provide for the extremities to which they will, I fear, be obliged to come. I am sorry to find that the people, sensible of the sufferings of the army, have not a proper idea of the method these mutinous people have taken to obtain redress. It seems that the soldiers expect a deputation from the Assembly, but nothing from Congress, who, therefore, are not obliged to commit themselves in any treaty. I am told General Washington is coming this way, and shall therefore wait for his orders.

With the most perfect regard and affection, I have the honor to be, dear sir, your most obedient, humble servant,

LAFAYETTE.

The following letter of Sullivan to the Minister of France, giving an account of the outbreak and its suppression, explains the part taken by the committee of Congress of which he acted as chairman. It has been said that more was conceded than the circumstances demanded. Lenity is often the part of prudence in dealing with large numbers of dissatisfied soldiers, especially when they have reason for their ill-humor;

and Wayne writes, a little later, that after going home for a while, as they claimed to be their right, they re-enlisted, and the line was stronger than before.

TRENTON, Jan. 13, 1780.

SIR, — The dispute with the Pennsylvania line being happily terminated, I take the liberty of giving your Excellency a short account of the rise and progress of this unexpected and surprising revolt. Many of the men were held by enlistments, which expressed the term of service to be for three years, or during the war.

As the three years began to expire about the first of January, they inquired of their officers whether they were to expect their discharges at the end of that period. The officers, in general, supposed the term of enlistment not to expire but with the war. This construction gave them much uneasiness, which was increased by some arrearages of pay, which they were to have received from the State, not being furnished; and, though the State had taken means for paying these arrears, unfortunately the intelligence had not reached them previous to the first of January. These were the real sources of the mutiny; for though there were some other grievances, common to the American as well as other armies, they never mentioned them as having any weight in their proceedings. The two first affected a great part of the divisions, who used every art to induce others to support them in their intended revolt, which they were the more encouraged to attempt, as they were sixty miles distant from the main army.

The affair was conducted with so much secrecy, that the officers had not the most distant suspicion of it till the evening of the first of January, when, hearing that the troops were in arms, they repaired to the parade, and, not supposing it was general, exerted themselves to quell the mutiny. The soldiers, in general, showed no disposition to injure their officers; though some, who were intoxicated with liquor, discharged their muskets, killed one officer, and wounded three or four.

Part of the divisions moved a few miles that evening, and the remainder followed them the next morning, when the whole assumed a military order, and marched without offering the least insult to the inhabitants, except in one instance, for which the culprit was immediately apprehended, and delivered over to the civil power. The inhabitants say, that, on their whole march, the soldiers were never suffered to enter their houses, even for water; nor was any article taken from them during this march. Upon their taking post at Princeton, it began to be suspected that their intention was to join the enemy; but they persevered in declaring their detestation of the British, and their attachment to the cause of their country. They said they were only seeking a redress of grievances, which when obtained, they would cheerfully return to their duty; and, if the enemy appeared in the interim, they would fight them with desperation.

This, however, was not fully credited, until they seized and brought to General Wayne, who, with Colonel Butler and Stuart, remained among them without command, two British emissaries from Sir Henry Clinton, with a written invitation, promising them great rewards if they would march to South River, about twenty miles distant from Princeton, where he would cover them with a body of British troops. The spies were delivered over to General Wayne, and, after Governor Reed's arrival, to him; but afterwards, at their request, returned to them. The Board of Sergeants, who had assumed the command, issued orders next morning, stating the facts, and declaring that the Pennsylvania line despised a treachery and meanness like that of Benedict Arnold; that their views were honorable, and their attachment to the cause of their country unalterable; and that they were only seeking redress of grievances from men of honor. When Governor Reed came to Princeton, they received him with every mark of respect and esteem. They mentioned to him the grounds of their complaints, which were principally the two first mentioned. He made them some proposals, and communicated others from the Committee of Congress, which were readily accepted.

They were then requested to march to Trenton, which they agreed to; and delivered to the Committee of Congress the spies sent from Sir Henry Clinton, who were tried by a board of officers, condemned, and executed on the 11th inst.

The Committee of Congress have appointed commissioners to determine respecting their enlistments, to discharge such as are entitled thereto, and give them the necessary certificates. This seems to be perfectly satisfactory to them; and many of those discharged are now offering to re-enlist, upon having a furlough for a short time. Thus, sir, has this surprising affair been brought to a happy issue.

Perhaps history does not furnish an instance of so large a body of troops revolting from the command of their officers, marching in such exact order, without doing the least injury to inhabitants, and remaining in this situation for such a length of time, without division or confusion among themselves, and then returning to their duty as soon as their reasonable demands were complied with.

This conduct ought to convince the British how much they mistake the dispositions of the Americans at large, when they assert that they would willingly join them, if not overawed by their tyrannic rulers. Here was a large body, composed as well of foreigners as natives, having no officers to command them, and no force to prevent them from joining the enemy, for which they had repeated invitations; yet, though they well knew they were liable to the severest punishment for their revolt, they disdained the British offers with a firmness that would have done honor to the ancient Romans; and, through the whole, have shown the greatest respect to the Committee of Congress, to the Governor and members of council from the State of Pennsylvania, expressed the highest confidence of their civil rulers, and have not, through the whole, deviated from that order and regularity which on other occasions must have done honor to military discipline.

His Excellency the Minister of France.

P.S. One circumstance ought not to be omitted, which, in my opinion, does the insurgents much honor. When they delivered up the British emissaries, Governor Reed offered them a hundred golden guineas, which they refused, saying that what they did was only a duty they owed to their country, and that they neither wanted nor would receive any reward but the approbation of that country for which they had so often fought and bled.

Similar discontents broke out into open mutiny, a few weeks later, in the Jersey line; but the Government, from its recent experiences, was better prepared to deal with it. Washington had had time to ascertain the temper of his other troops, and that he could depend upon them. He took vigorous measures to check the insubordination before it assumed formidable proportions, which proved effectual.

For the more efficient administration of the Government, on motion of Mr. Livingston, of New York, a committee of five had been appointed, in August, 1780, "for the revision and new arrangement of the civil executive departments of the United States under Congress." They recommended, in

January, the appointment of secretaries of foreign affairs, of war, of marine, and of a superintendent of finance. Sullivan wrote Washington, to ascertain his views as to the selection of Alexander Hamilton for the head of the financial department; a post which, ten years later, he filled in the Cabinet of Washington, with resplendent ability. The reply of Washington from New Windsor, above West Point, dated 4th February, 1781, discussed various other subjects of interest: —

DEAR SIR, — Colonel Armand delivered me your favor last evening, and I thank you for the several communications contained in it. The measure adopted by Congress of appointing ministers of war, finance, and for foreign affairs, I think a very wise one. To give efficacy to it, proper characters will, no doubt, be chosen to conduct the business of these departments. How far Colonel Hamilton, of whom you ask my opinion as a financier, has turned his thoughts to that particular study, I am unable to answer, because I never entered upon a discussion on this point with him. But this I can venture to advance, from a thorough knowledge of him, that there are few men to be found, of his age, who have a more general knowledge than he possesses; and none, whose soul is more firmly engaged in the cause, or who exceeds him in probity or sterling virtue.

I am clearly in sentiment with you, that our cause became distressed, and apparently desperate, only from an improper management of it; and that errors once discovered are more than half mended. I have no doubt of our abilities or resources, but we must not sleep nor slumber; they never will be drawn forth if we do; nor will violent exertions, which subside with the occasion, answer our purposes.

It is a provident foresight, a proper arrangement of business, system, and order in the execution, that are to be productive of that economy, which is to defeat the efforts and hopes of Great Britain; and I am happy, thrice happy, on private as well as public account, to find that these are in train. For it will ease my shoulders of an immense burthen, which the deranged and perplexed situation of our affairs, and the distresses of every department of the army, had placed upon them. I am much pleased to hear that Maryland has acceded to the confederation, and that Virginia has relinquished her claim to the land west of the Ohio, which, for fertility of soil, pleasantness of climate, and other natural advantages, is equal to any known tract of country in the universe, of the same extent, taking the great lakes for its northern boundary.

I wish most devoutly a happy completion of your plan of finance, which you say is nearly finished, and much success to your scheme of borrowing coined specie and plate. But in what manner do you propose to apply the latter? As a fund to redeem its value in paper to be emitted, or to coin it? If the latter, it will be one more added to a thousand reasons which might be offered in proof of the necessity of vesting legislative or dictatorial powers in Congress, to make laws of general utility for the purposes of war, that they might prohibit, under the pains and penalty of death, specie and provisions from going to the enemy for goods. The traffic with New York is immense. Individual States will not make it felony, lest, among other reasons, it should not become general; and nothing short of it will ever check, much less stop, a practice, which, at the same time it serves to drain us of our provision and specie, removes the barrier between us and the enemy, corrupts the morals of our people by a lucrative traffic, weakens by degrees the opposition, and affords a means for obtaining regular and perfect intelligence of every thing among us, while even in this respect we derive no benefit from a fear of discovery. Men of all descriptions are now indiscriminately engaging in it, Whig and Tory speculators. On account of its being followed by those of the latter class, in a manner with impunity, men who, two or three years ago, would have shuddered at the idea of such connections, now pursue it with avidity, and reconcile it to themselves (in which their profits plead powerfully), upon a principle of equality with the Tory, who, knowing that a forfeiture of the goods to the informer is all he has to dread, and that this is to be eluded by an agreement not to inform against each other, goes into the measure without risk.

This is a digression; but the subject is of so serious a nature and so interesting to our well-being as a nation, that I never expect to see a happy termination of the war, nor great national concerns conducted in peace, till there is something more than a recommendatory power in Congress. It is not possible, in time of war, that business can be conducted well without it. The last words, therefore, of my letter, and the first wish of my heart, concur in favor of it.

In response to the passage in the foregoing letter relating to the selection of a superintendent of finance, Sullivan says: "I am glad to find that you entertain the same sentiments of the virtues and abilities of Colonel Hamilton as I have ever done myself. After I wrote, I found the eyes of Congress turned upon Robert Morris as financier. I did not, therefore, nominate Colonel Hamilton, as I foresaw it would be a vain attempt." A few days later, Robert Morris was chosen without a dissenting voice, although Samuel Adams and General Ward, of the Massachusetts delegation, declined balloting. The establishment of the departments was not without opposition. A doubt existed as to the utility or expediency of placing them under the charge of individuals.

M. de la Luzerne wrote Vergennes: "Divisions prevail in Congress about the new mode of transacting business by secretaries of different departments. Samuel Adams, whose obstinate and resolute character was so useful to the Revolution in its origin, but who shows himself very ill suited to the conduct of affairs in an organized government, has placed himself at the head of the advocates for the old system of committees of Congress, instead of relying on ministers or secretaries, according to the new arrangement." Sullivan, in his letter to Washington, says: "The choice of a minister of war is postponed to the 1st of October. This was a manœuvre of Samuel Adams, and others from the North, fearing that, as I was in nomination, the choice would fall on me, who, having apostatized from the true New England faith by sometimes voting with the Southern States, am not eligible. They were not, however, acquainted with all the circumstances. I was nominated against my will; and, if chosen, should not have accepted. General MacDougal is appointed minister of marine." Another reason may have operated for deferring the election of a minister of war: the Board of War was filled with able and influential men, amongst them Samuel Adams, who did not wish to be displaced.

The vast disproportion in territorial area, and the claim of several of the States to extend indefinitely westward, under their respective charters, weighed, in Maryland, as an objection to adopting the Articles of Confederation. Upon a communication from that State in September, Congress had advised the several States to consider the propriety of relinquishing some portion of their claims. They passed a resolution, in October, that the land ceded should be disposed of for the general benefit, and formed into distinct republican States, of areas respectively of from one hundred to one hundred and fifty miles square, to become members of the Federal Union, and have the same rights of sovereignty, freedom, and independence as the other States. Virginia had already ceded her North-western territory, and New York now abandoned all pretensions west of her present limits. This was not consummated before 1784; but, as soon as the preliminary steps were taken, Maryland, on the 3d January, 1781, agreed to ratify the Articles of Confederation. The whole subject was, at the same time, referred to a committee, of which Sullivan was a member; and, on the 1st of March, the delegates of Maryland subscribed the articles, and the union of the original thirteen States, intended to be perpetual, was made complete.

The most important service rendered by Sullivan to the cause whilst a member at this time of the Congress, was that alluded to in the foregoing letter of Washington, — a thorough reform of the finances. At his suggestion, a committee of five, consisting of himself as chairman, and Bland, Matthews, Clarke, and Matlack, — Clymer being afterwards substituted in the place of the latter, — was appointed " to prepare, and lay before Congress, a plan for arranging the finances, paying the debts, and economizing the revenue of the United States." They made various reports, which were long under debate, and their recommendations were generally accepted. The old Continental currency, amounting to one hundred and sixty millions, had depreciated, until seventy dollars were worth less than one in specie. They determined upon a nearer return to specie basis, establishing rates of depreciation for whatever paper issues had been made. They urged measures for gathering in the old Continental bills in exchange for the new emission, forty for one; and most of them were either redeemed and destroyed, or disappeared from circulation. Their proposition, that six millions, in proximate equivalents to specie in the new emission, should be apportioned among the several States, to be paid in quarterly instalments, was adopted; and the delicate responsibility of apportionment was devolved on a committee of which Sullivan was chairman.

They also recommended an application to the States to make the new issue legal tender at its current value, and for power to impose a duty of five per cent on imports, to pay the public debt and interest. In April, 1781, an act of New Hampshire, authorizing such impost within its borders, obtained through the influence of Sullivan, was laid before Congress. The proceeds of the public lands were also pledged for the same purpose. An efficient system of auditing claims was devised, to prevent frauds and unreasonable exactions in the military service.

But time was needed to perfect these measures, and realize their fruits. Meanwhile, its treasury and credit alike exhausted, Congress possessed no means to defray ordinary expenses, much less supply the sinews of war. Coin had abandoned a country where it had ceased to be regarded as a circulating medium; and yet, in purchasing munitions from abroad, and for some other objects, a certain amount was indispensable. Its presence, even in small quantities, would serve as a standard to fathom the abyss into which the federal credit was sinking. It was for these purposes, and not from any sanguine expectation of restoring the currency to a solid basis, — one hardly to be sustained by the most opulent nations in a protracted war, — that an effort was now made, as intimated in the foregoing correspondence, to collect, for the use of the Government, some portion of the gold and silver remaining in the possession of individuals.

Confiding in the good sense of their countrymen to perceive that the crisis demanded extraordinary sacrifices, and perhaps reminded by their chairman of the generous application by Langdon of his gold and merchandise, to fit out Stark for Bennington, — a proximate cause of the victory of Saratoga, — associations were proposed in the several States, to encourage the deposit, in the treasury, of gold and silver plate and other articles, except watches, the place of which could be supplied by substitutes of iron, earthenware, or glass. Certificates for their value, bearing interest, together with a premium, were to be given in exchange. The associations were to be under obligation to sustain their credit, and discountenance and disclose every attempt, either of secret or open enemies, to depreciate their value.

This proposed form of association is followed in the Sullivan manuscripts by a plan for a Federal Bank, to be established by Congress. It is of too great length for insertion, but contains suggestions which might be useful in the existing condition of our currency. It is substantially the same as that adopted by Congress, and put in operation the following January, in the Bank of North America, which fully answered even the seemingly extravagant anticipations of those who projected it. The fifth section provided that the gold and silver collected in the country should be coined; the silver pieces to be of six shillings, three shillings, one and sixpence, ninepence, and fourpence halfpenny, — terms attaching, down to within a very recent period, to American coins and currency.

It is not pretended that Sullivan is entitled to the exclusive merit of either the measures proposed or adopted. He originated the committee, was its chairman, and his papers show that he took a leading part in maturing and bringing about these excellent measures. One of the early fruits of the system, now methodized, was the fitting-out of the ship-of-war "America," then on the stocks at Portsmouth, which was, on his motion, completed and put afloat.

It is certainly not designed to imitate that grave defect in Revolutionary biography, which arrogates to one, merit that belongs to many. Such a revolution could only be sustained, and carried to successful issue, by numerous men of noble purpose and marked ability, in the field and cabinet. Their elevated nature is wholly inconsistent with that pious zeal in their descendants, which heaps their altars at the cost of their associates. There is glory enough for them all; and the country must lose its best guarantee for its liberties when the foul breath of detraction dims the lustre of their example. All through the war, patriotic statesmen were indefatigable in devising methods to make it a success. But as the army was in rags, and for days with only such food as they could forage from an exhausted country; as credit was sunk beneath the weight of two hundred millions of dollars of federal debt, besides nearly as much more of the separate debts of the States; and that particular year that Sullivan was in Congress brought about so many important measures, emanating from committees of which he was a member, — he is justly entitled to some credit, where they proved effectual.

These reforms, whoever suggested or shaped them, or induced their adoption, infused new life and vigor throughout every department of the Government. They made hopeful a cause which, for supineness and discouragement, had well nigh been lost. The effect for good was instantaneous. Maryland adopted the Articles of Confederation. Greene's masterly campaigns at the South; Washington's able combinations, which entrapped Cornwallis on the Peninsula, and, with the help of Rochambeau, compelled him, with seventy-two hundred men, to surrender at Yorktown, October, 1781, — virtually ended the war. It led, the following winter, to a resolution on Conway's motion in Parliament, "that, in the opinion of the House, the further prosecution of offensive war in America would, under present circumstances, be the means of weakening the efforts of the country against her European enemies, and tend to increase the mutual enmity, so fatal to the interests both of Great Britain and America." Immediate steps were taken for a pacification, delayed, by the objection on the part of Mr. Jay to treat except on the basis of the recognized sovereignty of the several States, until the fall of 1782, when the preliminaries of peace were signed.

Thomas Burke, of North Carolina, who originated the accusations against Sullivan, for not having, with four thousand men, defeated ten thousand, at the Brandywine, in 1777, was still in Congress. It will be remembered, that when these charges were investigated, soon after the battle, he stood nearly alone in opposition, which pronounced these charges groundless. The correspondence between them had been acrimonious. Burke was not in Philadelphia when Sullivan took his seat, but made his appearance on the 15th of December. As Congress consisted of less than thirty members, and both of them were occasionally elected on the same committees, their intercourse was somewhat embarrassing. Sullivan was too magnanimous to harbor resentment, too conscientious to allow private feud to interfere with public duty. General MacDougal, his firm friend from before the war, was also a member for a special purpose, — the relinquishment of the New-York claims. At the suggestion of other gentlemen, mutual friends of both parties, he undertook to accommodate the subsisting differences between them, and bring about a reconciliation. This was happily accomplished. Burke declared that his opinion of General Sullivan had undergone a material change, and the latter withdrew the offensive expressions provoked by injustice. A letter from MacDougal describes the final pacification, and expresses his sense of the propriety of Sullivan's conduct throughout the transaction.

A report, made by Dr. Boudinot, on the 3d of August, may well have emanated from some suggestion of his. It was an earnest remonstrance against cruelties practised in the British prison-ships. Not long before, Daniel, the brother of

General Sullivan, had perished one of the victims. He had been active in getting up the attack on Castine in the summer of 1779; and the following winter, in February, a British frigate, commanded by Mowatt, was sent to Sullivan, on Frenchman's Bay, in Maine, where he resided, to seize him. A party landed at night, turned his wife and children out into the snow, burnt his dwelling, and, having first endeavored to persuade him to take the oath of allegiance, carried him to New York. He was imprisoned in the Jersey hulk. Disease, contracted from the frightful impurities, starvation, and neglect, terminated his existence, as he was on his way home.

Soon after Sullivan joined the Congress, he addressed to that body a communication praying to be allowed for the depreciation of the bills in which his allowance as a major-general — one hundred and sixty dollars each month — had been paid him. At seventy for one, the amount realized was inconsiderable. He also requested reimbursement of moneys expended in the service. The committee, to whom his letters were referred, reported in favor of both requests. But Congress, while voting fifteen hundred dollars in specie to reimburse him, declined to allow the depreciation, as it would open the door to similar claims from all others who had quitted the army. After the peace, in 1787, such an order was passed, allowing him forty-three hundred dollars for this depreciation, to be paid in the first instance by New Hampshire.

Sullivan, having now been a year absent from home, took his leave of Congress in August, and returned to his residence at Durham. The journal that announces his arrival, with commendations, in no stinted phrase, on his services, likewise mentions that, at the same time, of Commodore Paul Jones from Philadelphia. He had been appointed to the charge of the seventy-four-gun ship building at Portsmouth, which Congress, on Sullivan's motion, had ordered to be set afloat.

Sullivan resumed his professional employments, and was soon afterwards appointed Attorney-General of New Hampshire; an office held later, for many years, by his son George, whose eloquence and noble character are still held in honored remembrance in the State. George Sullivan was one of its leading lawyers when Daniel Webster and Jeremiah Mason were his competitors. He served, with distinction, in Congress in the war of 1812, and died in 1838. John, son of George, was also for many years, and to his death in 1860, Attorney-General; the office having been filled, by the three generations, at different periods, nearly half a century. Of John, it was said, when his professional brethren were lamenting his loss, and paying the customary tribute to his memory, "that, eloquent as were they who had made the name of Sullivan illustrious before him, no forensic effort of theirs ever surpassed, in force and beauty, the arguments of him whose voice had been so recently hushed for ever." James, the brother of General Sullivan, was Attorney-General of Massachusetts from 1790 to 1807, when he was elected to its chief magistracy.

It was the duty of General Sullivan, as Attorney-General, to attend the sessions of the Superior Court in the several counties; and the following incidents are related, in the Life of Governor Plumer, as occurring, on such an occasion, in the county of Cheshire. The towns along the Connecticut were still harassed by a double jurisdiction; their inhabitants, in some instances, being nearly equally divided in their allegiance.

"In October, 1782, as the judges of the Superior Court, accompanied by Sullivan, then Attorney-General, were approaching the town of Keene, where the general uneasiness was augmented by the controversy with Vermont, they were informed, that the village was full of people, whose object was to compel the court to adjourn without trying any cases.

"On the receipt of the information, the cavalcade halted in a small wood, to consult as to the course proper to be adopted in this emergency; and the result was, that Sullivan undertook to get the court, with as little loss of dignity as might be, out of the hands of the mob, who, if resolute, must, it was foreseen, have very much their own way, as the court had no armed force at its command, and the *posse comitatus* would in vain have been called to their aid, in the then excited state of the public mind. Taking from the portmanteau of his servant his uniform as a general officer, which it seems he had with him, General Sullivan mounted the powerful gray horse which he usually rode, and, preceding the court, conducted them into the town. A portion of the better-disposed inhabitants had come out in the saddle to meet them. These he ordered to fall in, two and two, behind the court; Arthur Livermore, then a youth of sixteen, acting as his volunteer aid on the occasion. The grounds surrounding the courthouse were filled with men, many of them armed, who, though giving way to the court as they entered, were sullen in their aspect, and resolute in their purpose to prevent the transaction of business. The judges having taken their seats, the court was opened, in due form, by the crier, while the crowd rushed tumultuously in, and filled the house.

"In the mean time, Sullivan, who was a man of fine personal appearance, dignified aspect, and commanding deportment, was seen standing erect in the clerk's desk, surveying the crowd calmly, but resolutely. In it were many who had recently served under him in the war. Turning slowly from side to side, he recognized among them, here perhaps an officer, and there a soldier; and returned, with a slight nod or motion of the hand, their respectful salutations. This mutual survey and recognition continued for some time, amidst the profound silence of all around; while the instinct of obedience was working strongly in the mass, who felt the presence, and involuntarily obeyed the motions, of their old commander. Slowly, and with composure, he now took off his cocked hat, disclosing a profusion of white powdered hair, and laid it deliberately on the table. Looking round again with an air of authority, he next unbelted the long staff-like sword from his side, and laid it by the hat. Perceiving, at this moment, some stir in the crowd, he hastily resumed the sword, drew the blade half-way from the scabbard, as if for immediate use, and then replaced it deliberately on the table. All eyes were now fixed intently on him, as he addressed the assembly, and demanded of them why they had come in this tumultuous manner before the court.

"A cry at once arose, 'The petition! the petition!' and a committee stepped forward with a huge roll of paper, which they were about to present, when Sullivan told them, if they had any thing to offer to the court, he would lay it before them. He accordingly received it, and, after looking it over, presented it to the court, saying, that it contained matter of grave import, which he recommended to their Honors' careful consideration. The court ordered it to be read by the clerk, and Sullivan then addressed the people, courteously but firmly, on the impropriety of any attempt to influence, even by the appearance of violence, the deliberations of that high tribunal; and, telling them that their petition would in due time be considered by the court, he directed them to withdraw. Some hesitation being at first shown, he repeated more sternly, and with a repellant gesture, the command to withdraw, which was obeyed, though not without some reluctance among the leaders. The court then adjourned to the next day, in the hope that the mob would leave the town. In the afternoon, Sullivan addressed them on the subject of their complaints, and advised them to return to their homes.

"On the opening of the court, on the next morning, the house was full of people impatient for the expected answer to their petition. Sullivan, now in his citizen's dress, rose, and, with mingled grace and dignity, said, that he was instructed by the court to inform them, that, finding that they should not be able to go through with the very heavy civil docket before them in the short time which they could alone devote to it before going to another county, they would continue all causes in which either party was not ready for a trial.

"On receiving this announcement, the people withdrew, amidst loud shouts of 'Hurrah for General Sullivan!' with here and there a faint cheer for the court, which seemed, on this occasion, to act quite a subordinate part in the scene. The mob thus carried, in effect, their main point,—that of postponing the transaction of business; but the presence of mind and authority of the Attorney-General prevented their breaking out in open violence, and saved the court from any personal indignity.

"I received the above account from Mr. Webster, a short time before his death; when, though occupied with current events, he seemed to have lost none of his interest in the past. He added, 'Put this into your book: it will show the character of the times, and the kind of men your father had to deal with.' I repeated the story, soon after, to Judge Livermore, who supplied the part relating to himself; and seemed inclined to give less prominence to Sullivan, and more to the court, than Webster had done. He retained, however, in extreme old age, a lively recollection of his youthful adventure, and of the skill and eloquence of Sullivan. 'I thought,' he said, 'if I could only look and talk like that man, I should want nothing higher or better in this world.'"

Three of the boldest of the ringleaders were arrested, and bound over to the next session of the court in October. This increased the ferment, and two hundred men formed an armed association to prevent the court being held. On the first morning of the session, a petition was presented to the judges "that the court might be adjourned; and that no judicial proceedings might be had whilst the troubles in which the country had been involved still subsisted." The petitioners were told the judges could come to no decision but in open court. When the court was opened, their petition was publicly read, and its consideration postponed to the following day. The court proceeded with its business, and the grand jury was impanelled. The doors of the house where they met were kept open, whilst Sullivan, as Attorney-General, laid before them the case of the rioters, against whom a bill was found. Arraigned, they pleaded guilty, and cast themselves on the mercy of the court, which remitted their punishment on condition of their future peaceable behavior. This well-judged combination of firmness and lenity, says Belknap, from whom we borrow the incident, disarmed the insurgents, and they quietly dispersed. From that time the spirit of opposition to government in that quarter gradually abated; and the people returned to their connection with New Hampshire.

In the spring of 1783, peace brought independence. If the eight years the war had lasted had been fruitful in feuds and rivalries, common dangers and sacrifices inspired, in the generous, sentiments of fellowship, — friendships to endure for life. At the moment of separation, when the objects for which they had so long been contending were accomplished, from a sense of the propriety of perpetuating these hallowed associations, it was determined to organize the Society of Cincinnati. To give it a permanence beyond the generation who served in the war, the privilege of membership was extended to lineal representatives, or, in case of their failing, to collaterals. The idea is said to have originated with General Knox, than whom no general of the Revolution seems to have been more universally popular. Washington, Steuben, and others favored it. In the sensitive jealousy that prevailed against orders of nobility, the society was, by a few, deemed repugnant to those principles of equality which should be cherished under republics. But this prejudice wore away, and it is now an honored institution in many States. Steuben, in July, 1783, thus brings the subject to the notice of Sullivan: —

I have the honor, as president of a convention for establishing the Society of the Cincinnati, to present you with a plan of its formation, together with several resolutions which have taken place relative to it.

The principles on which the society is founded will, I hope, meet your approbation, and engage you to become one of its members and supporters. Not only your character and station in civil life, but the superior rank you held in the army of the United States, point you out as the most proper person in the State of New Hampshire to whom the forming a society in that State can be committed.

Your friendship for the officers of the American army, with whom you were so long connected, induces me to believe you will embrace with pleasure the opportunity of joining them in an institution, the chief motive of which is to perpetuate that virtuous affection which, in so exemplary a manner, existed among them while in arms for the defence of their country.

At a meeting in November, at the house of Colonel Samuel Folsom, at Exeter, the State branch of the society was formed. General Sullivan was chosen its president; Colonel Dearborn, vice-president; Eben Sullivan, secretary; Colonel Cilley, treasurer; and Captain Cass, his assistant. All persons who had served three years in the army or navy were invited to sign the covenants and become members.

The State constitution, adopted in 1776, was provisional for the war, — not designed to endure longer. Several attempts were made in New Hampshire, as in Massachusetts, to agree upon a form that should be permanent. The latter State had established a government which, with slight modifications, still subsists as originally framed. New Hampshire, in 1779, had engaged in the same task; but, when completed, the result was so defective, that it was rejected when submitted to the people. Another convention, which held nine sessions, was for two years employed in the work, but long with no better success. When Sullivan returned from Congress, the convention was completing a draft, substantially the same as that adopted by Massachusetts in 1779, but with some modifications, to be submitted to popular vote in January. Prefixed to the printed draft was an able address. Objections prevailed to features of the plan, and it was rejected.

In August, 1782, another effort was made to meet public sentiment; and a modified plan, with the same address varied in a few passages, was ordered to be circulated, that the different towns might make their objections. Sullivan acted as Secretary; and the address is attributed both to him and Jonathan M. Sewall, who had preceded him in that office. Numerous alterations were proposed in the constitution submitted; and it was not finally perfected, to conform to the views of the people, before the fall of 1783. It went into operation in June, 1784. What part General Sullivan took in the work can only be inferred from his energy and influence, the interest he had always manifested in the subject. Tradition gives him credit for having been useful in its preparation, and also in securing its adoption.

One proposed innovation was, that the representatives should be chosen by conventions, not directly by the people. The effect would have been to legalize the primary meetings for selection,—all parties, however, being represented in the conventions. This and other points, about which existed differences of opinion, were canvassed in the public prints, over different signatures, with much ability. Some of these signatures were affixed, on other occasions, by Sullivan to his contributions, and his busy pen can be traced, by other indications, throughout the discussion.

Upon the organization of the State government under its new constitution, in June, 1784, Meshech Weare, who, as president of the Council, chairman of the Committee of Safety, and Chief-Justice, had been virtually the head of the State from the outbreak of the war, was elected President. From his long service and exemplary character, this title had become endeared to the people, and ten years passed before they were content to relinquish it for the more usual designation of Governor. Weare, when chosen, had already begun to experience the symptoms of a strong man failing, having lived more than his threescore years and ten, forty-five of which had been spent in public employments. He resigned towards the close of his term, and died two years later. According to Jeremy Belknap, the historian of New Hampshire, " though not a person of original or inventive genius, he had a clear discernment, extensive knowledge, accurate judgment, a calm temper, modest deportment, an upright and benevolent heart, and a habit of prudence and diligence in discharging the various duties of public and private life."

John Langdon followed him, — a man of pleasing address, noble presence, and large estate, — who served for several terms, at intervals, as Governor, and who, as member of the Senate from New Hampshire at the first Congress, presided over that body in 1789, when the present Federal Government was organized. Both in 1784 and 1785, Sullivan was in nomination for the Presidency, and the vote cast in Durham, where he resided, indicates his popularity amongst his own townsmen. They gave him in the former year all but six votes; in the latter, all but three; and, in 1786, when the successful candidate, the whole number cast, — two hundred and twenty-two. He was elected, in 1784, to the Council, and continued at the head of the military department.

Political opinions under free institutions are rather passions than principles; and whilst self-government continued a novelty, party spirit ran high. Whatever the question at issue, measures or men, either side strove with like zeal for the mastery. Personages of ability abounded in the State, popular favorites, eager for distinction. Their respective friends and followers labored to promote their preferment; lauding their favorites and decrying their antagonists with quite as much zeal as scruple. Less rancor and personality, however, were indulged than in other States, perhaps for the reason there were fewer journals. But with the Athertons, Atkinsons, Gilmores, Livermores, and Langdons; Bartlett, Folsom,

Dudley, Long, Pickering, Peabody, Whipple, the Wentworths, and many more contending for public honors, competition at times became animated, was often inflamed and imbittered.

As Attorney-General, it had become the duty of Sullivan to enforce the laws against refugee loyalists. John Pickering, afterwards Chief-Justice, and Woodbury Langdon reproached him in the "Gazette" for unseasonable lenity in their favor, whilst veterans from the war were in want. Since 1765, he had been the counsel of Colonel Boyd, a wealthy merchant, who, at the commencement of hostilities, went to Europe to take care of property there, and did not return. His wife and children had remained, and he had shown, in England, much kindness to American prisoners. When Sullivan received the appointment, he declined to accept it, lest its duties should interfere with his obligations to his clients. The Council agreed to exonerate him from official functions affecting his subsisting engagements, and he then consented. Chief-Justice Livermore and others, in reply to his assailants, certified that his conduct throughout the transaction was scrupulously honorable, loyal alike to his clients and the State. In his own justification to the people of New Hampshire, he referred to the treaty of peace, which provided that Congress should urge upon the States the passage of bills of amnesty and oblivion in favor of the loyalists. This policy was generally adopted. Indeed, throughout the war, extreme tenderness had been exhibited in all the States towards those who, from conscientious motives, sided with the Crown. In New Hampshire, seventy-five prominent individuals were placed upon the list of the proscribed. But few estates were actually sequestered, and of these a small portion confiscated. The whole amount realized by forfeitures was inconsiderable; and out of this the debts due by the loyalists were paid before the residue was applied to public uses.

Convinced from the lessons of experience that a people must not only be virtuous, enlightened, and brave, but accustomed to the use of arms, would they preserve their liberties, General Sullivan, from the close of the war, had exerted his influence to keep alive a military spirit. As a large portion of the adult population had been in the armies of the Revolution, this was more easily accomplished. Appointed Major-General, he had, with the assistance of a committee of the Legislature, in 1783, organized the twenty thousand men of military age, into from twenty to thirty regiments,—infantry, cavalry, and artillery,—and was indefatigable in bringing them into a good state of order and discipline; in perfecting them in their drill and evolutions. In February, 1785, he addressed to the freemen of New Hampshire two able communications on this subject, embracing incidentally other topics fraught with important consequences to their prosperity. Indeed, many reasons existed at the period why the States should not allow their arms to grow rusty.

England was exhausted by her late efforts, and not disposed to renew hostilities. But there were points of controversy which might at any time embroil us in war. Contrary to her treaty stipulations, she retained fortresses on the frontiers she had agreed to surrender. Weak in numbers, with a vast expanse of territory to defend, and no reliable elements of consolidation, America lay at the mercy of foreign powers. Discontents in Massachusetts, that were shortly to betray Shays and his misguided followers into open resistance to authority, were rife in various portions of the country. Vermont acknowledged no fealty to Congress. She was under no obligation not to return to British rule. Should recourse be had to the arbitrament of arms, New Hampshire was a border State, and might, unless on her guard, be taken at disadvantage. These considerations counselled preparation and encouragement of that loyalty to government apt to be engendered by bearing arms in her service.

He was aided in his efforts by Dr. Nathaniel Peabody, eminent in his own profession and in public affairs, and who attached the same importance as Sullivan to proficiency in arms as an element of national strength and security. His special charge was the cavalry, being appointed general of the horse. The frequent general orders in the journals exhibit the attention paid to every detail, and their pains were amply repaid. According to contemporary writers, all ages and ranks caught the infection, and displayed the utmost alacrity and ardor in accomplishing themselves for their duties. In the absence of other arrangements or objects to bring the people together, the field-days were festal occasions, and they flocked in from long distances to witness the movements, which closed with spirited repetitions of historical battles. Disorderly conduct or intemperance was of the rarest occurrence, and this is made subject of comment both in the general orders and public prints.

Arms of the same description and size were readily procured, as many remained from the war, in a good state of preservation. But it was more difficult to induce an unpaid soldiery to adopt uniformity of dress. This Sullivan earnestly urged, and with a success beyond expectation. In the addresses already mentioned, he proposed that the regiments should wear uniforms of home-made cloths, in order to encourage the agricultural and manufacturing industry of the State. At the reviews in 1786, most of them appeared in woollen garments of uniform shape and color, the material of which was raised and woven on their farms. Where such cloths were not to be obtained, at his suggestion rifle shirts were worn, of linen, of which large quantities were then made at Londonderry and neighboring towns, settled by Scotch-Irish, from flax they grew and spun. These shirts were bound and trimmed with ribbons to correspond in color with the facings of the several regiments.

The attention of General Sullivan had been early directed to the advantages possessed by New Hampshire for growing and manufacturing wool. Although engrossed in his professional duties, he had established at Packer's Falls, a few miles from his dwelling at Durham, fulling as well as grist and saw mills. Cloths were then made both of linen and woollen by hand-looms, and cotton was not known. It was at that period, as now, the mistaken policy of England to discourage useful arts in her dependencies. But when emancipated from this colonial thraldom, the new States proceeded at once to improve the field. Many articles previously imported were made at home. During the six years that intervened between the peace and the organization of the Federal Government, this was a frequent subject of discourse with Sullivan in his contributions to the press. When inaugurated President, he was attired in garments of which the materials were raised, woven, and dyed on his own estate. His zeal was further exemplified by his importing skilled artisans from France; and he seems to have had a prophetic sense that his neighborhood was to become one of the busiest manufacturing centres of the world.

When the time approached for the annual election, in 1785, he was regarded as an eligible candidate, and put in nomination. His friends, among his claims for the Presidency, urged that he had, at the earliest period of the contest, asserted the rights of his country with perseverance and unremitting ardor, regardless of personal consequences; in the darkest times, redoubling his exertions instead of relaxing them, giving life and vigor to our laws and operations; and been greatly instrumental in relieving the public credit, on which the political safety depended. His independent fortune, experience in political affairs, extensive correspondence abroad,— abilities that would give energy to the wheels of government,— should make him the choice of every freeman. Uniting to the virtues of a citizen the accomplishments of a soldier, his acquaintance with mankind and complete knowledge of the laws, would enable him to support the first office in the State with becoming dignity; the laws would be duly administered; the militia trained to arms and evolutions; the State made respectable at home, and reverenced abroad.

His principal competitor, John Langdon, was justly popular from his character and talents. He, moreover, was possessed of great wealth, and exercised the most generous hospitalities in the commercial and social capital. His brother Woodbury Langdon and John Pickering zealously promoted his election. They assailed, with the greater acrimony, General Sullivan, that his friends had reproached Langdon with lukewarmness in the cause of independence, and, besides, with having repaired to England in 1775, and returned to New York in a British frigate. Sullivan, as was his wont, when attacked, vindicated himself with warmth and vigor, and, in an appeal to "the Impartial Public," thus proved the charges groundless : —

Although I have no desire to satisfy, or even to answer, a writer who has endeavored to wound my reputation by a publication in the "New-Hampshire Mercury" of the 19th ultimo, yet, as I am conscious of having acted with uprightness in every part of my political conduct, I shall, for your satisfaction, answer the three charges which his malice has suggested, and which his knowledge of their falsity has prevented being signed by his proper name.

The first charge is, obtaining a considerable sum from Congress by false representations respecting the taking powder from Fort William and Mary; secondly, giving up the fishing-ground; and, thirdly, receiving a bribe in my office of Attorney-General, which prevented my complying with my duty in endeavoring to confiscate a valuable estate; by which, I suppose, he means Colonel Boyd's.

To answer the first, it will be necessary to relate the manner of taking the stores from the fort. When I returned from Congress, in 1774, and saw the order of the British King and Council, prohibiting military stores being sent to this country, I took the alarm, clearly perceived the designs of the British ministry, and wrote several pieces upon the necessity of securing military stores; which pieces were published in several papers.

On the 18th of December, some gentlemen belonging to Portsmouth went to the fort and took sundry barrels of powder, and sent, in a gondola, one hundred and ten barrels into my care; which myself and others deposited in places of security. The next day a report was spread that two vessels of war were coming from Boston to take possession of the fort and harbor.

I went down with a large number of men, and, in the night following, went in person with gondolas, took possession of the fort, brought away the remainder of the powder, the small arms, bayonets, and cartouch-boxes, together with the cannon and ordnance stores ; was out all night, and returned to Portsmouth next day. I might here add that I bore the expense of all the party. These gondolas, with the stores, were brought to Durham, after several days spent in cutting the ice; Durham River being then frozen over. The cannon and other articles were then deposited in places of security.

These are facts known to almost every person in the State and to all who were concerned, that almost the whole expense was borne by me, notwithstanding which I never applied for a single farthing to Congress, or any other body, for this service ; and when a committee of Congress, who were appointed to report what was due for my allowance in separate departments when I commanded, reported one hundred dollars for this service, I warmly opposed it, and told Congress I never expected or desired a single farthing for it. For the truth of this I appeal to the Hon. Judge Livermore, who was with me in Congress at the time, and knows every fact relating to it. He is now on the circuit through the State ; consequently any gentleman may satisfy himself, by asking him, whether these facts are true or false.

But to prove whether Congress have been generous to me in their grants, I beg leave to mention that, by a resolve of Congress of the 15th of June, 1775, general officers in separate departments were to be allowed one hundred and sixty dollars per month, over and above their wages. I served thirty months in separate departments, and Congress made me a grant of fifteen hundred dollars only, in lieu of four thousand eight hundred, which was my due. It is true, one hundred of it was reported for the above-mentioned service, but, upon my objecting to it, it was not in reality granted in that light ; and further, to prove the generosity of Congress to me, I now say, that for near five years' service I have never received only the nominal sum in paper for my services, and am the only officer in America that has received no depreciation or allowance therefor.

With respect to the second charge, I can only say, that the general and secret instructions to our ministers respecting the fishery remained the same as they were first formed, years before I went to Congress, in 1780. The secret instructions made the independence of the thirteen United States, and every part of them, — the grand ultimatum of a peace ; and the general instructions, among other things, directed them to secure our right of fishery on the banks.

When I was in Congress, Dr. Franklin, Mr. Jay, Governor Jefferson, and Mr. Laurens were added to Mr. Adams. New instructions were framed, but no alteration made respecting the fishery. It was indeed moved by a member that the fishery should be made an additional article of the ultimatum, to which I, among others, objected, and thought our general instructions to our ministers on that head were sufficient to show the wishes of Congress; that their own inclinations would prompt them to use every possible effort to secure it; and that it would be dangerous for Congress, at so great a distance, who could not possibly know the disposition of the European powers, to dictate positively the articles of peace, and thereby fetter ministers who, in my opinion, had as much zeal for the American interest, and had more knowledge of what we could or could not obtain, than all Congress together. Besides, let the articles agreed to, be as they might, they could not be binding on Congress until ratified by them. Every person must know that the capture of General Lincoln and his army was owing to the positive orders of Congress to keep possession of Charlestown.

And I confess myself to be one of those who had rather trust the command of an army to a good general on the ground than to a Congress at five hundred miles' distance; and the making a peace to five of the greatest characters in America than to a Congress at three thousand miles' distance; especially as, after all, Congress could approve or disapprove, as they thought proper.

There never was a question in Congress whether the fishery should be given up; and if there had, I should have been the last man in America to have yielded it to Britain; but I could not see the necessity of making it an additional article in our ultimatum. Our right to fish on Jaffrey's Ledge, and off Boon Island and the Isle of Shoals, were not articles of the ultimatum, yet we were never in danger of losing it.

When the instructions "Honestus" alludes to were made out, great part of New York and Virginia, and the whole of Georgia, were in possession of the enemy; we were without money, our paper currency had vanished, and our army was revolting; a change against us, even before our instructions arrived, was at least possible. Had Arnold's plan succeeded; had Greene been defeated in the South; had Washington been unsuccessful against Cornwallis; had the

French fleet been blocked up in the Chesapeake by the British; had Britain obtained a decisive naval victory over our allies; had Russia and Germany, or even the former, declared in favor of Britain, — we might have been compelled to accept terms less favorable than we obtained. Either of those events was possible; and yet our ministers obtained not a single point but what they were instructed to insist on. But as the events of war were uncertain, I acknowledge, and glory in the confession, that I was one of those who objected to fettering our ministers, and positively to dictate orders of peace, to five gentlemen who were, in my opinion, more than equal in the business of negotiation to all the members then on the floor of Congress.

Had the refugees, with the very sagacious and candid "Honestus" at their head, had the power of dictating terms, I dare say that our having possession of Great Britain would have made one article of the ultimatum to prevent a peace which Tories detest and Britain laments.

As to the third charge, I would only observe, that, in March, 1782, Mrs. Boyd sent to me, and informed me, that, as I had ever been attorney for Colonel Boyd, was then engaged in several important matters pending, and was expected to take charge of all affairs relating to the family, she wished to make me some satisfaction, and offered me a chariot, which I then agreed with her for. In the last of June following, I was, without my knowledge or expectation, appointed Attorney-General. John Smith, Esq., then clerk of the House, gave me the first information of it, and I informed him it was not possible for me to accept. In July following, at Dover, I was called upon to act as Attorney-General, and refused to take the oath, because I was previously engaged against the State in some matters. In September following, I was called upon by the Superior Court — President Weare being present — to take the oath, and refused for the reasons aforesaid; and particularly mentioned my previous engagement with Mrs. Boyd and others, which I could not break through. The Court agreed to excuse me in all matters where I was previously engaged; and even at that term appointed Mr. Bradbury to act as Attorney-General in some matters where I was engaged against the State.

When the votes came to be counted, it was found there was no choice by the people. The names of Langdon and Atkinson were selected by the House from the four candidates having the largest number, and Langdon was chosen by the Senate. General Sullivan, who had been returned from Durham, was elected Speaker, and chosen a member of the Council, which latter office he declined. He was continued as Major-General, and appointed Attorney-General, both of which offices he resigned on the fourth of March, 1786. He was again put in nomination for the Presidency, and was elected.

In May, 1786, soon after his election as President, appeared, a statement under his signature, as agent of the Allen claimants. It is well known that the Plymouth Company, in 1629, issued a patent to John Mason, confirmed in 1635, of a tract bounded by a line running from the mouth of the Piscataqua to its head, and thence north-westerly sixty miles, and by another line up the Merrimack, and running west sixty miles; thence to head of the line first mentioned. This constituted the grant under which New Hampshire was settled. John Mason devised to his sons John and Robert, who, in 1691, conveyed to Samuel Allen, a merchant of London, for twenty-seven hundred and fifty pounds sterling, under which Allen took possession. This claim under the Allens, who fell into poverty, not being improved, a number of persons, in 1747, purchased of a descendant of John Mason, for seven hundred and fifty pounds, his right to the territory; and their representatives were designated as the Masonian Proprietors.

The heirs of Allen applied to Sullivan to represent their claim. He declined, unless they agreed to confirm all grants to the purchasers from the Masonian Proprietors already made, limiting the points in controversy to the lands still waste and unsold. One motive was, to quiet titles bought from the Masonian Proprietors liable to be divested, if the adverse claim were established. His advocacy of the Allen title provoked the resentment of the Masonians, who were among the most wealthy and influential of the State.

Competition for popular preferment, under republics, exposes character and antecedents to rigid scrutiny; and the robe must be pure and spotless as of the candidate in the better days of Rome when the term originated, to stand the ordeal. The canvass, for five or six years, between Sullivan and Langdon, for the chief magistracy of New Hampshire, was warmly contested, and whatever could be advanced to the prejudice of either, with any shadow of plausibility, found its way into the prints. For an intelligent view of public personages, and especially for the preparation of their biography long after the generations that best knew them have passed, the journals of the day afford indispensable aid. At that particular period they professed,— to use the motto of the " Gazette," — to be " Open to all, influenced by none, aiming to be just; " and anonymous writers were allowed the widest latitude of discussion on either side, in the same columns. There was no delicacy or forbearance. The struggle for party supremacy was a fiery furnace. Praise and blame were alike subjected to the test, and truth eliminated from the dross.

From the " Gazette," in May, 1786, is taken the following vindication of General Sullivan from an aspersion there shown to be undeserved, and believed to be wholly inconsistent with his habits of thought. There may not be as frequent proof of the constant ascendancy of religious sentiment over his mind as over that of his brother, Governor Sullivan, of Massachusetts; but abundant trace is found in his published writings of his reverential spirit, familiarity with the Scriptures, and respect for the observances of religion. He may not have been sanctimonious: his mind was not of a nature to receive dogmas upon authority without investigation; but he was too enlightened not to reconcile revelation with reason; and if, after the bad habit of the times, occasionally using a stronger term than is ever heard now from people of education, it was only a mode of expression.

Having lately perused a piece in the Newbury paper, wherein, under the notion of a dream, a representation is given of a dialogue between three persons at Mr. Brewster's, at Portsmouth, in which the Christian religion and the whole of the sacred Scriptures are treated with contempt and ridicule, — although I am at no loss to discover the characters meant to be pointed at, I confess, it gave me great pain to hear that some persons, to gratify their malice, have ungenerously whispered that the Hon. Major-General Sullivan was one of the party, because he happened to lodge at Mr. Brewster's the last session of the General Court, and because he is interested in Allen's claim ; but, though he lodged at that house, he was in a separate apartment, and had no connection with the three persons alluded to.

Although interested in Allen's claim, it is a well-known fact, that fraud and deceit make up no part of that gentleman's private or public character; consequently it cannot be supposed that he joined in any plan to deceive the good people of this State. But, to suppose him to be one of those who joined in reviling the sacred writings, is most unjust and ungenerous. It is a fact well known to all who have the pleasure of his acquaintance, that he has ever been a zealous and able advocate in favor of the divinity of the Scriptures, and particularly of the truth of the Christian system.

It is well known to a number of worthy officers who served under him, that, while the army which he commanded, in 1779, lay at Wyoming, he wrote a most learned and ingenuous treatise against Deists, which was highly applauded by all the chaplains in that army, among whom was the Rev. Dr. Evans, then chaplain to the New-Hampshire troops; and even those who professed to be Deists acknowledged that it contained the most powerful and conclusive arguments in favor of divine revelation and the system of Christianity they had ever seen. This piece, though many copies of it were given out, he would not consent to have published, lest it should be said he was acting out of his sphere.

Not long after his inauguration, Sullivan, finding the " Gazette " and " Mercury," published at Portsmouth, and the " Freeman's Oracle," at Exeter, not quite impartial, but disposed at times to favor the views of his rival rather than his own, persuaded his friend George Jerry Osborne to establish the " New-Hampshire Spy." Osborne had been an officer in the Revolution, commanding a company of artillery long stationed at Portsmouth, where he had married Olive, the daughter of John Pickering. The earliest number of the "Spy" was issued at Portsmouth, October 24, 1786, and it appeared Tuesdays and Fridays; the first paper in the State published oftener than once a week. It was continued some six years, and during the administration of General Sullivan was made the official paper. "It was edited with spirit and ability, and many of its articles bear the impress of his vigorous mind."

Although inaugural addresses are too frequent and familiar to be of much general interest, some few of General Sullivan's may be of service in connection with our present object, as indicating the condition of affairs in New Hampshire at the time of his administration. That of June, 1786, had certainly the merit of brevity. It was as follows: —

The free and unsolicited suffrages of my fellow-citizens, having called me to the chief seat of government, at a time when our trade is in embarrassment, our finances deranged, and, for want of a sufficiency of circulation, even the requisitions of Congress but in part complied with, duty and inclination lead me to recommend for your consideration those measures which appear to me most likely to promote the public good; and to join you in adopting and enforcing such as you shall judge best calculated to preserve the public faith, to encourage industry and frugality, and to relieve the people from their present difficulties. To answer which purposes, if any measures more effectual than promoting agriculture, discouraging the consumption of foreign luxuries, encouraging the manufactures of our own country, and giving a free course to the exportation of those articles which our soil or industry may produce, had offered themselves to my view, I should have proposed them for your deliberation; but, as these will probably prove the most efficacious, I beg leave to call your attention to objects so worthy of your notice, in full confidence that your wisdom will direct to such laws and regulations as will answer the expectations of your constituents, and advance the interest of our common country. The laws now in force respecting navigation and commerce, being thought by some to militate with public commercial treaties, and supposed by others not calculated to answer the good purposes for which they were intended, may deserve your serious consideration. The unfortunate events which prevented the sale of lumber the last year occasions large quantities, manufactured before passing the late act for regulating the size thereof, to remain still in the hands of the industrious laborers and honest purchasers, and cannot now be exported or disposed of without violating said act.

Perhaps the injury which individuals must suffer by the operation of that law at this time, may merit a supervision of it at some future period. The opening roads, and encouraging an intercourse, between the several parts of this State, are objects which, I persuade myself, will be deemed too important to pass unnoticed. As our national character, and even our political existence, depends in great measure upon a punctual compliance with requisitions of Congress, nothing can be more necessary than the adopting measures which will answer the demands and wishes of that honorable body, with as little delay as the nature of things will admit. As a well-regulated militia is the most safe and natural defence of this country, and, from its importance, merits every possible attention and encouragement, perhaps a review of the military system in this State may deserve your notice at this time. A revision of the laws of the States, and particularly those which relate to duties on articles imported, are too important to escape your observation. Gentlemen, the well-known abilities and patriotic spirit of the members in the respective branches of the Legislature afford to the public the most pleasing prospect of the happy effects of their wise deliberations in this session; while their candor encourages me to hope for every necessary and constitutional support which the nature of my office may require. Permit me to assure you, gentlemen, that the happiness which I feel in meeting members of such knowledge and integrity in this Assembly, will be augmented by every opportunity which I may have to prove my readiness to join you in any measures for advancing the interest of the State, and relieving the distresses of our fellow-citizens.

JNO. SULLIVAN.

Given at the Council Chamber in Concord, the 10th of June, 1786.

The reference to distress to be relieved was not without its significance. The war had interrupted trade and industrial pursuits, and left the country impoverished. No uniform imposts had been laid by the different States, and no power been delegated for this purpose to Congress. Taxation on estates and polls for State and Federal obligations harassed beyond endurance a people who, engaged in tillage and lumbering, found no market for their products. Coin, which during the last two years of the war had been abundant, went abroad to pay for imports. The circulating medium, composed chiefly of State issues, and commanding but sixty per cent of their nominal value, was in excess of the requirements of trading centres, yet rarely reached the pockets of the farmers. Debts accumulated, suits at law wasted their substance, tender laws led to fraudulent conveyances. Discontent was the more general and poignant that the anticipations of prosperity to follow independence had been extravagant, and were necessarily disappointed.

A large portion of the adult population had been in the army. In contrast with the stirring incidents and companionships of the camp, ordinary occupations had lost their zest, and desultory habits unfitted for patient labor. It was quite as much a yearning for excitement, as any grievance or actual distress, which produced the insurrectionary spirit rife at the period. If this disaffection assumed less formidable proportions than in the neighboring State of Massachusetts, it still was widely extended in New Hampshire, and, gathering fresh fervor from the turmoil across the border, created at times alarm among the timid as to the stability of free institutions.

Conferences were held among the disaffected, who inveighed against courts and lawyers; but their principal clamor was for paper money. A convention was called to meet at Concord in June, 1786, when the Legislature was to meet, and President Sullivan to be inaugurated. It was supposed that the presence of so large a body of men, from all parts of the State, would induce the Assembly to accede to their demands. This project was defeated by some young lawyers and others, who, when but a portion of the delegates were in attendance, professed to be also members, and called a meeting to organize. They persuaded them to adopt an address, complaining in the most extravagant terms of their grievances, praying for a loan of three millions of dollars, funded on real estate; the abolition of inferior courts, and all lawyers but two in each county; and for free trade with all the world. They went in procession to the Assembly, some of whom had been let into the secret, and presented their petition, which was laid upon the table. Other delegates to the convention arrived, but it was too late to repair the mischief.

In the hope of better success, recourse was had to county conventions, as in Massachusetts; and from two of them petitions were presented to the Assembly at their session in September at Exeter. To ascertain the real sense of the people as to an increase of paper currency, the Assembly submitted to the several towns a proposition for an emission of fifty thousand pounds, at four per cent, on landed security. The insurrection at this time in Massachusetts was at its height; one-third of its population being disaffected to the government, and several thousand men in different parts of the State in arms to prevent the courts from sitting. The object in New Hampshire was not so much to subvert the government as to overawe the Legislature.

Not satisfied with the concessions made, and inflamed by the example in Massachusetts, on the 20th of September from two to four hundred men from the westerly part of Rockingham County assembled at Kingston, six miles from Exeter, and by the help of some militia officers formed into companies, armed with muskets and swords, — growing in numbers as they went, — marched to Exeter where the Legislature was assembled. They sent a paper demanding an immediate answer to their petition. They then marched through the town, parading before the meeting-house where both branches were assembled. The doors were open, and as many as were disposed entered. President Sullivan, who by the Constitution presided over the Senate, in a cool and deliberate speech explained the reasons on which the Assembly had proceeded in rejecting the petitions; exposed the weakness, inconsistency, and injustice of their request; and said that if it were ever so just and proper in itself, and if the whole body of the people were in favor of it, yet the Legislature ought not to comply with it while surrounded by an armed force. To do this would be to betray the rights of the people, which they had all solemnly sworn to support. He concluded by declaring that no consideration of personal danger would ever compel them to violate the rights of their constituents.

When he ceased speaking, the rioters, disappointed and exasperated, left the building. Orders were given to load their muskets with ball, sentinels were stationed at the doors, and the members were assured that they should not be permitted to retire until they had complied with the demands contained in the petitions. Nowise intimidated, the Legislature proceeded with their business. In the evening, at the usual hour, they adjourned. As the President was leaving the building, his progress was barred at the steps by a close column of the rioters. A cry was raised among them to fire upon him; but he, with great composure, told them that he had had too much experience of powder to be afraid of theirs. He then expostulated with them upon the madness and folly of their course; assuring them it could only bring ruin on themselves, without tending in the slightest degree to accomplish their object, and that they should be resisted by the whole force of the government so long as he continued at its head.

Their answers were full of menace and reproach. The burden was a demand for paper money, an equal distribution of property, and release from debts. At this moment a drum was beaten at some little distance by well-disposed citizens of Exeter, who had beheld with dismay this insult to the

Legislature, but were at a loss what to do, having no authority to act. Alarm was given that a body of artillery were approaching, upon which the whole force of insurgents speedily withdrew, scarcely heeding the direction of their leaders to assemble again at nine the next morning.

The Legislature forthwith resumed its session, authorizing the President to suppress the insurrection by military force. His orders were issued promptly, and so well obeyed, that companies of militia arrived in Exeter in the course of the night. Early in the morning, two thousand had assembled, horse and foot, with several field-pieces, and the President ordered them to attack the insurgents in motion about a mile distant. Those who were unarmed withdrew beyond the river, the rest holding their ground till a party of light horse appeared in view, when the whole body retired. Some of them were taken; others gained the bridge at King's Fall, and were disposed to dispute its passage. An order given to fire was fortunately disobeyed. A rush was then made upon them, and forty, including their leader, were taken. The rest fled with precipitation. The prisoners were examined before the President and Council; but, the authority of the government being vindicated, lenity was deemed the best policy. Six were detained; and two others, who had been among the most active, but had gone home, were taken from their beds, and brought to Exeter.

They were forthwith arraigned on an indictment for treason before the Superior Court, then in session in the town, and ordered to recognize for their appearance at the next court; but there the process was dropped. Some of the insurgents belonging to the Presbyterian churches were cited before ecclesiastical tribunals, and censured as opposers of just government. Others, being militia officers, were tried by a general court-martial; of these some were cashiered, but not incapacitated for future service, some reprimanded, and others acquitted. The insurrectionary spirit, which in other States carried its point triumphantly, was effectually subdued by this generous forbearance, and the disaffected submitted with cheerfulness to a government which they had themselves established, and found not only able to assert its authority, but mindful of their rights.

The conduct of President Sullivan throughout this emergency was such as to receive the entire approbation of his constituents. It was prudent and dignified. The House of Representatives had shown some disposition to temporize, and appointed a committee to confer with the insurgents. When the order came up to be joined in the Senate, where Sullivan by law presided, this was not concurred in. To this firm and decided course of the President and Senate may be justly attributed the seasonable crushing-out of a rebellion, which, had it gained any early headway, with such numbers of discontented in the State, would have set law and order at defiance.

In the foregoing narrative of the insurrection, we have followed closely the relations of Belknap and Peabody, using their language freely where it served the purpose. It seemed hardly worth while to seek new phrases where they had selected the best; and their opportunities of ascertaining the truth were far better than any to be had at this distance of time. Many additional particulars might be gleaned from the records and public prints, but would occupy too much space in these pages.

A few weeks later, the President issued the following proclamation, addressed to the freemen of the State: —

Whereas, a number of the good people of this government have formed conventions in different parts of the State for the purpose of consulting with each other on the best measures for relieving our countrymen from their present distresses, and with a view of petitioning the General Court to adopt such as promise to be most speedily effectual; and crafty and designing persons, wishing to make these conventions, however innocent in their first formation, a cover for the most injurious and unjustifiable conduct, and, under color of conventional authority, to subvert the constitutional power of the State, have even with arms demanded from the legislature an immediate compliance with the measures proposed by one of these conventions, and threatened an immediate dispersion and dissolution of the General Court in case of neglect or refusal, —

The good citizens of New Hampshire, of every rank and denomination, are earnestly exhorted not to join or give countenance to such conventions in future, as these assemblies have, by experience, been found in this and one of the neighboring States to have a tendency to overturn and destroy all constitutional authority and government. The voice of every town in the State may be given in town-meetings, agreeably to the thirty-second article of the Bill of Rights, upon any point that respects the interests of the public or the rights of individuals ; and the sentiments of the people at large may be collected with more certainty in that way than in conventions, where, at best, only those of a few individuals can be obtained.

I am well convinced that many wealthy citizens joined in these assemblages without the most distant thought that government would be thereby endangered ; but, since events have proved the danger of setting up even the resemblance of a government or authority within a constitutional government to which the former is unknown, I most ardently entreat my fellow-citizens to have their " consultations upon the common good" in regular, orderly, and constitutional town-meetings ; that they will freely instruct their representatives upon the most interesting points that may come under consideration of the legislature, that so the desire of all may be known, and the wisdom of the whole united in selecting and pursuing those measures which may tend to promote the public good, secure our constitutional rights, and lead us in the true path of political happiness.

Given at the Council Chamber in Durham, the thirtieth day of September, 1786. JOHN SULLIVAN.

The rebellion in Massachusetts was far more extended, embracing one-third of the whole population. It raged with great violence for several months. In January, 1787, an army of four thousand men marched to Springfield, and, on the third of February, General Lincoln, who commanded it, learning that Shays, the rebel leader, had marched to Petersham, left Hadley at eight in the evening, and, after a night march of thirteen hours, — part of the way over high hills and in a violent snow-storm, — reached that place, more than thirty miles distant, at nine the next morning. Many of his men were frost-bitten, and all by exhaustion unfitted for combat. But the rebels were panic-stricken at their unexpected appearance, and dispersed without a shot. The same clemency was shown as in New Hampshire. Eight hundred acknowledged their error, and, upon taking the oath of allegiance and giving promise of future good behavior, were released. Fourteen of the ringleaders were convicted of treason, and many more of sedition. Large numbers took refuge in Vermont and New Hampshire, and President Sullivan issued a proclamation for their apprehension.

The autumn was busily occupied by General Sullivan in reviews of the troops; a duty the more important from the civil war across the border. He improved every suitable occasion not only to stimulate their ardor in the line of their duty, but to disseminate sound views of loyalty to the government. How far his influence was of any avail can only be conjectured. But it is believed there never afterwards was exhibited in the State the slightest disaffection. The Legislature, under some solicitude as to the possible course of events, had adjourned to January, and when they assembled he opened their session with the following address: —

> Perhaps nothing could be more fortunate than your meeting, by your own adjournment, at a time when Congress calls for your immediate attention to matters which respect the safety of the Union ; and which are of so interesting a nature, that, in case your adjournment had been to a more distant period, I should have been compelled, by the request of that honorable body, to have called your attendance at an earlier day. The conduct of the Indians on the Western frontiers indicates an intention on their part to break through the most solemn treaties, and to prevent our taking possession of that territory which was intended to be applied to the payment of our foreign debt. An immediate augmentation of the troops of the United States has consequently become necessary. The requisition, with the sev-

eral letters from the Secretary of Congress and the Secretary of War, will be laid before you for your consideration. Among other public papers which I have the honor to submit, are some letters from the Board of Treasury, with their inclosures, which cannot fail to engage your attention.

Whatever may appear to be the opinion of the several towns respecting the plan sent out by you, at the last session, for the consideration of the people, I cannot persuade myself that such part of it as respects turning the produce of the country, by the intervention of a State agent, to the payment of our foreign debt, ought to be neglected, as it will render the payment of taxes less burdensome, give a spring to industry, prevent our coin from being drawn away, and be a means of making those payments which are demanded from us at least practicable, and perhaps seasonable and certain.

I am happy to inform you that the military force in this State is in a most promising situation, and, through the exertions of the officers and activity of the soldiers, cannot fail to become in a short time truly respectable.

It is no less pleasing to have the opportunity of assuring you, that, notwithstanding the machinations of a few interested, designing, and unprincipled men, the people are generally determined to support and maintain the constitutional authority of the State against every attempt of seditious insurgents.

I have also the satisfaction to acquaint you that individuals, in most parts of the State, are engaged industriously in fabricating articles with which we have hitherto been furnished from foreign countries, and of which the purchase has constantly drained us of coin, and kept us in a state of poverty and dependence. And should it be thought worthy the attention of the legislature of this State to encourage the manufacturing of glass, steel, and a variety of other articles, — which have seldom arrived to a pitch of perfection in any country unless aided in the first instance by the supreme power, — we might experience national advantages which would soon enable us to become a flourishing and a happy people.

Among the various measures which may offer themselves to your consideration for promoting the public interest, perhaps none can be more successful than attempting to raise a revenue upon particular articles of foreign growth and manufactures imported into the State, and adopting indirect, in lieu of direct, taxation, in all cases where it may be found practicable. The former will probably have a double effect in favor of the country, and the latter cannot fail to yield a revenue for payment of our public debt which will be more certain, less burdensome, and more equitable and productive, than can be obtained in any other way.

The requisition of Congress of the 2d of August last will undoubtedly come again under your consideration at this session; and I am convinced that you will use every possible exertion to grant such aids to Congress as are necessary for supporting the Union, and are within the abilities of your constituents to comply with.

Should it be thought inconvenient to have another session prior to the next election, the necessary grants for defraying the expense of our domestic government will of course come under your consideration. And the interest of the public, as well as that of individuals, will require that as much of the business now before the Court as can possibly be done should be completed at this session; in the despatch of which you may rely on every aid and assistance in my power.

Given at the Council Chamber in Portsmouth, the seventh day of December, 1786.
JOHN SULLIVAN.

One topic of the foregoing address claims passing comment. Some portion of the Federal foreign debt was falling due. The several States were jointly bound for its redemption. Credit in the money-markets of Europe, precious to young republics, perhaps to be called upon again to defend their dearly bought independence, might be jeoparded, should they fail to meet their obligations. There were, besides, considerations in the circumstances under which the loan had been effected, which made it peculiarly sacred. The apportionment to New Hampshire of the Federal burdens was not large, less than one-thirtieth of the whole; but she was in no condition for additional assessments. Her late difficulties had proceeded from the intolerable weight of the taxes. It was proposed that the several towns should contribute a part of the yield of their inexhaustible forests, to be shipped abroad by a State agent. Already vessels from foreign ports were loading with lumber at Portsmouth, and it was thought the few hundred thousand dollars constituting their share of the sum to be paid, might be thus raised without distressing the people. Timber of suitable quality was very equally distributed among the settlements, and could be economically brought to the seaboard by watercourses which abounded throughout the State.

If productive of no other result, discussion would relieve solicitude as to the public burdens, and incline the people to a central government exclusively charged with such obligations. If no substitute for the articles of confederation proved feasible, New Hampshire might thus, by combined efforts of the people and the government, find means to redeem its faith.

Although opinions on questions of public policy were about equally divided, — political prejudices and preferences fervent and intense, — party lines were not as distinctly marked as since. When Langdon, in 1785, with less than a majority of the popular vote, was sent up to the Senate by the House as its preferred candidate for the Presidency of the State, and elected, the latter body chose Sullivan as its Speaker. When he in turn took Langdon's place as President, and by virtue of that office presided over the Senate, his unsuccessful competitor was chosen to preside over the popular branch. The temper exhibited by their respective adherents in the canvass did not disturb their friendly relations; and in January, 1787, James, the brother of General Sullivan, afterwards Governor of Massachusetts, married, at Portsmouth, Martha, the sister of Langdon, and the widow of Captain Simpson, who had commanded the continental frigate "Ranger," built at Portsmouth. Judge Sullivan had resigned his seat on the Supreme Bench, and resumed the practice of his profession in Boston. Whilst studying law with John, at Durham, before the war, he had become engaged to his first wife, Hettie Odiorne. Her recent death had left him with a young family requiring maternal care.

As the time approached for the annual election, there was manifested a general disposition to re-elect Sullivan. His bold, judicious, and effective course had won respect from all parties, and this often assumed in the canvass the measure of panegyric. While some allowance must be made for unqualified terms of praise usual in recommendations for office, as in obituary tributes, they serve to afford, at least, a proximate view of actual character. Praise undeserved or glaringly extravagant would defeat its design in attracting the wavering. The following, from the "Freemen's Oracle," is selected as indicating the estimation in which he was very generally held at the period: —

Our present commander-in-chief is possessed of those shining qualities which form the scholar, the statesman, and the soldier. His genius seems admirably adapted to our needs and for times like the present. When a gentleman is raised to an important trust, who pays unwearied attention to its duties, and whose conduct in every respect is unexceptionable, he does the highest honor to the understanding of those who have elected him, while it proves their confidence is not misplaced. They should not be forgetful of his services nor insensible to his virtues, but reward them by re-election until his eligibility ceases.

He who now presides over you more than answers this description. His unremitting endeavors to regulate the militia of the State, and to make it appear formidable and respectable, must make a pleasing impression upon the mind of every friend to his country.

In him we see no opposition to acts of utility, but readiness to adopt and enforce every measure which aims at the public good. Such as view his popularity with an envious eye object that his political principles are not of a republican nature. If calling forth the powers of the State and animating them by his spirited exertions to support the present government; if an anxiety to comply with the requisitions of Congress, who are guardians of these republics; if unwearied pains to fix upon each individual only his fair proportion of the foreign debt, and pointing out the most easy and expeditious mode of discharging it, are proofs of it, we shall be perfectly secure in wishing for more of them. But so opposed is he to the very idea of a change which must tend to disorder and confusion, that when any public calamity is impending, his eloquent appeals inspire even unbelievers in republicanism with a saving faith in its doctrines, and arouse them to a sense of its value by his works.

These eulogiums some perhaps may construe as savoring too much of adulation. But gratitude and a desire to speak well of our rulers, especially of those that do well, are motives too prevalent to hide or suppress. The truth, when set forth in all its colors, will have weight with the candid and judicious. If an unwearying application to business, a head to contrive and a heart to pursue the best interests of the State, are the necessary qualifications for a candidate to that office, it would seem that the man who now presides over you will preside over you again.

It so indeed proved; and Sullivan was elected, although not without opposition. Many whose cherished schemes he had thwarted bore him ill-will and voted against him. His inaugural was chiefly occupied with discussion of the financial condition of the State and nation. He recommended that, to supply currency for ordinary transactions, those who held State securities should be allowed to exchange them at the treasury for smaller denominations, which should be received for a portion of the taxes. He suggested amendments in the imposts and excises. One rule, now general, but not then usual, he urged should be adopted, — the appropriation of every part of the public revenue to particular objects of expenditure. The convention for framing a Federal constitution was sitting at Philadelphia, and he called their attention to the expediency of sending delegates. The revival and continuance of laws expired or that were expiring, as also some enactments for a full and ample compliance with the treaty of peace, claimed consideration. As the busy season of the year was approaching, he hinted at the propriety of a short session.

His address to the council betrays a sensitiveness to the expedients to which his political opponents had resorted to defeat his election and secure that of Langdon. Had he lived at a later day, when misrepresentation of facts, impeachment of motive, gross exaggeration, and opprobrious epithets are the ordinary weapons employed in political warfare, he would have heeded them less. But as it was not in his own nature to pervert the truth for a purpose, and he was keenly alive to any reflections upon his honor or integrity, he felt sorely aggrieved. These reproaches seemed especially aggravating, inasmuch as he had had the past year extraordinary difficulties with which to contend, and was acknowledged to have acquitted himself wisely and well. On meeting his new council, he thus addressed them: —

At a time when the greatest stretch of human wisdom is requisite to extricate our country from the most trying embarrassments, to restore public and private credit, and to secure and maintain national honor and dignity, the appointment of gentlemen in whom the advantages of political experience are happily united with patriotic virtue and acknowledged abilities, to advise with and direct me in the executive part of the government, cannot fail to afford me unspeakable pleasure.

Although taught by experience that artful and designing men will multiply their attacks against me in proportion to the endeavors which I may use for promoting the interest and happiness of my country, this confidence, however painful, cannot in the smallest degree lessen my exertions for the public good; while I am consoled by the pleasing assurance that I may at all times avail myself of your friendly hand to conduct me in the path of political rectitude.

Deeply affected with the disagreeable aspect of our public affairs, fully sensible of my own unenviable situation, yet unalterably determined to fulfil with integrity and firmness the duties of my office, nothing could yield me so much satisfaction as a well-grounded confidence, that, through the whole course of my administration, I shall receive from you every advice, direction, and assistance which the nature of my office may require.

His official position as President did not admit of his being a candidate for the convention which was called to meet in June, 1787, at Philadelphia, to revise the articles of confederation. Langdon, Atkinson, Livermore, and Bartlett were elected delegates to that body and to the Continental Congress then sitting at New York; the two former being subsequently selected to represent the State in the convention. As they did not make their appearance at the opening of the session, General Knox wrote Sullivan as follows, to hasten their coming: —

MY DEAR SIR, — As an old friend, a number of gentlemen, members of the Convention, have pressed me to write to you, soliciting that you urge the departure of the delegates from New Hampshire.

Impressed most fully with the belief that we are verging very fast to anarchy, and that the present Convention is the only means of avoiding the most flagitious evils that ever afflicted three millions of freemen, I have cheerfully consented to their request, and beg leave to have recourse to your friendship for an excuse, if any is necessary. There are here a number of the most respectable characters from several States, among whom is our illustrious friend, General Washington, who is extremely anxious on the subject of the New Hampshire delegates. A number of States sufficient for organization and to commence business will assemble this week. If the delegates come on, all the States excepting Rhode Island will be shortly represented. Endeavor, then, my dear sir, to push this matter with all your powers. I am persuaded, from the present complexion of opinions, that the issue will prove that you have highly served your country in promoting the measure.

I am, affectionately, your most obedient humble servant,

H. KNOX.

His Excellency President SULLIVAN.

The Convention, of which Washington was President, after full deliberation, agreed upon their plan, and submitted it to the people of the several States for ratification. That Sullivan never wavered in his faith that it ought to be adopted, is shown by the decided stand taken by the "Spy" in its support. Several of the States had ratified it, but not the requisite number to give effect to the instrument; and the following letter from Knox to Sullivan intimates how anxious were its friends that New Hampshire should adopt it: —

MY DEAR SIR, — The new Minister of France, the Count de Moutiers, who arrived yesterday, brought the inclosed letter from our common friend, the Marquis de La Fayette. It was addressed to you, on the supposition of your being in this city, and President of Congress. But, alas, there is no Congress, although two months have elapsed since one ought to have been assembled, agreeably to the Confederation. The new Constitution! the new Constitution! is the general cry this way. Much paper is spoiled on the subject, and many essays are written, which perhaps are never read by either side.

It is a stubborn fact, however, that the present system, called the Confederation, has run down; that the springs, if it ever had other than the late army, have entirely lost their tone, and the machine cannot be wound up again. But something must be done speedily, or we shall be involved in all the horrors of anarchy and separate interests. This, indeed, appears to have been the serious judgment of all the States which have formally considered the new Constitution; and therefore they have adopted it, not as a perfect system, but as the best that could be obtained under existing circumstances. If to those which have already adopted it, Massachusetts and New Hampshire should be added, a doubt cannot be entertained but that it will be received generally in the course of the present year. If Massachusetts and New Hampshire reject it, we shall have to encounter a boisterous and uncertain ocean of events. Should you have leisure, I shall be much obliged by a confidential information of the disposition of New Hampshire on the subject; and you may rest assured that your confidence will not be misplaced.

I am, my dear sir, with great respect and affection, your most obedient humble servant, • H. KNOX.

His Excellency JOHN SULLIVAN, Esq.

In the uncertainty as to the event, curiosity was naturally felt as to the course likely to be pursued by leaders, to whose guidance in critical conjunctures the citizens were accustomed to trust. The "Freemen's Oracle" of the 15th of December says, "It can with pleasure announce the sentiments of his Excellency, President Sullivan, to be perfectly federal. He has been heard to express himself in nearly the following terms: that, although he did not doubt New Hampshire, singly considered, might have formed a better constitution for themselves; yet when the whole of the thirteen States were considered,—that it was to unite them, jarring in interest, in politics, and prejudices,—he was bold to say it was one of the best systems of government that ever was devised, and that all the objections which have been raised against it are no more than may be brought against any form of government whatsoever."

That same month the subject was thus brought to the notice of the Legislature in the opening address of the President: —

> Some important despatches which have come to hand since the close of the last session having rendered it necessary to call the General Court together at an earlier day than that to which it stood adjourned, I have by advice and order of Council directed your attendance at the place where by your appointment you were to hold the winter session ; and, although it is much earlier than you proposed to meet, I can see no reason why all the business necessary to be transacted may not as well be completed now as at any other period.
>
> Among the public papers which I have the honor to lay before you, the Report of the National Convention respecting a plan of Government for the people of the United States, with the resolves of Congress accompanying the same, will undoubtedly claim your attention.
>
> The important question whether the proposed form shall be received or rejected, can no farther come under your consideration at this time than as it stands connected with, or may be affected by, your determination respecting the propriety of appointing delegates to decide upon it.
>
> The proposed plan undoubtedly has its defects. The wisdom of man has never yet been able to furnish the world with a perfect system of government. Perhaps that which claims the attention of America is liable to as few exceptions as any which has hitherto been produced.
>
> I have considered the plan, and endeavored to weigh the objections which have been raised against it; and have not as yet been able to discover any of more weight than might be urged against the most perfect system which has been offered to mankind ; or perhaps might be alleged against any which human wisdom may ever contrive.

The Convention of New Hampshire met Feb. 13, 1788, at Exeter; and Sullivan, who had been returned from Durham, was elected President. The rules adopted for their government embraced the provision now more usual than regarded in deliberative bodies, that no member should speak more than twice to any subject in debate until each member had had an opportunity to offer his opinion. The session lasted ten days, including Sunday, and at this and at the subsequent adjournment in June there was a very general attendance. Each section in turn was discussed, and on the last day the whole instrument made subject for debate. It was then determined to adjourn, to meet again at Concord on the third Wednesday of June, in order that the popular sentiment might be ascertained, and so important a step might not be taken without due deliberation.

What part General Sullivan took in the debates does not fully appear. The "Journal of the Convention" affords no clue, but in the "Freemen's Oracle" of March 7 is the following report of his remarks on the clause defining the jurisdiction of the Federal courts: —

Every part of the Constitution exhibits proof of the wisdom of those that framed it; and no one article meets my approbation more than the one under consideration. All acknowledge that causes wherein ambassadors, other public ministers or consuls, wherein citizens of different States are parties, or foreigners are interested, ought to come under cognizance of the Federal jurisdiction; and, if this be just and reasonable, it is equally so that causes between different States should be tried by the same tribunal. There are few of us who have not been witness to the bias the most upright judges have upon their minds in deciding causes between their own citizens and foreigners or citizens of another State. The limits of the eastern boundary of this State were formerly disputed by Massachusetts. Towns upon or nigh the line had been granted by both. The Massachusetts grantees commenced actions of trespass against the New-Hampshire settlers in the county of York; and the court held, upon consideration, that the lands were within that county. Similar actions were commenced by the New-Hampshire settlers within their own province, and the courts determined the actions were well brought. The controversy was long continued, till at length the parties observing the inefficiency of the laws of either province to determine a question of this kind, compromised the dispute.

The mode pointed out by the constitution remedies these evils. Tribunals upon the adoption of this government may be instituted where the grants of different States will have no more weight than their intrinsic goodness will warrant; where it will not be so much considered whether a party belongs to Massachusetts or New Hampshire as whether his cause be just. And all this we may certainly predict without any party being ruined in the prosecution or defence of his rights. Justice will be administered without any extraordinary expense to the subject; and Congress, under such regulations as they are empowered by the constitution to make, provide for the easy and expeditious dispensing of law. It seems singular that gentlemen who considered the British king was as eligible as that of any people could be, complain of this regulation as a hardship, and destructive of the rights of the people. They quietly suffered an appeal to Great Britain in all causes of consequence. They then boasted of their liberties, boasted of the liberty of appealing to judges ignorant of our situation, and prejudiced against the name of an American. And will they now object to this provision in the constitution? Could they be content under their former bondage; and will they now reject a constitution because an unprejudiced American court are to be their judges in certain causes, under such limitations and regulations as the representatives shall provide?

The following fast proclamation, not for any peculiar excellence, when compared with the numberless similar productions annually issued by State executives, sheds light on the religious sentiments of Sullivan, whose duty it was to prepare it. New Hampshire was as orthodox and observant of religious rites as any other part of New England. It was even more intolerant, not, until within a comparatively recent period, allowing Roman Catholics to hold office. It contains a seasonable reference to the action of the Convention:—

As the constant dependence of man upon the Supreme Ruler of the universe for life and all its enjoyments, is undeniable, while his natural disposition to wander from that line of rectitude which divine Revelation clearly points out, is no less certain; the laudable and pious example of our ancestors, in setting apart certain days for imploring the pardon and protection of Almighty God, is well worthy of our imitation. The General Court have, therefore, thought proper to appoint the tenth day of April next, to be observed as a day of general humiliation, fasting, and prayer throughout the State.

And, in consequence of such appointment, I do by and with the advice and consent of Council issue this proclamation, earnestly recommending to the religious societies of every denomination, that they assemble themselves together on that day, and offer up their supplications to the Father of mercies for the pardon of our numerous transgressions, and a continuance of those favors which he of his infinite goodness has hitherto been pleased to make us partakers of; to entreat him to avert those judgments which our sins have justly merited, and save the land which his own arm has delivered from oppression; that he will graciously inspire our rulers with wisdom, integrity, and love of virtue; crown the labors of our husbandmen, by causing the earth to yield her increase; prosper our trade and manufactories; bestow upon us the blessing of health; preserve us from foreign wars and intestine commotions; grant to the members of our convention that wisdom which is necessary to direct and lead them to those measures which may promote the interest and happiness of the United States; and, above all, that the Gospel of our blessed Saviour may spread throughout the world, and that the ambassadors of his kingdom may have reason to rejoice in the success of their labors.

All servile employments and recreations are strictly forbidden on said day.

Given at the Council Chamber at Durham, 29th February, A.D. 1788, and 12th year of American Independence.

The following letter — dated April 9, 1788 — from General Knox at New York, presents a comprehensive view of the condition of the great question before the country: —

I have hitherto deferred, my dear Sir, answering your esteemed favor of the 27th of February, in hopes of being able to give you a satisfactory statement of public affairs. But the unfortunate check the new constitution received in New Hampshire, has given new life and spirits to the opponents of the proposed system, and damped the ardor of its friends.

The Convention in South Carolina is to meet on the 12th of next month. The general tenor of the information is, that it will be adopted there, but not without considerable opposition. North Carolina is not to meet until July. The general opinion seems to be that they will follow the example of Virginia, the convention of which meets in June. The Constitution in that State will meet with opposition, indeed, and the issue is extremely doubtful. As far as information has been received of the elections — which were finished in March — the complexion is favorable. The arguments urged against its adoption there are mostly local, although many ostensible ones will appear. Impositions by the Eastern States on their commerce, and treaties being made the supreme law of the land, thereby compelling the payment of the British debts, will be the real objections of the greater part of the opposers, — while some others apprehend the consolidation of the Union as a real evil.

In Maryland it is highly probable, according to information that has been received, the Constitution will be adopted by a great majority. Their convention will meet the last of this month. In the State of New York, the interests pro and con are divided, and it is impossible for an impartial person to say which way the scale will turn. Both sides appear confident of victory, and are industrious in preparing for the elections, which are to take place in about a fortnight.

I am happy that you have such confidence in the future conduct of your convention. I hope in God you may not be disappointed. The business of electioneering runs high. We cannot judge who will be the President, you or Mr. Langdon. But in either case your friends, who are the friends of the Union, rest assured that you are both too good patriots to suppose your ardor for the Constitution will be abated. A man possessing all the virtues of an angel, may not have the majority of votes in States where the choice very frequently may depend on mere trifles, not more important than the color of a man's hair, eyes, his size, or carriage.

I hope to have the pleasure to see you the ensuing summer in New Hampshire. In the mean time I shall be happy to learn from you the fate of the Constitution.

I am with great respect and affection, your humble servant,

H. KNOX.

It would have seemed that, by his devotion to the public interests during the two years he had been President, he had richly earned a renewed expression of confidence from his fellow-citizens. But power was then guarded with a watchful eye, and rotation in office considered the best safeguard of popular rights. The friends of Langdon were indefatigable in promoting his election, and the cluster of able men at Portsmouth, who were identified with him in interest and social ties, brought to bear against Sullivan every influence that could be used with effect. A contemporary print informs us, "faction was exerting itself to hurl from the Presidential chair the brightest patriot that ever illumined the councils of New Hampshire."

Langdon was elected by a majority of one vote, a few hundreds being divided among various candidates. Sullivan was again chosen Speaker of the House, having been returned from Durham. But for reasons not assigned, and which can only be conjectured, he declined that position, considered the second in the State. This may have been from disappointment in not being re-elected President, but more likely proceeded from the state of his health, which already began to show symptoms of being greatly undermined. An accident in the campaign against the Iroquois had produced the incipient stages of spinal disease, the development of which, a few years later, incapacitated him for bodily effort.

Had he been firmer in health, and, trusting to the favor his fellow-citizens had uninterruptedly manifested towards him from his entrance upon public life, accepted the speakership, he would have been a more prominent candidate in the distribution of offices under the federal government. This was soon to be established. The instrument to create it had several months been subject for anxious consideration, and the moment was at hand when the State was either to accept or reject it.

Engaged in defence of their chartered rights and political liberties, the American people had, for a generation, been called upon both to study and discuss the subject of government. Emancipation from foreign control, protection of property, preservation of order, what constituted free institutions, were constant topics of discourse. The several efforts to frame a State government, and the nine sessions of the convention for settling the form recently established, which had been repeatedly submitted for their deliberation in town meetings, had prepared the citizens of New Hampshire to comprehend the questions involved in the proposed federal constitution. They were frequently discussed in the press and wherever men congregated; and, as often the case in political issues, when the time approached for the convention to re-assemble, opinions were about equally divided. The preponderance, however, was seemingly adverse. This created much uneasiness throughout the country, as eight States had ratified, and one more was needed to render the instrument obligatory even upon those which had already adopted it.

Pursuant to its adjournment, the convention met at Concord, on Wednesday, the 18th of June. The following day was employed in a general discussion of controverted points. A motion was offered, towards its close, that a committee of fifteen should be appointed to consider and report such amendments as they judged necessary in alteration of the constitution, which motion was the following day adopted. This committee consisted of Langdon and Sullivan, Bartlett, Badger, Atherton, Dow, Bellows, West, Severance, Worcester, Parker, Pickering, Smith, Hooper, and Barrett. As their report was made that same afternoon, the twelve amendments reported were probably prepared before the opening of the session, as had been the case in Massachusetts. A motion by Mr. Atherton, that the constitution should not operate in New Hampshire without said amendments, was lost, and the course pursued in the other States, recommending their adoption under the fifth article providing for amendments, adopted in stead.

The first of these proposed amendments, that powers not expressly delegated should be reserved to the several States, was subsequently adopted in the tenth amendment, with the additional words "or to the people." The second and third, that the number of representatives should be one for every thirty thousand until the whole number was two hundred, and prohibiting any regulations by Congress contrary to a free and equal representation: the fourth, that Congress should not lay any direct tax, so long as the impost, excise, and other resources were sufficient; nor then, before neglect of the States upon requisition to pay their proportion as fixed by the census: the fifth, that Congress should erect no company of merchants with exclusive advantages of commerce, — were not adopted. The sixth, that no person should be tried for crime unless indicted by a grand jury, except in the government and regulation of the land forces, was embodied in the fifth amendment. The seventh, that actions at common law between citizens of different States should be commenced in the State courts, and appeal permitted thence to the federal, was not acceded to. The eighth, that civil actions at common law should be tried by jury, was incorporated in the seventh amendment. The ninth, that Congress should not consent that any person holding office of trust or profit under the government, should accept a title of nobility, or any other title or office from any king, prince, or foreign state; and a part of the tenth, that no standing army should be kept up in time of peace, unless with consent of three-fourths of the members of each branch of Congress, were not adopted; but a provision that no soldiers in time of peace should be quartered upon private houses, forms part of the third article. The eleventh, that Congress should pass no law touching religion or infringing the rights of conscience, forms part of the first article; while the twelfth, that Congress shall never disarm any citizen unless such as have been in actual rebellion, is virtually enacted in the second. The first six, and the eighth were nearly *verbatim* the same as in Massachusetts.

On Saturday, the twenty-first, on motion of Mr. Livermore, seconded by Mr. Langdon, the main question was put. Fifty-seven voted in favor of ratification, forty-six against it.

There were gentlemen of character and ability on both sides; but the names most familiar were enrolled in the affirmative. It is recorded that General Sullivan was, at the time, suffering from hoarseness, arising from a severe cold. When some plausible objection was started, in the course of the debate, and no other member seemed disposed to answer it, the President, expressing his regret that no one would relieve him of the task, addressed them with decisive eloquence and power. It was generally conceded that, but for his efforts in rendering it popular, and explaining away objections, the Constitution would have been rejected.

With the exception of an eloquent and well-timed remonstrance by Mr. Atherton against any constitution which tolerated or in any way recognized slavery, but little trace is to be found in Eliot, in contemporary gazettes or correspondence, of what took place in the convention. The Journal has been this present year for the first time given to the public in the "Historical Magazine;" and contains the document of ratification by which New Hampshire entered the Union.

Whatever differences of opinion had existed as to the expediency of the measure in the convention or among the people, no sooner was it decided, than the event was everywhere hailed with enthusiasm, as the harbinger of political blessings. The ministers announced the event to their congregations as subject for devout acknowledgment. Days were set apart in the chief towns and cities for festal jubilee. There was a general disposition to indulge in the most sanguine expectations of prosperity, public and private, to flow from a government founded on justice and equal rights for a nation, which was destined to become, as then already predicted, one of the most powerful on the earth.

As the ratification by New Hampshire would give vitality to the instrument, and it was supposed the other four States which had not yet given in their adhesion would be governed by the course she should take, it had been thought desirable that the result, if favorable, should be communicated as speedily as possible to Richmond and Poughkeepsie, where the conventions of New York and Virginia were respectively assembled. Generals Knox and Sullivan consequently arranged expresses through the country to transmit the intelligence; but Virginia had voted to adopt before the courier arrived. North Carolina ratified soon after; and Rhode Island, the last of the original thirteen, entered the Union in 1790.

The following letter from Knox, at Poughkeepsie, alludes to the services rendered by Sullivan in bringing about the result: —

MY DEAR SIR, — I thank you for your kind favor of the 21st, from Concord, announcing the highly important and satisfactory information of the decision of the Constitution by New Hampshire. I hope that the news of this event may reach Richmond previously to the decision of the question in the Virginia Convention. The last letters from Richmond were dated on the 19th. The main question would either be put on the 21st, or the Convention would then make a short adjournment (perhaps a week), for the purpose of accommodating the Legislature, which had been called to assemble at the same place the twenty-third. In either case, it appears to be the opinion of the Federalists and Antifederalists that there would be a small majority for adopting the Constitution, in the same manner as by Massachusetts and New Hampshire. The express, with the New Hampshire information, will probably reach Richmond this day, as it departed from the city on Wednesday last, one o'clock.

If the adjournment should have taken place, the majority in favor of the Constitution will probably be increased. I cannot well state the politics of this State. It is sufficient to say they are opposed to the Constitution without previous amendments. The Convention have been sitting since the 17th; the majority greatly on the side of Anti-federalists. However, as the noble conduct of your State has secured the Constitution, it is possible the Antis may think the ground changed, and may, instead of stipulating for previous amendments, accept the Constitution on the terms you have. If this should be the case, with which, however, I do not in the least flatter myself, the Antis will take care to show their power by some declaration that the acceptance is from expediency, and not from conviction.

Your friends attribute much of the success in your State to your unremitted exertions, and hope that your country will eminently reward your patriotism.

Few indications are afforded by the public journals, or is any private correspondence accessible, to show what combinations in New Hampshire controlled the distribution of offices under the new government. Much has since transpired of what took place in other parts of the country to secure for prominent individuals or shades of political opinion all they could reasonably demand. No evidence, whatever, is to be found that Sullivan was self-seeking, or allowed his tranquillity to be disturbed by any aspirations for place or power. His wish for posts of public duty had been chastened by disappointments attending the most prosperous career; and, while disposed to accept the place assigned him, he neither weighed nor urged his claims. Langdon, as President, possessed a strong hold on public favor, and his ample means and generous hospitalities at the social and political capital made him popular, not only with the eminent men who resided at Portsmouth, but with all classes throughout the State.

Durham was a small village, remote from any populous centre. Sullivan had declined the speakership, and was but a member of the house. The conservatives, for the most part, favored Langdon; while the anti-federalists, who had voted against the Constitution, were alike opposed to both him and Sullivan. There were, besides, arrayed against the latter Masonian proprietors and their grantees, late insurgents, and also refugee loyalists, who had little love for any one who had been active in bringing about independence. It was remarkable that, with so many obstacles in his way, and a dignity of character that did not condescend to seek popularity, he should have received so many tokens of public favor. He was straightforward and careless of self in the performance of duty; and his frankness and fearlessness often engendered animosities, working secretly to his disadvantage, and which it was not always possible for his friends to disarm or counteract.

Langdon and Bartlett were elected senators; West, Wingate, and Livermore to the House; and, Bartlett declining, Wingate was chosen to the Senate, Gilman taking his place in the lower branch of Congress. Sullivan, with Bellows, Pickering, Thompson, and Parker, constituted the electoral college that gave the five votes of the State for Washington and Adams. There was an opposition ticket for the House on which Sullivan was a candidate. What were his own wishes, in the absence of evidence, is mere matter of conjecture. But his health, limited means, and the condition of his family, were incompatible with his assuming duties obliging him to leave home. His friends no doubt anticipated that he would receive a cabinet, diplomatic, or judicial appointment; but other considerations than past services weighed with those who were dealing the honors, and even John Hancock and Samuel Adams were overlooked. Sullivan was chosen a third time President of the State, and, when the General Court met, in June, 1789, thus addressed them: —

Neither my own inclination, nor the state of my health, led me to expect the honor of being called to the chair of government the present year, or even to hazard a wish of embarking on an ocean far from being smooth and pacific even in the best of times. But, having long accustomed myself to obey with cheerfulness every call of my country, I have ventured once more to attempt performing the duties of an arduous and important office, with a firm reliance on your great experience, integrity, and long-tried abilities in the political field, and under a full persuasion that your kind and friendly assistance will never be wanting to support me in its discharge.

I have now to entreat your acceptance of my most cordial thanks for this additional mark of your regard, and to assure you in your separate branches, and, through you, my fellow-citizens at large, that, if faithfulness and integrity in discharging my duties will in any measure compensate for the want of those abilities which are more amply possessed by others, you shall have no reason to complain of your having misplaced the confidence with which you have honored me. Under the present situation of our public affairs, it is almost impossible for me to say much with regard to them : so many matters of national importance are now in agitation before the Federal Government, and the event still remains so uncertain, that it cannot, in my opinion, be prudent at this time to attempt what under other circumstances might be both beneficial and necessary.

The militia law has often been supposed to need amendments, and those respecting schools very material alterations.

Some acts that were laid over from the last session for consideration may now meet your further examination. The judicial department is of so much importance to every individual, that surely nothing will be wanting on your part to pursue every possible measure for keeping up the due administration of justice. Permit me, also, to hint, that, unless measures are taken to prevent it, our fellow-citizens may be subjected to duties by authority of Congress, and, at the same time, to others collected by the laws of the States, and remain under this double burden until the General Court is called to remedy the evil. The busy season of the year, and the imprudence of attempting at this time to decide upon measures, which seem rather to wait the action of the Federal Legislature, will render it unnecessary to protract the present session for any considerable length of time. You may rest assured, that, on my part, nothing shall be wanting to assist you in whatever you deem necessary to promote the welfare of our common country.

Washington, as will be remembered, soon after his inauguration as President in 1789, visited the Northern States; and, while he was on his way, Sullivan received from him the following communication, inclosing a commission as Federal judge of New Hampshire, the only position in the appointment of the President his health permitted him to accept : —

UNITED STATES, Sept. 30, 1789.

SIR, — I have the pleasure to enclose to you a commission as Judge of the United States for the District of New Hampshire, to which office I have nominated, and, by and with advice and consent of the

Senate, appointed you. In my nomination of persons to fill office in the judicial department, I have been guided by the importance of the object, considering it of the first magnitude, and the pillar upon which our political fabric must rest. I have endeavored to bring into the high offices of its administration such characters as will give stability and dignity to our national government; and I persuade myself that they will discover a due desire to promote the happiness of our country by a ready acceptance of their several appointments.

The laws which have passed relative to your office accompany the commission.

I am, sir, with very great esteem, your most obedient servant,

GEORGE WASHINGTON.

The Hon. JOHN SULLIVAN.

Early in November, Washington reached Portsmouth, and it devolved upon Sullivan to extend to him the hospitalities of the State. The following was his address of welcome in behalf of the Executive of the State, which term embraced also the Council: —

Amidst the applause and gratulations of millions, suffer the Executive of New Hampshire, with grateful hearts, to approach you, sir, and hail your welcome to this Northern State, — to a government whose metropolis was, at an early stage of the late war, by your vigilance and attention, saved from destruction, and the whole of which was, at an after period, rescued from impending ruin by that valor and prudence which eventually wrought out the salvation of our common country, and gave birth to the American empire.

Deeply impressed with the remembrance of these important events, you will permit us to say, that, among the vast multitude of your admirers, there is not a people who hold your talents and your virtues in higher veneration than the inhabitants of New Hampshire. We beg you, sir, to accept our most cordial thanks for the honor done to this State by your more than welcome visit at this time, and that you will believe we shall not cease to unite our most fervent prayers with those of our American brethren, that you may be continued a lasting blessing to our nation, and long, very long, be suffered to rule in peace over those whom you have protected and defended in war.

The tenure of his judicial office not requiring the immediate assumption of its duties, he continued in the Presidency of the State till towards the close of the term for which he was elected. No event of importance occurred to demand any particular comment. The custom, since universal in New England, and in later years very generally adopted in all the States, had been initiated by his predecessor, of setting apart in the autumn a day of thanksgiving for the bounties of Providence; and his proclamation for its observance deserves a place in these pages: —

The season returning loaded with the bounty and manifesting the munificent hand of the great Creator, who hath been the constant and merciful protector and supporter of us and our ancestors, to render him our annual and public tribute of gratitude and praise, in pursuance of a vote of the Legislature, appointing Thursday, the twenty-sixth day of November next, to be observed as a day of thanksgiving throughout the State, I do by and with the advice of Council issue this proclamation, earnestly exhorting ministers and people of every denomination to assemble on that day, and with devout and grateful hearts to adore the unmerited goodness of Almighty God in causing the earth to yield her increase and crowning the labors of the husbandmen with plenty; inclining the hearts of the people to adopt a plan of general government happily calculated to secure and perpetuate the peace and prosperity of America; inspiring them in the choice of rulers who justly merit and have their confidence; to give thanks at the remembrance of his goodness in continuing peace within our borders and health in our habitations, while discord, war, and pestilence have ravaged many other parts of the world; to bless His holy name for the preservation of our civil and religious privileges, and sparing the important life and restoring the health of the President of the United States, so justly dear to the citizens thereof; to supplicate the continuance of his favors and implore the forgiveness of our sins, which render us ill-deserving of his mercies; and to beseech Him that the Redeemer's name and religion may be spread, known, and revered throughout the world.

As the Federal Court was about to be organized, in June Sullivan took leave of the Legislature in the following address: —

The General Court being now properly organized, and only a few members not qualified, and it not being of absolute necessity that

I should remain here until they have taken the oaths, I beg you to permit me, being called to act in a different department, to take my leave of the two branches of the Legislature at this time.

Will you allow me, gentlemen, at this moment of my quitting the chair of government in the State, and probably bidding a final adieu to all posts and offices within the same, to entreat that you, as a body, in particular, and, through you, the citizens of the State in general, will accept my most cordial thanks for the repeated marks of confidence with which you have so repeatedly and variously honored me, and to assure you, that, in whatever department of life Providence may place me, I shall retain a grateful remembrance of the generous conduct of New Hampshire.

To this the Legislature made the following response:—

SIR,— The Senate and House of Representatives, having received your letter of this day, wherein you very affectionately take leave of the two branches of the Legislature, beg leave to express the high sense they entertain of your military talents, and past exertions in the many and important offices you have been called by the suffrages of your fellow-citizens to sustain, and to assure you that the repeated marks of confidence the good people of this State have from time to time reposed in you have been but faint testimonials of their gratitude and your merit. They congratulate you on your appointment to an honorable office under the United States, and sincerely wish that your health may be restored, and that you may long continue, by dispensing equal justice, a great blessing to this people; and, while they anticipate future, they will ever retain a pleasing remembrance of your past exertions for the public good.

His court was opened by Chief-Justice Jay and himself, and it is found recorded that Sullivan made to the grand jury an address which was eloquent and appropriate. Trace is found from time to time of its sessions at Portsmouth; but the business of the district did not require they should be either frequent or protracted. His health was already failing. The ministerial duties of the court were acceptably performed by his son-in-law, afterwards Judge Steele of the Supreme Court of New Hampshire, who held the office of clerk; and his judicial functions occasionally by Judge Lowell, when illness prevented his attendance. The fatal malady which was slowly sapping what had once been a remarkably robust constitution, after a few years confined him wholly to his house, and he was obliged to move from room to room on a wheeled chair. When some person over eager for the advancement of a friend to the post which seemed likely in the natural course of events soon to be vacated, applied to Washington for the office, he replied there was no man in the country he would not sooner remove than General Sullivan.

The hope was indulged that time would conquer or greatly alleviate a disease of which the patient is generally the last to perceive the inevitable progress. It had been contracted in the public service, and what fortune remained to him was moderate, and his family had claims upon him which he felt ought not to be disregarded. As there was little admiralty business in his district, or any other, for the cognizance of a Federal tribunal, he was governed by the advice of his friends in not tendering his resignation.

At so distant a day, little remains in the shape either of correspondence or tradition to afford any indication how these last few years were passed. His three sons had graduated in 1790 in the same class at Cambridge. The eldest, John, became an officer in the army, and did service on the Western frontier and in Louisiana. George, the youngest, inheriting the virtues and strength of character of his father, was preparing for a career of distinguished professional success. Mrs. Steele resided in Durham, near the residence of General Sullivan. His parents were at Berwick, not far away, and Master Sullivan, although more than a hundred years of age, occasionally came over in the saddle to visit his son. His brother Eben was practising law at Kittery near Portsmouth; and James, Attorney-General of Massachusetts, passed every year through New Hampshire to and from his Maine circuits.

Towards the close of 1794, his complaints assumed a more

decided character, and a brief period of prostration and pain preceded his death. This took place on the 23d of January, 1795, in his fifty-fifth year. As it was the depth of the severe winter of New Hampshire, and Durham was far remote from Exeter, Portsmouth, or other of the larger towns, his obsequies were attended by his friends and neighbors, but there was no military display or funeral honors. Some feeling was expressed in the public prints that no escort was ordered out for the occasion; but intelligence, at that period of sparse population and few public conveyances, travelled slowly through the deep snows of New Hampshire, and, when his mortal remains were committed to the earth, time permitted little preparation.

Behind the house where he had resided for thirty years, and which still in the best of preservation is occupied by one of the most respectable and affluent of the inhabitants of Durham, is a small cemetery, in which his own family and that of his friend, William Odiorne, — whose daughter was married to his brother James, — are interred. It is now well filled with monuments, and due care is taken by their kindred to prevent dilapidation. On the marble slab over his tomb is an appropriate inscription. It is to be hoped that at some future day the State, as she grows in prosperity, and is more disposed to value the services which established her independence and free institutions, will erect in her capital or near their sepulchres, statues or monuments to the memories of her distinguished revolutionary worthies.

Of these, several of the most intimate associates of Sullivan, who had borne with him the heat and toil of the contest, had preceded him to the tomb: Weare and Atkinson in civil life, advanced in years; Poor, Scammell, and Sherburne, gallant soldiers, in their prime. Greene and Sterling were gone; Hancock and Franklin. But dying at the early age of fifty-four, many of his companions in arms or in Congress survived, by further services to take deeper hold upon the respect and affection of their country, to occupy a more distinguished place in its annals. How far his public career entitles him like them to be remembered, is for the reader from the foregoing pages to determine. It certainly was too honored and useful for obloquy to taint, or for misconception to remain uncorrected. He was permitted to take an active and, it is fearlessly asserted, an efficient part in bringing about American independence; and it is fortunate for his memory that the closest scrutiny discovers nothing either in his character or conduct which was not honest and estimable.

In the political arena popularity is not always the test of merit. The great body of the people are generally wise enough to perceive who best deserve their confidence, yet in periods of excitement often make men of little character their idols. Ability and eloquence and skill in pandering to prevailing prejudices wins favor which modest worth is too proud to seek or too honest to retain. The avenues to preferment are beset by intrigue, and swayed by passion fomented for a purpose, the community yields without reflection to pressure and pretension. This is discouraging. But if an inseparable concomitant of self-government, those who believe in free institutions as the best social condition accept the evil with the good. Political experience exhibits frequent instances where past services are overlooked, capacity still to be useful thrust aside in the feverish struggle for power and place.

General Sullivan had too firm a faith in the system which it had been the principal work of his life to establish, to experience, when consummated, either mortification or disappointment that others should be preferred to himself. He no doubt sincerely felt what he frequently had occasion to express, that the marks of public confidence he received were the free gift of the people, to be extended or withheld as they pleased. He gladly accepted every occasion that presented to further their interests according to his judgment, and this was his governing principle throughout his public life; but he willingly gave way to others whose zeal and qualifications were an equal claim to his own. He believed in rotation in office as the best guarantee for fidelity, and, while glad to be elected, was not fretted by defeat. He had no reason to complain; and the numerous offices conferred upon him were flattering proofs of the estimation in which he was held.

He had given up a lucrative practice to enter the army; and, when compelled by the wants of his dependants to resume it, it had lost much of its charm. He could not rest contentedly idle; and he found in public affairs an agreeable substitute for professional occupations. But no evidence is found that he was self-seeking, or swerved from the right by any yearning for office. On the contrary, tradition bears witness to his independence, his readiness to sacrifice his hold on the favor of the people, to turn them from paths which were leading to error. It was this directness of purpose, fidelity to principle, that secured confidence which politicians, sacrificing conviction to expediency or advancement, do not merit, though they sometimes obtain. His sphere was limited, but our institutions were forming, and his official responsibilities were attended by many embarrassments. His public life furnishes valuable lessons to chasten ambition, in a country where to participate in the administration of affairs is alike the birthright of all.

However insignificant the population or armies of America, compared with the multitudes engaged or represented in more recent conflicts, its struggle for independence is not to be measured by numbers either in interest or importance. For the first time mankind was instituting the experiment of self-government, based on equal rights. The leaders, in sagacity and elevation of character, were worthy of the cause; and not only here, but wherever there exists a disposition to emulate their example, what is known of them will engage attention. A few who boldly assumed the responsibility of inducing their countrymen to throw off a yoke, no longer to be borne, commanded in the field, took part in the councils, and were subsequently called upon to administer the governments which they aided to form. Washington, although not like him a member of the Continental Congress, was distinguished both in civil and military life; and this also was the case with Sullivan, if not in so exalted a sphere.

When sovereignty vested in the people, its noblest prerogative, that of promoting the public welfare, was zealously exercised by all in whom the people placed trust. Their eagerness to develop the resources of the country was only limited by opportunity. Commerce and manufactures, roads and canals, the public safety, a sound currency, reforms in jurisprudence were of general concern. Sullivan was not the less ardent that his motives were sometimes impugned, and his public spirit mistaken for ambition, in exerting whatever influence he possessed in furthering these objects. His brother James in Massachusetts projected the Middlesex Canal, and John lent his aid to similar improvements, which promised to benefit New Hampshire. As already stated, he encouraged manufactures, and at one time imported skilled artisans from France. This enterprise was not a financial success, but served its purpose in stimulating others. Works for making duck and other coarse fabrics were started in various parts of the State. A long period was destined, however, to elapse before this branch of industry, to which New Hampshire owes so largely its present prosperity, was fully developed.

His energy of character, and desire to be useful, found also other fields of employment. Durham, a century since, as now, was attractive for its agreeable scenery, cultivation, and commodious abodes. Among other branches of industry it prosecuted with success, was the building of vessels, for which its proximity alike to the forest and the sea afforded facilities. He actively engaged in all that would promote the general prosperity, and his ardor in whatever he undertook was an example and incentive to others. He was frequently about in the woods in pursuit of lumber for his saw-mills, or for game. When Jefferson was minister in Paris, the idea was advanced in his presence that both man and beast degenerated in America. The well-known anecdote of the Shenandoah men at his table corrected the prejudice as to the human species. And, to remove any doubt as to the latter, he wrote Sullivan to send him specimens of our moose and deer. Sullivan formed a party in the depth of winter, and went off beyond Lake Winnipiseogee towards the White Mountains, and killed or captured what, sent out to Paris, convinced the French savans that our beasts of the forest were quite equal to their own.

Before the war his professional emoluments had been large, and, by prudent investments, at the early age of thirty-three, he was already, as mentioned by John Adams in his diary, in affluent circumstances. He owned, besides his beautiful farm along the shores of the river at Durham, valuable water-powers and extensive tracts of territory. His liberal expenditures and generous hospitality during his campaigns exceeded his allowance as a general, and he was compelled to draw largely on his private resources. It was not in his nature to economize, and he lent his aid freely to those in need. Payment made him by his creditors was in depreciated currency, so that his fortunes were greatly reduced by the war. When he left the army and resumed practice, he was again possessed of competence, if not of wealth. His official recompense was of little amount, but his house was always open to friends and strangers; and his widow, who resided there till 1820, when she died, is said to have been, in proportion to her means, hospitable like himself.

His farm consisted of much fertile land; he conducted it himself, and took a lively interest in all its details. His experiments in stock and tillage were not for his own benefit alone, but for that of his neighbors. A fine dairy-house stood near his dwelling; there were beehives near the river; and he had what is not probably to be found anywhere, certainly not in that neighborhood, in these days, a rabbit warren on one part of the estate. Numerous communications on agricultural and horticultural topics, on the keeping of bees, in the public prints bear internal evidence of having proceeded from his desire to diffuse information that might be of use.

Farming, to be profitable, depends, especially in New England, upon rigid economy. This was not in his nature. But a blessing attends a generous spirit, and, though liberal in all his expenditures, he came not to want. A gentleman of the neighborhood writes of him, —

He kept in his employment a large number of workmen, and his farmer, coachman, carpenters, wall-builders, and others in his service, are said to have been much attached to him. He was considerate of their welfare, and paid them liberally. Being constantly engaged in official and other public duties, he was much from home, and he left to their charge the management of his farm and domestic affairs, having no reason to regret the confidence he placed in them. His coachman [Stephen Noble] was accustomed to speak of his generosity to himself and others as he traversed the country on his way to the courts or the capital.

At Durham he was generally popular, though, for some reason not known, an alienation existed at one period between himself and the head of an influential family of the place. This was made up before his death. He was courteous and cordial in his social relations, and when at home it was much the custom of the leading men of Durham to assemble about eleven o'clock in the forenoon in his parlor, where, refreshed from a capacious bowl of punch, cold in summer and steaming hot in winter, they passed an hour in pleasant chat. These habits, brought from the camp, were not conducive to health or longevity, but added much to the good-fellowship which marked the intercourse of the period. He was convivial, but careful not to exceed the bounds of moderation. Possibly from his French associates he acquired a taste for snuff; and his use of it in his latter days is said to have impaired a voice remarkable originally for its depth, flexibility, and sweetness.

Another account says he was of a gay and happy temperament, fond of a joke, quick at repartee, and companionable with all with whom he chanced to be thrown. He was sufficiently dignified, and, when occasion demanded, ceremonious; but this proceeded from a sense of propriety, and not from pride. It never chilled. All felt at ease in his presence. Though attentive to his dress, as was the custom of the day, far beyond the social or official requirements of our own, though he was often attended, as then usual, about the country on State occasions by escorts of cavalry, and although his equipage was handsome, his adherents were from all classes, and they did not like him the less for a display many of them had witnessed under similar circumstances in other parts of the country on their campaigns. He was very fond of fine horses, and he mentions one shot under him at Brandywine as the finest horse in America.

His kindliness of manner, readiness to consider others, disregard of his own comfort where he could contribute to theirs, explains in a degree the attachment felt for him by Greene, Knox, and Lafayette, by Laurens and Hamilton, and many of the noblest characters of the war. It certainly won the regard of the soldiers. On the western campaign, when necessary to move with expedition, from some oversight valuable packages were left unprovided with transportation. Unwilling to impose unusual hardship on others he was not ready to assume for himself, he dismounted, had his own horse laden, and proceeded on foot. His example was followed by other officers, and what would have been a serious loss to the army, was preserved.

It was charged against him that he was not republican in his sentiments; the term being used not in a party sense as now or half a century ago, but in its original purport. This seems to derive some force from his addresses on the military organization of the State, to be found later in the volume. He was no theorist, and took a practical view of the actual condition of society. He believed in the equality of man before the law as before the altar and the judgment-seat; but was too sensible to undervalue the claims to respect of character and intelligence, or the homage due to authority. His military life had trained him to habits of subordination, and the distinctions of social life in all parts of the country then were more marked than now. He was willing to level up but not down, and frequently manifested his sense of the importance of popular education, which, as President of the State, he did all in his power to promote. His writings prove that no one was more decided in his views than himself that America should be a republic.

With many others who apprehended the growth in our country of similar social distinctions to those of Europe, he was at first opposed to the foundation of the order of Cincinnati; but he had reason subsequently to change his opinions, and became one of its officers. He inherited a dislike of British institutions, and all his sympathies were with France. He was on terms of intimacy with Lafayette; and his descendants possess mementos, which were sent to him after the war, from French officers who had been his companions in arms. He undoubtedly sympathized with the struggle in France so long as its object was the establishment of republican liberty. But he was not a disorganizer; and his vigor in suppressing the rebellion of 1786, which extended into New Hampshire, shows his sense of the importance of maintaining law and order. His professional pursuits, his extended experience in the camp and in Congress, his official responsibilities at home, all tended to make him a wise and prudent statesman; and the frequent marks of public confidence reposed in him testify the sense that was entertained by his fellow-citizens of his merit.

His brother James was more devoted to literary pursuits, but he also had the pen of a ready writer. His letters and public documents evince much command of language, are expressed with force and clearness, and, where occasion demanded, were earnest and eloquent. They prove that his classical studies were not suffered to grow rusty, and in his frequent allusions to ancient history, considerable scholarship. His letters in French, indicate a familiarity with that language, which he both wrote and spoke with facility. From early manhood he was a frequent contributor to the press, and throughout his career are to be found numerous essays in the columns of the journals, chiefly on political questions, but extending over a great variety of other topics, — social, economical, and military.

Among his papers are various letters from Jeremy Belknap, affording evidence of the friendly relations that subsisted between himself and the accomplished historian of New Hampshire. It was in his power to lend much assistance to Belknap in the prosecution of his principal task, and this he gladly improved. There was at that period but slight encouragement for literary productions, but the work referred to was of rare excellence, and has always maintained a high rank among American historical publications.

Like Washington, he was a freemason. There were many lodges during the Revolution in the American army, as well as in the British. The fortunes of war placed at one time the regalia of one of the latter in the possession of Washington, whose action in returning them will be remembered. The favorable influences of masonic institutions, in cherishing kindly feelings and a high standard of Christian character in officers and men, have often been remarked. After his return from the army he was instrumental in establishing a masonic organization, and it has been said he was the first grand master of the State. How extensive its brotherhood may have been is not known; but, to a genial and sympathetic nature like his own, the association must have proved the source of much social enjoyment.

His nature was ardent and impulsive. He was quick to take offence, impatient under affront, but generous and placable, and too noble to seek revenge by any indirection. He had a high sense of honor, was faithful and loyal to all his obligations, and, if he took exception at the course of others towards him, he was frank and open in seeking redress. His resignation from the army has been generally attributed by himself and others to the state of his health. This probably was the true and sufficient reason. But it has also been ascribed to his sense of the injustice of Congress in refusing to allow an equivalent for the half-rations given up by his army in New York, and which he had given assurance, so far as he had any influence, should be made up.

Where there were so many aspirants for official distinction, there were natural rivalries; but among the high-toned men of that day they rarely degenerated into selfishness or animosity. During the canvass their respective adherents indulged in exaggeration and abuse. When the election was decided, both sides met too constantly in public and social relations for alienation or resentment. Sullivan was on friendly terms with Langdon and his other competitors for popularity. His friendships were deep and constant, but he was somewhat noted for the steadfastness of his dislikes where he considered himself unfairly treated, or saw any thing to disapprove.

Despotisms rest on fear, monarchies on honor and a sentiment of loyalty, republics on virtue and intelligence. If the latter qualities are indispensable to their maintenance, public and private integrity in the body of the people is essential to free institutions in their foundation. Their traditions, laws, religious obligations, a public opinion unusually exacting, tempered and chastened the character of the Americans when they vindicated their right to self-government. Their leaders in the field and civil life gained confidence by their exemplary character, and, actuated by the most elevated motives, commanded respect even from their enemies. Dignity of bearing, refinement of manner, were the habit of the period, and highly educated officers from abroad, who took part with them in the contest, insensibly moulded their modes of thought and social intercourse.

All that is known of them confirms the faith we are prone to cherish, that they were remarkable men. Energetic, capable, self-sacrificing, they proved their claims to confidence by fidelity and zeal to promote, not the special object alone for which they were contending, but whatever tended to the public good. Their public documents and official writings, their printed works and private correspondence, were fitting accompaniment for their heroic deeds, are their imperishable monument. Their names and lives are familiar to old and young. Lapse of time but places their memories in bolder relief, and, so long as we continue to value the liberties they established, will mould political sentiments throughout the land. To lessen its lustre by unjust disparagement, works a double wrong.

Three score years and ten have passed since his career ended, and probably very few survive who have any personal recollection of General Sullivan. But materials abound in which stand recorded in authentic form his leading traits. Much has perished, both of incident and anecdote, which would have been of interest. Much, no doubt, yet remains to be collected. The following selection from what has at different times been said of him will serve to indicate in some measure the impression he made upon those who knew him: —

" General Sullivan was an eloquent lawyer, a good writer,

and, as a man, just and sagacious. He was generous, high-spirited, and intrepid; and, in his bearing, graceful and dignified. He conversed freely and with fluency; and his engaging address made the stranger at once at ease in his presence. He had the faculty — invaluable to an advocate — of making each one in a company of many persons think he was an object of his particular attention. He was hospitable, fond of the elegancies of life, prodigal of money; but in his dealings honest, generous, and honorable." " His temper was ordinarily mild and tranquil, and as far removed from petulence as any man could be, but when irritated he was stormy and violent." " He took a lively interest in military preparations for defence, and his writings on that subject are sensible and comprehensive. His religious sentiments were deep, though he shrank from display; and a manuscript defence of Christianity — written in camp and circulated amongst his brother-officers — is alluded to in a subsequent notice of him, though not known to have been preserved." If not tall, his presence was commanding; he was erect, his shoulders were broad, his chest full, his movements quick and elastic. His eyes were black, piercing, and of remarkable brilliancy; his hair dark and curling; his complexion embrowned by constant exposure; he had a rich, warm color on his cheeks. His portrait was painted once or oftener during the war. Several engravings exist, and one of them, colored in his lifetime, was in possession of his widow and daughter for more than half a century after his death, and pronounced by them to have been a good likeness. His picture was also painted by Trumbull in 1783.

Experience proves how little it is safe to leave reputation unguarded, where duty or circumstance calls from private life to take part in public affairs of moment. Unless there is at hand for reference an orderly statement of events, supported by documentary evidence, the unscrupulous who delight in detraction take advantage to distort or impugn. This has been particularly exemplified in the history of the Revolution; and often to give variety to a story of which the incidents need no embellishment, or to borrow laurels for some favorite, much is stated which is pure invention. The grandson of General Sullivan, late Attorney-General of New Hampshire, in an able vindication of his grandfather for not having more precise intelligence of the British movements at Brandywine, reviewed every fact and circumstance connected with that battle. He evidently had never heard of any such imputation as that now made of disobedience of orders in not crossing the river, which it has been one principal object of this publication to refute.

It may seem quixotic for one of less literary pretensions to controvert such a charge, however ungrounded, when advanced by a voluminous author. Those who on the battle-field established our liberties were never discouraged by odds or calculated personal consequences, and they certainly earned a right to be defended when misrepresented or traduced. So long as our institutions are preserved, the Revolution must remain the most interesting epoch of our history. Americans will draw from its memories more fervent devotion to their political faith. Other biographies will be written to keep aglow the fire on its altars, each successive generation produce historians to present its characters and events in forms more attractive and exact. Whoever to magnify himself or from other illaudable motive would dull the fame of these illustrious personages, which is not only our glory but our safeguard, will be remembered, but only for his perversity and injustice.

This work has grown in the press far beyond its original design. Had its present dimensions been anticipated, it would have assumed the usual form of biography, and, divided into chapters, been more convenient for perusal or reference. Should the subject commend itself to favorable consideration, another edition, differently arranged, will be prepared.

Numerous interesting incidents and anecdotes, not falling within the scope of the present volume, have been reserved. There remains, besides, much correspondence in letters, both from and to General Sullivan; and it seems reasonable to believe that yet more will be collected. A few documents are given in the Appendix, for which no fit place was found in the preceding pages.

APPENDIX.

APPENDIX.

PARENTAGE OF GENERAL SULLIVAN.

PAGE 9.

MENTION is occasionally made of the father of General Sullivan, in connection with his sons, four of whom took an active part in the Revolution. These statements have not always been precisely accurate; and, as what is known of his history explains in part what was remarkable in theirs, it may not be out of place to correct them. For nearly half a century he was an instructor of youth at Somersworth, in New Hampshire, and Berwick, in Maine, towns separated by the Salmon-Falls River. Highly educated himself, his sons were indebted to him for a training which their subsequent career proves to have been unusually thorough. Measured by their general information, development of mental power, or the ability which they exhibited in their writings, it compared favorably with the collegiate culture of the period.

A native of Ireland, and in birth not far removed from the chieftainship of a once powerful sept, he came to America cherishing little loyalty to the government that had dispossessed them of their inheritance. All true friends of Ireland deplore recent forcible demonstrations, as calculated to frustrate proposed measures of reparation, expose to aggravation of wrong. Yet there exists but one opinion, even amongst

Englishmen, unless where the judgment is distorted by interest or prejudice, — that, in the condition of that unfortunate country, much is discreditable which can and should be reformed. All are candid enough to admit that the confiscations and discriminations which brought it about, were justified neither by law, humanity, nor sound policy. Sturdy resistance against oppression, which no people of any spirit could patiently endure, is too generally respected for any motive that led to American Independence not to be applauded.

At the request of the wife of General Sullivan, his father, then late in life, prepared the following statement: —

"I am the son of Major Philip O'Sullivan, of Ardea, in the county of Kerry. His father was Owen O'Sullivan, original descendant from the second son of Daniel O'Sullivan, called Lord of Bearehaven. He married Mary, daughter of Colonel Owen McSweeney, of Musgrey, and sister to Captain Edmond McSweeney, a noted man for anecdotes and witty sayings. I have heard that my grandfather had four countesses for his mother and grandmothers. How true it was, or who they were, I know not. My father died of an ulcer raised in his breast, occasioned by a wound he received in France, in a duel with a French officer. They were all a short-lived family; they either died in their bloom, or went out of the country. I never heard that any of the men-kind arrived at sixty, and do not remember but one alive when I left home. My mother's name was Joan McCarthy, daughter of Dermod McCarthy, of Killoween. She had three brothers and one sister. Her mother's name I forget, but she was a daughter to McCarthy Reagh, of Carbery. Her eldest brother, Colonel Florence, alias McFinnen, and his two brothers, Captain Charles and Captain Owen, went in the defence of the nation against Orange. Owen was killed in the battle of Aughrim. Florence had a son, who retains the title of McFinnen. Charles I just remember, He left two sons, — Derby and Owen. Derby married with Ellena Sullivan, of the Sullivans of Baunane. His brother Owen married Honora Mahony, daughter of Dennis Mahony, of Dromore, in the barony of Dunkerron, and also died in the prime of life, much lamented.

"They were short-lived on both sides; but the brevity of their lives, to my great grief and sorrow, is added to the length of mine. My mother's sister was married to Dermod, eldest son of Daniel O'Sullivan, Lord of Dunkerron. Her son Cornelius, as I understand, was with the Pretender in Scotland, in the year 1745. This is all I can say about my origin; but shall conclude with a Latin sentence: —

> ' *Si Adam sit pater cunctorum, mater et Eva :*
> *Cur non sunt homines nobilitate pares ?*
> *Non pater aut mater dant nobis nobilitatem ;*
> *Sed moribus et vita nobilitatur homo.'* "

Not long after the decease of both father and son, the following letter, addressed to the latter, reached New Hampshire:—

A granduncle of mine having gone to America about sixty years ago, his relations have suffered greatly from being without the means of finding out his fate, till now, by great good fortune, I am informed that you are a son of his. If you find, by the account below, that I have not been misinformed, I shall be glad to hear from you.

Mr. Owen O'Sullivan, son of Major Philip O'Sullivan, of Ardea, in the county of Kerry, Ireland, by Joanna, daughter of Dermod McCarthy, of Killoween, Esq., in said county. They were connected with the most respectable families in the province of Munster, particularly the Count of Bearehaven, McCarthy More, Earl of Clancare, Earl Barrymore, the Earl of Thomond, the Earl of Clancarty, McFinnen of Glanarough, O'Donoughu of Ross, O'Donough of Glynn, McCarthy of Carbery, and O'Donovan, &c.

I am, sir, yours respectfully,

PHILIP O'SULLIVAN.

ARDEA, May 16, 1796.

In explanation of the above documents, some passages are presented from an account of Master Sullivan and his progenitors, prepared for another purpose by the present writer. They contain information, obtained not without labor, which many may gladly possess. This would have been reserved for the more extended biography contemplated; but life is precarious, and that may never be accomplished. Inasmuch as character is in some measure affected by transmitted traits, it has a direct bearing on our subject. No apology is needed for the distant starting-point or particularity of detail. The recital will be as brief as a clear view of the circumstances which shaped the incidents of his lot will admit.

The southerly portion of Ireland, consisting of the present counties of Cork, Kerry, Limerick, Clare, Tipperary, and Waterford, forms what is known as the province of Munster. It extends about one hundred miles in either direction, embracing an area of nearly twelve thousand square miles. In an old manuscript of the College Library at Dublin, McCarthy More,* King of Desmond, bearing sway at Cork, O'Sullivan More of Dunkerron, and O'Sullivan Beare of Dunboy, are mentioned as the principal chieftains of Munster not long subsequent to the English invasion. For many centuries prior to that period, the O'Sullivan More chief of the Eugenian nobles, so called from their descent from Owen More, had his principal residence at Knoc Graffon, a strong castle near Cashel and Clonmel on the river Suir, in Tipperary, at the eastern extremity of Munster. After long but ineffectual resistance against the English forces, they withdrew from the more exposed portions of their inheritance to their mountain strongholds at

---

* More, or, in Erse, Mogha, was the customary designation of the eldest lineal representative of the line of chieftains of the different septs or nations. O'Sullivan More was the head of his sept, though the ruler, after the invasion, only over his own principalities at Dunkerron and Iverah, comprising an area of seven hundred square miles. The O'Sullivan Beare was the chief of Beare, Bantry, Ardea, and Glanerough; and his territories, land and water, extended over about one thousand square miles. McCarthy More, Earl of Clancarre, who died in 1596, was Prince of Desmond, and was succeeded by Florence, son of McCarthy Reagh, who married the daughter of the Earl of Clancarre, and passed forty years a prisoner in the Tower of London. The McCarthy Reaghs ruled over Carberry. Another branch of the name possessed the principality of Duballo, and their chief abode was the castle of Kanturk. The most prominent in later days was a younger branch, Lords of Muskerry, whose principal residences were Blarney Castle, built about 1450, and Macroom. There were other branches of the O'Sullivans, independent chieftains. A cadet of the Dunkerron line, resided at Drominagh Castle. Another branch were styled of the Reeks, the high mountains near the lakes of Killarney. The castle of Ardea was on the east side of the river Kenmare, about five miles from the castle of Dunkerron; the castle of Dunboy, still occupied, was at Castletown, on the west side, about twenty miles to the south.

the southwest in the counties of Cork and Kerry, where, in the principalities of Iverah, Dunkerron, Beare, Bantry, and Glenarough, they erected the castles of Dunkerron, Cappanaacuish, Dunboy, Ardea, and Bearehaven, as well as many other places of strength. In these wild regions, remote from the English Pale, and protected on every side by friendly septs or the sea, they were less frequently disturbed than their more exposed neighbors, and longer retained their property and independence.

The circumstances attending the English invasion are generally familiar, and need but a brief allusion. About the middle of the twelfth century, Henry II. obtained from the sovereign pontiff Adrian IV.* the permission of the Catholic Church to add the island to his dominions. A few years later, in 1169, Dermot Macmurrogh, Prince of Leinster, exiled by Roderick, King of Ireland, at the instigation of O'Rourke, whose wife Dermot had abducted, solicited the intervention of the English. This was the beginning of a long and imbittered struggle, — on the one side for supremacy, on the other against subjugation, — which still at times seems smouldering in its ashes. Superiority of numbers and resources finally triumphed; and Ireland, exhausted and overwhelmed, succumbed to her conquerors.

Seven centuries earlier, Christianity had been introduced by St. Patrick, and under St. Columba, in the sixth century, took the place of druidical rites. Monastic institutions were liberally endowed; flourishing schools and colleges became the resort of students from other countries; and, in the eighth and ninth centuries, the scholars of Ireland were among the most distinguished at the courts of the Saxon kings and of Charlemagne. If the general enlightenment were not in all respects equal to that of more centrally situated portions of Europe, its chiefs and rulers compared favorably in culture with any

---

* Adrian IV. was an Englishman, the only native of the British Isles ever Pope. His name was Nicholas Breakspere. His pontificate began in 1154.

persons of the period of similar rank. After the Danes, who had long ineffectually striven to gain a foothold, were finally defeated at Clonfert, Good Friday, 1012, by Brian Boru, its forty-fourth Christian King, Ireland was for a time but little disturbed by the presence of the stranger. Under the seven succeeding monarchs, ending in Roderick, already mentioned, important reforms in secular and ecclesiastical administration promised to insure the blessings of good government, quiet, prosperity, and progressive civilization.

These hopes were destined to be disappointed. Lust of conquest had few scruples, and inherent defects in social condition tempted aggression. In the middle ages, and down to a comparatively recent period, everywhere throughout Europe, under various modifications, could be recognized the feudal system in some of its leading features. If less complicated than in France and Germany, there existed in England, both under the Saxon heptarchy and Norman rule, subdivision of authority and territorial rights, subordination of parts to a whole. In Ireland, the prerogative and authority of the monarch depended much on personal character; but under him were inferior kings, as they were called, who were the actual rulers. Unfortunately for the general safety, feuds and jealousies amongst these chieftains produced dissension, and prevented union in maintenance of independence. They fell in consequence a more easy prey to adventurers from abroad, to whose rapacity common interests lent direction and strength. Before the Reformation, English authority, though always aggressive, commanded little obedience outside the Pale, then embracing the counties of Dublin, Louth, Meath, and Kildare. Under Elizabeth, Cromwell, and William of Orange, it took a wider sweep over the land; and coercive measures against the Catholics, instigated by the prevailing intolerance of the times, and animosities craftily provoked, afforded convenient pretext for stripping the native septs of their possessions.

This was more easily accomplished, from the fact, that Englishmen, who had participated in the early invasion, had established themselves in various portions of the island ; and Burkes and Butlers, and the various branches of the Geraldines, intermarrying with the leading families, and identified with them in sentiment and interests, disarmed their jealousy, and equally themselves opposed to English domination, which interfered with their exercise of power, became, as it was said, *Hiberniores Hibernis,* more Irish than the Irish themselves. By matrimonial alliances, successive conquests, or grants from the English monarchs when their arms were in the ascendant, they gained accessions to their territories, interspersed with those of the Milesian chieftains, who were thus precluded from offering any effectual barrier against the steadily progressive encroachments on their rights and liberties, or to the settled policy of England to destroy their distinctive nationality.

Our present purpose warrants no detailed account of much that is interesting in the laws and customs of Ireland under its native princes ; but one of its more marked peculiarities ought not to be overlooked. In different climes or at different periods, various forms of social organization, despotisms, or states feudal, aristocratic or republican, have been established. But the patriarchal system of the Irish septs, similar to that of the Gaelic clans of the Scottish Highlands, — one which has not yet wholly disappeared, — had in some respects the advantage of them all. Large numbers of the same name, derived from a common origin and occupying distinct portions of territory, were gathered together in separate sovereignties.

Rarely having occasion to wander far from their homes, intermarrying much amongst themselves or with the septs in their immediate neighborhood, attachment to their natal soil, pride in their traditions, the necessity in troubled times of union for mutual protection, drew constantly closer the ties that bound them. These ties were political and military, as well as patriarchal and social. The head of the sept was not merely its representative by right of primogeniture, but the arbiter of its quarrels, the leader in its wars, lands and castles vested in him as the feudal sovereign, but were held as a sacred trust for his people, who, whilst they paid him accustomed tribute and were obedient to his rule, regarded him and his immediate family with affectionate loyalty, shared his hospitality, and never forgot they were his kinsfolk.

Each individual participated in the honors of his race. No sense of social inferiority fretted his temper, or lessened self-respect. The power of his chieftain, limited by established usage, protected him in his rights; and, in default of nearer claimants to the headship of the clan, the supreme control of its affairs might devolve upon himself or his descendants. Courage, loyalty, and other chivalric virtues, sprang from congenial soil; and all the resources of the sept being combined for its general welfare, and likewise directed to work out the prosperity and enjoyment of each member, however lowly, their social condition, adapted as it was to the circumstances in which they were placed, seemed peculiarly calculated to ensure both security and happiness.

From the vicissitudes of war and consequent confiscations, their various marriages whereby lands were acquired or granted away, the limits of their territories varied at different periods. The province of Munster, originally divided for the most part between the O'Briens of Thomond and their cognate septs, the McCarthys More of Desmond, Duhallow, Carberry and Muskerry, and the O'Sullivans More, Beare, of the Reeks and McFinnen, was, after the twelfth century, encroached upon by the Fitzgeralds, Earls of Desmond, Fitzmaurices of Kerry, and families nearly allied to them, and the limits of the O'Sullivans were considerably reduced. At one period in the fourteenth century, after some reverses, the Barnewalls, under grant from the English Crown, took possession of a part of their domains; but the wars of the Roses, attracting home the Butlers, who declared for York, and Fitzgeralds, who sided with the house of Lancaster, the hold of the proprietors of

English race on their conquests was weakened, and the O'Sullivans put to the sword the usurpers of their inheritance, not a living male surviving. For the next three centuries, they remained, if not unmolested, still able to maintain themselves in possession of their territories.

At the beginning of the seventeeth century, their limits are described in a manuscript in the British Museum * as follows: The O'Sullivan More is bounded upon the west, the ocean; upon the east, on McCarthy More; upon the south, O'Sullivan Beare; upon the north, Kerry. The O'Sullivan Beare, upon the west, the ocean; upon the east, Muskerry; upon the south-east, Carberry; upon the south, O'Driscol; upon the north, O'Sullivan More. According to an ancient map in Boswell's Antiquities, the territories of O'Sullivan Beare, including Glanerough, extend fifty miles from north-east to south-west by twenty in greatest breadth. Those limits embrace the Bay of Bantry, which in some places is ten miles wide. Dunkerron and Iveragh, the country of the O'Sullivans More, measured together about thirty-five miles by twenty.

A glance at the map of Munster, with the graceful indentations of its shores, its ranges of lofty mountains, its lakes and streams, makes it easy to credit the enthusiastic descriptions of its wild and romantic scenery, as presented by the magic pens of the Halls, Macaulay, and other gifted writers. If not rich in mineral wealth or agricultural products, this lovely region was eminently suited for the abode of a patriarchal people, who, in the chase of the elk and red deer that abounded in its forests, in the fisheries in its bays and rivers and along its coasts, found manly occupations in the intervals of war. The character of their institutions was social, and occasions frequent for assembling together for religious ceremonial, festive entertainments, or the transaction of affairs. They are often described by the English as inferior to themselves in civilization.

---

* Harleian MSS., 1425, pp. 24, 25.

Constant resistance to encroachment was not favorable to the refinements of life, or to the useful arts; and ignorance and impoverishment must always suffer in comparison where there is ampler opportunity for cultivation.

How numerous were the inhabitants of these several countries, as the separate territories of the clans were designated, can only be conjectured. When at the close of the Catholic War, at the beginning of the seventeenth century, a general amnesty was offered to the people of Munster, who had been very generally engaged in the recent strife, of four thousand pardons granted, five hundred and twenty-eight of the principal followers of O'Sullivan Beare, four hundred and eighty-one of those of the O'Sullivan More, five hundred and forty-two of Muskerry, two hundred and ten of McCarthy Reagh of Carberry, are stated to have received them. Many of the former had previously left the country with their chieftain, and more had perished in these desolating wars. Notwithstanding this show of forbearance, and disposition manifested on the part of the conquered to avail themselves of the proffered amnesty, there were many who were subjected to pains and penalties, exiled and proscribed; and laws of the most aggravating character kept alive their resentment, and prevented any cordial reconciliation. Every opportunity was improved to throw off what all candid Englishmen now readily admit to have been an intolerable tyranny, and Munster was finally reduced to subjection by the destruction or impoverishment of the larger number of its inhabitants.

It is idle to mourn over events growing directly out of human infirmities, and constantly paralleled in other lands and ages. But a candid consideration of the past yields the most valuable lessons to statesmen who control the destinies of nations. Had England been governed by a wise and more generous policy towards Ireland, and respected the rights and liberties, civil and religious, of its people, she would have been spared a vast effusion of blood and waste of treasure, a heavy responsibility for infinite misery and wretchedness. For centuries, Ireland was an expense to her treasury. If its inhabitants had been permitted the same privileges as Englishmen, they would in process of time have become loyal, and, advancing in prosperity and civilization, contributed in a larger measure to her strength. To heap upon a favored few immense wealth, which added little to their enjoyment, the masses were reduced to a condition of predial servitude. The immunity of both countries from foreign assailants has at times been dependent upon their political consolidation, but persecution has only served to strengthen the attachment of the Catholics to their faith; and there can be no loyalty to a government felt only in oppression. More liberal measures have already been adopted. Should tenures be made more permanent for those that till the soil, education universal, and suffrage extended to all who read and write; if the funds set apart for the support of religion were enlarged, so that, without infringing on vested rights, more than one-sixth of the ecclesiastical revenues were applied to the religious instruction of three-fourths of the people,—pregnant sources of discontent would be removed. Rancor for ancient wrongs throws obstacles in the way of reparation, renders more insupportable existing restraints. Religious toleration, equality before the law, blending of nationalities, are indispensable to tranquillity, progress, and strength.

Whatever obligations of fealty may have at times been recognized to the monarchs of Ireland, these septs, during the long period of resistance to English subjugation, were virtually independent. What was known as the Brehon law had been from time immemorial established for their government, and was administered by their own courts and judges. They had schools for instruction, bards, and historians; and, devoutly attached to the tenets of their church, monastic institutions were founded, and religious rites observed. By this Brehon law, when the heir of a deceased chief was incompetent, from youth or infirmity, the headship devolved on the nearest of kin, possessed of sufficient experience, prudence, and ability to administer affairs as Tanist. Incessantly engaged in feuds amongst themselves, or in hostilities with foes from abroad striving to subject them to a hated yoke, warfare was their most usual employment, and demanded a leader in full vigor of mind and body. Such a life, if not favorable to mechanical employments or agricultural pursuits, fostered habits of hardihood, activity, and subordination, rendered them thoughtful and devout, and also encouraged a taste for song and record, by which to preserve and transmit historical incidents.

During the lapse of centuries of strife, many of their more precious chronicles perished. Their destruction was at one period the settled purpose of the invaders, in order to break down that traditional pride which rendered them united and formidable. Fortunately, enough have been preserved to throw much light on their early history. Romance necessarily mingles with the remoter annals of every people, and historical criticism has to discriminate what may be received with confidence from statements obviously improbable, or which are not susceptible of proof. The compilations of the Four Masters from manuscripts transcribed from age to age, which had been carefully preserved by the Druids, or, later, in religious houses, are entitled to respect as they rest upon authority as reliable as that on which we depend for our knowledge of other nations. Faith may be at a loss how much to believe of the successive migrations and struggles for the mastery from the tenth century before the Christian Era, when we are told that the sons of Miletus by Scota, daughter of Pharaoh, wrested the island from the Tuatha de Danaans, its previous possessors. But, as we approach the epoch of authentic history, these records inspire greater confidence. They were submitted by the senachies of the various septs to the triennial assemblies of Tara, and the incidents they relate cannot be reasonably questioned.

Solicitude to determine with accuracy the lines of descent of such as may possess or transmit hereditary rights, being a characteristic trait in feudal and patriarchial communities, it was likewise the duty of the senachies to enter upon record births, deaths, and marriages, and furnish proof in all questions of disputed succession or inheritance. It is consequently possible to trace with comparative confidence the progenitors, from generation to generation, of these Irish chieftains. As their matrimonial alliances were for the most part confined to a few neighboring families, comparison of their several records insures greater exactitude. For many generations, the McCarthys, O'Briens, Fitzgeralds, Fitzmaurices, and O'Sullivans were closely allied by marriage in the immediate families of their respective representatives; and connections with the Roches, Barrys, Butlers, Burkes of Clanrickard, and Brownes of Kenmare, were frequent among them. Our present purpose is limited to some brief account of the O'Sullivans of Bearehaven, including whatever promises to be of interest connected with their origin.

From records reasonably authentic we can trace far back their lineage, as also that of most other Milesian families. Keating's "History of Ireland," the Harleian Manuscripts in the British Museum, give their names, and of many of them historical incidents have been preserved.* What early civilization existed in Ireland is said to have been derived through Spain, from the Scythians. According to Epiphanius, quoted by Keating, "their customs and manners were received by the other nations as the standards of polity, civility, and polite learning; and they were the first after the flood, who attempted to refine mankind into notions of courtesy, into the art of government, and practice of good manners." They are mentioned with respect by Justin and Horace, for their courage, purity of life, and noble traits of character. Several centuries earlier, a portion of them, crossing the continent of Europe, or

---

* Harleian MSS., No. 1425, pp. 24, 25.

passing through the straits into the Mediterranean, established themselves — as did also the Phœnicians, from whom the Greeks derived their letters and literature — in Spain, where, five centuries before the Christian Era, they are said to have attained a considerable degree of civilization, being in constant intercourse with Rome and Carthage. They were celebrated for their works in metal, the excellence of their swords and armor, for their musical attainments, and progress in refinement. They early passed into Ireland, and carried with them their language, laws, and customs.

In the second century, Conn reigned over Ireland; but Owen, likewise descended from Heber Fionn, son of Miletus, was his competitor for the throne. Owen, defeated, sought refuge in Spain, where he remained nine years employed in the military service of the king of that country, who gave him his daughter Beara in marriage. Returning into Ireland with a Spanish army, he landed at a harbor in the southwesterly part of the island, which, in honor of his wife, he called Bearehaven. He was soon joined by a numerous body of kinsmen and followers, and, defeating Conn in ten successive engagements, compelled him to resign his authority over the southerly part of the island. His son Olioll, in 237 King of Munster, had by Sabia, daughter of Conn, seven sons, and by will settled the crown of Munster by alternate succession upon the two eldest; Desmond, or South Munster, being the separate dominion of Owen, from whom descended the McCarthys and O'Sullivans; Thomond, or North Munster, of Cormac Cas, from whom derive the O'Briens, McMahons, and MacNamaras.

Owen, son of Olioll, married Moncha, daughter of Dill, a Druid of noble birth, and in 260, their son Fiacha Muilhethan succeeded, and established himself at Knoc Graffon, near Cashel, in the easterly part of Munster, "where his moat and extensive intrenchments are still to be seen." This was the birthplace of many of the early kings, and long continued

APPENDIX. 277

the abode of his descendants, being the chief seat of the O'Sullivans at the time of the invasion. In 489, Angus, the first Christian king of Munster, who had been converted and baptized by St. Patrick, was killed in battle. He was the common ancestor of many families of note, including the O'Keefes, O'Donovans, McCarthys, and O'Sullivans, although these names were not at that time adopted as family designations.* O'Sullivan More, in 909, was slain at the battle of Maigh Ailbe, and in 943, another O'Sullivan More, with other great chiefs of Munster, assembled and attacked the Danes, whom they defeated. O'Sullivan acted as general of the confederacy, and, in personal conflict, slew Moran, son of the King of Denmark. Donel More, eighth from the first who assumed the name of O'Sullivan, and a lineal descendant from Eogan More, was the ancestor of both branches of the O'Sullivan More and O'Sullivan Beare and Bantry. In the fifth volume of Sir William Betham's Baronetage will be found the pedigree of the elder branch, to which belonged various personages distinguished in the British civil service at the beginning of the century. The first Baronet,† long a member of Parliament, published several works on historical and philosophical subjects. In various historical and genealogical collections are found materials for the history of the O'Sullivan Beare.

---

* From Aodd Duff, tenth generation from Olioll, great-grandson of Angus, the first Christian king of Munster, sprang the McCarthys and O'Sullivans; the latter, according to authorities mentioned by Keating, being descended from Florence, or Fynen, the elder brother. Sullivan, whose name was attached to his descendants, was the eighteenth from Olioll. The elder branch of the McCarthys, of Desmond, terminated in the male line in 1596, in Donel More, Earl of Clancare, whose daughter Ellen married Florence, a younger son of Sir Donogh McCarthy Reagh, of Carberry. This Florence, recognized as McCarthy More, was an able leader, but, defeated, passed forty years as a prisoner in the Tower of London. He had four sons, of whom Daniel was his heir.

† The elder brother, Sir Benjamin O'Sullivan More, born 1747, was judge of the Supreme Court at Madras, married a daughter of Sir Digby Dent, and left three sons. The second brother, John, born 1749, of Richings Park, married Henrietta Hobart, daughter of Earl of Buckinghamshire. Henry Boyle, the fourth, died unmarried.

Donnel More, the common ancestor of the two branches of O'Sullivan More and Beare, was the twenty-fifth generation from Olioll; and his great-grandson Anra-ny Lacken,— according to the pedigree from the British Museum, Lord of Desmond, and the first Lord of Beare and Bantry, in Munster,— flourished sometime in the thirteenth century. Our limits forbid any detailed account of this long line of chieftains. Our object is simply to direct the attention of any who are interested, to what is recorded of them.

Dermod, eleventh Lord of Beare and Bantry, came to an untimely death from an explosion of gunpowder in his castle of Dunboy, in 1549. He is described in the ancient chronicles as " strong in war, formidable to his enemies, and dear to his friends." His wife was Julia, daughter of Donnel, Prince of Carberry, by Elinor Fitzgerald, daughter of Gerald, eighth Earl of Kildare ; the mother of Donnel being daughter of Donnel, ninth Lord of Bearehaven, who died in 1520. He left four sons, mentioned in the Harleian Manuscript, already cited.

1. Donnel, thirteenth Lord, killed in 1563, married Sarah O'Brien, daughter of Sir Donaugh, Prince of Thomond, by the daughter of the first Earl of Thomond. He was the father of Donel, the fifteenth Lord of Bearehaven, who was inaugurated as chief of his country in 1593, and was the leader of the Catholic armies in 1600. Overpowered by superior numbers, and discouraged by the defection of some of his allies too ready to make peace, after many battles with various fortune, he went into Spain, where he entered the Spanish service, and was created Count of Bearehaven. He was killed in 1618, aged fifty-seven. He married Ellen, daughter of Owen O'Sullivan More, seventh Lord of Dunkerron. Their son Dermod, second Count of Bearehaven, was page to the King of Spain, Philip IV. In Thurloe's State Papers, vol. i. 479, will be found a letter from the Bishop of Cork, O'Sullivan Beare and O'Sullivan More, dated 1653, at Paris,

in reference to a landing of troops, estimated from eight to fourteen thousand, in Munster. Smith, vol. ii. p. 236, ed. 1774, says, that, in his time, there was an O'Sullivan Beare in Spain, ennobled as Count of Bearehaven, who was hereditary governor of Groyne. There is reason to believe that this line is now extinct.

2. Sir Owen, fourteenth Lord of Beare and Bantry, married Ellen, daughter of James, Lord Barry, and died 1594. In 1563, he succeeded his brother as chief, and, in 1570, received a patent from the Crown, of the territories of his sept; but his nephew Donnell, when he came of age, claimed as his rightful inheritance, Beare, Bantry, Ardea, and all other castles and demesnes, including the castle and haven of Dunboy. It was finally decreed that the castle of Beare, its haven and demesnes, should be allotted to Donnell; Bantry, about twenty miles to the north-east, to Sir Owen; saving to Sir Philip, younger brother, and Tanist to the son of Sir Owen, the castle of Ardea and its dependencies on the river Kenmare in Glenarough. Dermod, son of Sir Owen, married a daughter of Cormac, Lord Muskerry, and died Lord of Beare and Bantry, in 1617. Their son Dermod married Joan, daughter of Gerald Fitzgerald, sixteenth Earl of Desmond, and, succeeding his father, died in 1618.

3. Dermod, born 1526, married Johanna MacSweeney, granddaughter of McCarty More, Prince of Desmond. He was in all the wars against the English in the reign of Queen Elizabeth, at the head of a large force from Beare, and in the Catholic War was the adviser of his nephew Donald, with whom he went into Spain about 1602. He received a pension of six hundred pieces of gold from the Spanish king, and died at Corunna, at the age of one hundred years, about 1626, his wife dying the same year. His son Don Phillip published soon after a history of Ireland in Latin, reprinted in 1850, to which is prefixed a Latin elegy, giving an account of his family. Another son, Daniel, was slain in fighting against the

Turks. His daughter Helena was drowned returning from Spain, and another, Leonora, became a nun.

4. Sir Phillip, of Ardea, who, as Tanist to Sir Owen's son, exercised the supreme authority, and held the castle of Ardea appertaining to Tanistry, married a daughter of Cormack, Lord of Duhallow, who built the celebrated castle of Kanturck, still remaining in possession of the Earls of Egmont, — the completion of which Queen Elizabeth ordered to be stayed as too strong for a subject. He is mentioned by Betham as residing at the castle of Ardea in 1613, with his son Donnel. He is stated to have been the ancestor of Master Sullivan of Berwick.

According to information procured from Ireland in 1860, the three generations which connected Sir Phillip of Ardea with Owen, mentioned in the statement of Master Sullivan, are as follows: Donnel, son of Sir Phillip, residing in the castle of Ardea in 1613, is described in the pedigree from the Ulster College of Arms as having married a daughter of O'Sullivan More; in another account, the daughter of Earl of Clancarthy; Phillip, son of Donnel, Honora, daughter of Lord Muskerry, of the castles of Macroom and Blarney;*

---

* Cormic Laidir, Lord of Muskerry, who held the chieftainship of Muskerry from 1448 to 1495, built the famous castle of Blarney, about three miles from the city of Cork. It is still standing in ruins, and the Blarney Stone, which endows all who kiss it with the faculty of persuasion and the gift of eloquence, is near the top of the rampart, now only to be approached at considerable peril. The son of Laidir, Cormac Oge, died 1524, having married a daughter of the ninth Lord Kerry. His son and heir, Teigue, died 1536, leaving Sir Cormac, friend of Sir Henry Sydney, who died 1583, and who married Ellen Roche, daughter of Lord Fermoy; and Dermod, who died 1570. Sir Cormac, son of Dermod, died in 1616. Cormac Oge, created Lord Blarney and Viscount Muskerry, married Margaret, daughter of Donogh, fourth Earl of Thomond; and his son Donogh, marrying Ellena Butler, sister of James, Duke of Ormond, was created Earl of Clancarthy, and died in 1666. His eldest son Charles, Lord Muskerry, married Margaret Burke, daughter of Clanrickard; and their son dying young, Callaghan, his second son, who married Elizabeth, daughter of George, sixteenth Earl of Kildare, by a daughter of Richard Boyle, Earl of Cork, succeeded as second Earl of Clancarthy. Donogh, his son, the third Earl, married Elizabeth Spencer, daughter of the Earl of Sunderland, and, becoming involved in the ruin of the Stuarts, was forced into exile, and lived on the Continent.

Donnel, son of Sir Phillip, Ellen, daughter of O'Sullivan More, by Mary, daughter of Sir Edmond Fitzgerald of Cloyne, Ellen through the Lords of Kerry and Earls of Desmond, descended from Edward I.* These frequent connections by marriage between the branches of Ardea and Dunkerron may be explained by the circumstance, that the castle of Ardea was about five miles, on the other side of the river Kenmare, from the principal abode of the elder line.

If there should be any disposition to question the appropriateness of these references to the remote ancestry of General Sullivan, in connection with his military and civil services, in another land, it will be admitted, on reflection, that whatever circumstances connected with the subject of biography are in themselves suggestive may well be stated. These circumstances, in this instance, are neither matter for pride nor for humility; but will afford many information, not without interest, nowhere else to be obtained without labor.

From the close of the Catholic war, in 1602, during the reign of James I., and a portion of that of his unfortunate son, the people of Munster were unmolested. This period of tranquillity naturally disposed them kindly towards the Stuarts; and, in 1641, they rose in mass against the Parliament forces. From divided counsels, false-hearted friends that betrayed

---

* Burke in his "Landed Commoners," Vol. IV., xix., note to p. 563, speaking of a daughter of Philip O'Sullivan of Glenarough, says, "She was a lineal descendant of the Fitzgeralds, Earls of Desmond; Barrys, Viscounts Buttevant; Butlers, Earls of Ormond; Fitzmaurices, Lords Kerry; O'Briens, Kings of Thomond; De Burys, Earls of Clanrickard; McCarthys, Princes of Desmond; McCarthy, Reagh, and Clancarthy; and through Joan Fitzmaurice, her direct ancestress, daughter of Thomas, eighth Lord Kerry, and Lady Honora Fitzgerald, descended from Humphrey De Bohun and Elizabeth, daughter of Edward I. and William the Conqueror." This implies also descent from Alfred and Charlemágne. Clares, De Courcys, De Lacys, and other well-known names, honorably connected with the early history of England, largely intermarried with the Munster families, many Scotch chiefs with those of Ulster. The broader culture of the stranger, the restlessness, greed, and coolness of calculation, which have produced the highest civilization the world has attained, tempered and strengthened the more generous and impulsive traits of the Milesian.

them, insubordination, and a want of prudence which placed trust and confidence in weak-minded men who could not keep their secrets, they were overpowered after stubborn resistance by Cromwell's veterans. O'Sullivan of Drominagh, and his son, were slain n defence of their castle, and many more of the leaders of the sept lost life and property in the strife. Cromwell, in conformity with the views of Harrington, in his "Oceana," that political power vests in the owners of the soil, made sweeping confiscations, and directed that all who opposed him should be forced from their possessions, and driven into Connaught, and that their estates should be distributed amongst his soldiers and the adventurers who had supplied him with means for the war.

Upon the restoration of the Stuarts, in 1660, hope was indulged that this wrong would be repaired. But Charles II. knew no policy but his own selfishness, and quieted the dispossessed with promises not even intended to be kept. What little religious sentiment ever gained ascendancy over him through his fears prompted toleration of the Catholics. His brother James was an avowed member of that church. The septs of Munster shed their blood like water at Aughrim and in numerous other hotly contested encounters for his cause. It ended in disaster; and, exhausted and overwhelmed, what remained to them of their territory was confiscated, and those who were left in the land reduced to a condition of destitution and dependence.

All who were able sought in the military or civil service of foreign lands the independence no longer permitted them in their own. Major Phillip lived many years in France. The son of his wife's sister by O'Sullivan More was, in 1745, the friend and companion of Prince Edward, the son of the Pretender. His rank in the service was Adjutant-General; but, during the earlier and more fortunate part of the enterprise, the prince was guided by his counsels. Later, when the forces collected by the government were too numerous for any rea-

APPENDIX.   283

sonable hope to be left them of success, the Scottish chieftains had exclusive control of the movements. Sullivan accompanied the prince from the fatal battle of Culloden, and remained with him until the chance of escape was diminished by so many being together. Having done all he could to aid the flight of the prince, he went over to the Continent.*

What part the family of Ardea took in the Catholic War or subsequent strife under Cromwell, in defence of their property and religious rights, does not appear. O'Sullivan More lost a large portion of his territories in the latter period. In 1653, he was in Paris with the Count of Bearehaven from Spain, making preparations for a descent on Munster, as mentioned above, with money furnished through the French king. After 1660, all branches of the race enjoyed a brief respite of quiet and prosperity; but, taking part with James II. against William of Orange, they were proscribed and banished. Major Phillip was with the garrison of Limerick, that, after a stubborn resistance, surrendered in 1691.

By the terms of surrender, such of the Catholics as were unwilling to abandon their religion, and take unconditional oaths of allegiance to the English Government, were to be furnished with transportation to France; and amongst those who preferred poverty and exile to this humiliation was Major Phillip. He had married Joanna, daughter of Dermod McCarthy More, descended from the Earl of Clancarre, — who died in 1596, — by Ellen, daughter of McCarthy Reagh and Elinor, daughter of Lord Muskerry, who thus united in her

---

* Lord George Murray, in order to justify himself, attributes the want of success to his having been thwarted in his plans by the counsels of Sullivan and Sheridan. This view has been taken by Scottish writers. It is not without precedent that fault seeks vindication in the accusation of others. Murray, with much talent for command, was overbearing, and, no doubt, offended those who opposed him. But, when he assumed command, the forces gathering under Cumberland had rendered the enterprise hopeless; and, though Lord Mahon entertains the idea that the march on London would have replaced the Stuarts on the throne, Murray was probably wise in dissuading a rash procedure, which would, in all probability, have been a futile waste of life.

person the three principal branches of McCarthy More, Reagh, and Muskerry. Their property was confiscated, though some part of it seems to have been restored. The date of his death, from the wound received in a duel in France, as mentioned by his son, is not known. He appears to have left another son besides the subject of this notice, who was born on the seventeenth of June, 1690, at Ardea, in the county of Kerry.

Little is known of his education. From its extent and thoroughness, it was probably at some one of the seminaries on the Continent, where his family in their prosperity had endowed, as was customary at the time, scholarships for the benefit of its members. He returned to Ireland to find even the terms of the surrender disregarded, and entered upon life under many discouragements. His original destination was for the priesthood, but this appears to have been early abandoned. Different traditions have been handed down with regard to his coming to America; but that which connects him with the efforts to restore the Stuarts after the death of Queen Anne would seem the most probable. The first, in 1716, was soon suppressed. Another in 1721, under the lead of the Duke of Ormond, was equally unfortunate; and it was in 1723 that he left his native land.

Seeking a retreat from calamities and persecutions that environed him at home, he came over the sea, trusting to find in the rapid development of our newly settled country, then as now the refuge of the unfortunate, opportunities to acquire independence. He brought with him the advantages of a good education, and had not been long in America before the circumstance that he was a good mathematician, and acquainted with several languages besides his own, attracted the attention of an estimable clergyman of the period, Dr. Moody. This kind-hearted man immediately took measures to his being engaged as a teacher, which to an advanced period of life continued his principal vocation. Several generations of the youth of a large section of country on the borders of Maine and New Hampshire grew into life, prepared for its duties by a training, which, according to the traditions of the neighborhood, was not confined to the ordinary rudiments of grammar and arithmetic, but partook in a degree of the varied and substantial accomplishments of his own.

The farm which he occupied consisted of nearly eighty acres of land, in South Berwick, on the bank of the river, opposite Great Falls, now a large and thriving manufacturing village. When he established himself, more than a century ago, in this beautiful spot, there were saw-mills on the streams, but all else was wild or rural; the primeval forest having been but partially encroached upon by the fields and pastures of recent settlers. Nothing now remains of the dwelling, where he resided for fifty years, but some slight excavations, with a portion of the cellar-walls. The barn was destroyed by fire about seven years since. His tomb and monument, surrounded by an iron fence, erected by his descendants, Governor Wells and others, stand in good preservation, not far from the bridge to Great Falls, on the farm near his former abode; a usage of ancient date in sparsely peopled parts of New England.

In an obituary notice, he is stated to have died at Berwick on Saturday, June 20, 1795, at the age of one hundred and five years and three days. " This respected and extraordinary character was employed till he was ninety in teaching public or private schools, and perhaps few persons ever diffused so much useful learning. At this advanced age he retired, lamenting that he could no longer be beneficial to mankind." " He wrote a good hand till he was one hundred and two, and " is said, after he had reached that age, to have occasionally ridden in the saddle from Berwick to Durham, thirty miles as the roads then were, to visit his son, General Sullivan, and to have returned the same day. " His chief amusement, until the last year of his life, was reading, at which time he almost totally lost his eyesight. This he called the most afflicting stroke he ever met with. Worn down with the weight of years, and cut off from his favorite amusement, he seemed desirous to meet his approaching dissolution. He was a stranger to pain till within a few months of his death.

"He bore its infliction with becoming resignation, giving such evidence of his belief in the Christian religion, and of a well-grounded hope of future happiness, as to make his transit appear more to be wished than dreaded. He continued to converse sensibly till seven days before his death, when his speech failed him. In an apparent state of devotion, buoyed up above every fear, and apparently insensible to pain, he met the king of terrors with a fortitude that must have appeared surprising to any one who had not himself experienced the happiness of a well-grounded hope.

"His integrity, uprightness in his dealings, his benevolence and hospitality, together with his instructive conversation and desire to be useful, insured him the veneration and esteem of all that knew him." Generations have passed since he died, but the traditions of his worth and services are not yet wholly effaced.

Mrs. Sullivan had come with him to this country as a child, and when she grew up to womanhood became his wife. She possessed great personal beauty and force of character; and to her influence, as well as to that of their father, may be ascribed the energy and vigor which made their children distinguished. She survived him several years, dying in 1801, at the age of eighty-seven.

Their children were, —

1. Benjamin, an officer in the British navy. He was lost at sea, some years before the separation of the colonies from the mother country.

2. Daniel, born about 1738, was married at Fort Pownall, in the town of Prospect, in the county of Waldo, June 14, 1765, to Abigail, daughter of John Bean, by James Crawford, Esq. Daniel Bean, of York, with others his associates, obtained a grant of what is now Sullivan, and a part of Hancock,

a tract about six miles square, from the provincial government; and here, with some of his neighbors in York, of the name of Preble, Gordon, Plaisdell, Johnson, and Hammond, he had established himself about the time Daniel was married. After his death, June 21, 1785, the town, under the name of Sullivan, was confirmed to the settlers upon their payment of £1,205 consolidated notes into the treasury, a small portion of the territory, nine thousand acres, being reserved in 1800, when the Legislature remodified its grant, to Bowdoin and Williams Colleges. Before the Revolutionary War, there were forty families within the limits of the town. These, at its close, had been reduced to twenty. At the present time, it is a flourishing seaport, building many vessels, manufacturing many articles of value, and sending far and wide excellent granite, which has been used in the fortifications of New York, and elsewhere for docks, custom-houses, and other edifices.

Sullivan is situated at the upper end of Frenchman Bay, a wide sheet of water, often compared, from its graceful outlines, lovely islands, and the lofty mountains rising from its shores, to the Bay of Naples. The island of Mount Desert, which forms its westerly bound, is annually visited by artists and persons of taste from all parts of the country. Extending southerly from the main part of Sullivan is a neck of land stretching into the bay, called Waukeag Point, from the name attached by the Indians to the neighborhood. On the southerly end of this Point, about four miles from the harbor, Daniel erected his dwelling, built several saw-mills, engaged in navigation, and here were born to him five children, — one son and four daughters. For the ten years following his marriage he was eminently prosperous; but when hostilities commenced with the mother country, finding his residence exposed to predatory attack from British cruisers, he removed his saws, and discontinued his works.

Throughout the war he was energetic and devoted, raising and commanding a force of minute-men, and, by his activity and fearlessness, did good service to the cause. In 1779, he was with his company at the siege of Castine, and, after returning home, he kept them in readiness for action, inflicting many heavy blows upon the enemy. The English and Tories made several attempts to capture him, which, from the constant vigilance of the patriots, were ineffectual. But one stormy night in February, 1781, a British war vessel, the Allegiance, commanded by Mowatt, who burnt Falmouth, now Portland, anchored below the town, and landed a large force of sailors and marines. The house was silently invested; and Captain Sullivan aroused from his slumbers, to find his bed surrounded by armed men. He was hurried to the boat, and his dwelling fired so suddenly that the children were with difficulty saved by their mother, and a hired man who lived in the family. Taken to Castine, his liberty and further protection from harm were tendered him, on condition he took the oath of allegiance to the king. Rejecting these proposals, he was carried prisoner to Halifax, and thence sent to New York, where he was put on board that vessel of infamous memory, the Jersey hulk, where he remained six months. Exchanged, he took passage for home, but died on the Sound, not without suspicion of having been poisoned, though probably, like many others, he was the victim of the barbarities of the British provost, who, either of his own accord or by instruction, subjected his prisoners to unparalleled privations.

James, his only son, born December, 1775, married Hannah Preble, of York, who deceased 1857. He resided at Sullivan, on the estate of his father, at the Point, in the house that was rebuilt after the conflagration by Mowatt in 1780. He was engaged early in life in navigation, and afterwards in the care of his farm. He was a man of good sense, fond of reading, took a lively interest in public affairs, and in his political affinities was an ardent Democrat. He died 30th August, 1830, without issue. His sister Lydia, born March, 1774, also resided at the Point with her brother, and died there, nearly eighty

APPENDIX. 289

years old, in 1852. From the other daughters of Daniel are descendants of many names in Maine and neighboring States.

4. James, born at South Berwick, 22 April, 1744, was educated by his father, studied law with his brother John at Durham, and first established himself in his profession at Georgetown, at the mouth of the Kennebec. In 1770, he was appointed King's Attorney for York; in 1774, he was sent delegate to the Provincial Congress; in 1775, elected Judge of Admiralty; in 1776, Judge of the Supreme Court; 1783, 1784, 1785, he was chosen delegate to Continental Congress, and also member of Massachusetts Legislature; in 1787, he was in Governor's Council; in 1778, Judge of Probate; 1790 to 1807, Attorney-General; 1796, on commission for determining boundary between Maine and the British Lower Provinces; in 1804, elector of President when the electoral college of Massachusetts cast its votes for Thomas Jefferson; in 1807, 1808, Governor of Massachusetts, in which office he died.

His principal writings, besides numberless addresses, official documents, and contributions to the public journals, were his "History of Maine," 1795, and "Land Titles," 1801. Among his many papers in the Collections of the Massachusetts Historical Society is a "History of the Penobscots." An answer to a publication of Mr. Thacher, on the subject of the pastoral relation, in 1784, was his earliest separate work. In 1791 appeared his "Observations on the United-States Government;" in 1792, "Path to Riches," on money and banks; in 1794, "Altar of Baal;" in 1798, "Letters on the French Revolution;" in 1801, "Constitutional Freedom of the Press." A work on Criminal Law, if completed, was never published. "An Address to Young Men on the Dangers of a Vicious Life," is in the list of works to be included in an edition of his writings proposed in 1809.

He was one of the original members of the Massachusetts Historical Society, and its first president from 1791 to 1806. With the Massachusetts Congregational Charitable and the

Humane Societies, with that for Propagating the Gospel, and the Academy of Arts and Sciences, he was long associated as member or presiding officer. Of the Middlesex-Canal and Boston-Aqueduct Corporations he was the president till he died, and among the most energetic in their projection and construction.

An interesting obituary was published of him by President John Quincy Adams; a funeral sermon, by Rev. Joseph Buckminster, his pastor; a memoir of him, by James Winthrop for the Historical Collections; a sketch of his character and professional life, by Knapp, in his "Lives of Eminent Statesmen;" and a biography, in two volumes, by his grandson, Thomas C. Amory, which was published on the 10th of December, 1858, fifty years after his decease.

5. Eben was also educated to the bar. After the surrender at the Cedars, in 1776, he volunteered as a hostage among the Indians, who would have put him to torture and death, but for a British officer, who interposed to save him after the fagots had already been kindled to burn him. Discovering that the enemy refused to comply with the stipulations, and the conduct towards him of the savages being contrary to all rules of civilized warfare, as his life was constantly threatened, and he was subjected to indignities, he came to the conclusion he was under no further obligation to remain. Watching his opportunity, when the Indians, on some festive occasion, after their games, dances, and carouse, had sunk at night into profound slumber, and the two sentinels, cheated out of their vigilance by his pretended sleep, were taking their repose, he glided silently out of the camp, and made for the bank of a neighboring river, in order to swim across to a Dutch settlement which he knew to be on the opposite shore.

The shout of his pursuers was heard as he entered the water, and when near the middle of the stream, the plash of their dog, a large and ferocious animal, as it entered the river.

APPENDIX. 291

He turned, and as the dog approached managed with one hand, while he supported himself by the other, treading water, to press its head beneath the surface, and, having drowned it, to effect his escape. Some days later, fearing that, having volunteered as a hostage, his honor might be implicated by his flight, he surrendered himself to a British officer, and was taken to Montreal. It was many months before his exchange could be regularly arranged so as to admit of his resuming active service, much to his chagrin, as shown by various of his letters in print. He served at Rhode Island and on other occasions, leaving behind him a very honorable reputation as a gallant officer.

Mary, the only daughter, married Theophilus Hardy, and was the ancestress of Governor Samuel Wells, of Maine, who died July 15, 1868; of the late John Sullivan Wells, of Exeter, N.H., who was in the Senate of the United States, Attorney-General, of New Hampshire, and who presided over both branches of the State Legislature; of Joseph B. Wells, formerly Lieutenant-Governor of Illinois; and of Frederick B. Wells, who was many years consul at Bermuda.

II.

ANECDOTES OF EARLY LIFE.

The following version is given by Mr. Brewster, in his "Rambles about Portsmouth," of Sullivan's early connection with his profession: —

It was not far from the year 1756 that a lad of fifteen years, with a rough dress, might have been seen knocking at the door of Judge Livermore, and asking for the Squire.

"And what can you do, my lad, if I take you?"

"Oh, I can split the wood, take care of the horse, attend to the gardening, and perhaps find some spare time to read a little, — if you can give me the privilege."

John Sullivan — for that was the name he gave — appeared to be a promising lad, and so he was received into Mr. Livermore's kitchen, and was entrusted with various matters relating to the work of the house and stable. Mr. L., finding him intelligent, encouraged his desire to read, by furnishing from his library any books he wished; and with this privilege he improved every leisure moment. Libraries then were not so extensive as now; but the position of Mr. L. gave him a very good one for the times, and among them the most choice legal works of the day. John was permitted at times to take a seat in the library room, and he had the care of it in Mr. Livermore's absence.

One evening there had been some trouble in the town, which resulted in a fight. As has been the custom in later days, so then, the party which received the greatest drubbing prosecuted the other for assault and battery. The case was to be brought before Deacon Penhallow, at his house on the south-east corner of Pleasant and Court Streets. The best legal talents were needed for the defence to save the culprit from the stinging disgrace of being placed in the stocks, — not squeezed in corporation stocks, but in those formidable pieces of timber which were standing for years near the south-east corner of the Old North Church. The defendant at once resorted to the office of Mr. Livermore. He was absent, and John was reading in the library room. The man, supposing that any one from an office so celebrated might answer his purpose, asked John if he would not undertake his case. John, on the whole, concluded to go; and, leaving word in the kitchen that he should be absent awhile, trudged off with his client. He soon learned the merits of the case, and having given some attention to the law books, and acquired some knowledge of the forms of trial, he had confidence that he might gain the case. The charges were made, the blackened eyes and bruises were shown, and the case looked awful for John's client.

While this trial was going on, Mr. Livermore returned from his journey; and, on inquiring for John to take care of the horse, was told that he had gone off to Deacon Penhallow's to defend a suit. Mr. L.'s curiosity was excited. He put the horse in the stable, and, without awaiting his supper, slipped into a room adjoining the court, and, without being seen by the parties, listened to the trial. John had just commenced his argument, which was managed with good tact, and exhibited native talent and as much knowledge of law as some regular practitioners. John was successful, his client was acquitted, and John received here his first court fee.

APPENDIX. 293

Mr. L. returned as obscurely as he entered. The next morning, John was called into the library room, and thus addressed : " John, my kitchen is no place for you : follow on in your studies, give them your undivided attention, and you shall have that assistance you need from me until you are in condition to repay it."

The result is well known. John Sullivan became eminent at the bar, became conspicuous as General in the army of the Revolution, and, after the peace, was for three years President of New Hampshire. He was afterwards District Judge. He died at Durham in 1795, at the age of 54.

General Sullivan was of Irish descent. His father was born [in Ardea in 1691], came to Berwick, Me., as early as the year 1723, and died in 1796, aged 105 years. His mother came over several years after from Cork. She was born in 1714, and died in 1801, aged 87. She was of a rough though noble-minded cast. The father's education was good, and together they enjoyed honorable poverty in early life.

The tradition is, she came over with her future husband. Another account states, " Her peculiarities of temper are still remembered ; but all speak with respect of her devotion to her family, and constant acts of kindness to her neighbors. If they were ill, she watched by their bedsides; and if in sorrow, was ever ready with kind words of consolation."

An incident which occurred a few years later has been thus related ; many additional particulars which have been transmitted in print or correspondence being omitted: —

" At the time of John's first settlement at Durham, a town rich in fertile farms, its inhabitants were devoted to the peaceable pursuits of rural life. There prevailed among them a strong prejudice against lawyers. It was believed that they were a class not required in the community ; that they fomented litigation for their own purposes, and craftily devoured the substance of their neighbors. Resolved, if possible, to secure their village from the presence of all such promoters of discord, some energetic young men gave the newly settled counsellor notice to quit Durham, threatening personal coercion if this peremptory order were not speedily obeyed. Nothing daunted by this open and decided show of hostility, John Sullivan informed them that he should not think of it ; and, if they cared to resort to force, they would always find him ready. The people of the town became greatly excited, and took different sides in the quarrel; collisions occurred between the parties, and, in the progress of the dispute, one of the assailants was severely though not dangerously wounded by an over-zealous adherent of Mr. Sullivan. The affair already wore a serious aspect, when a truce was called, and it was finally determined to settle the question by a personal conflict with any combatant the assailants should select. Their chosen champion not being considered a fair match for the elder brother, who possessed great physical strength, James, at his own request was substituted to do battle for the law. The encounter took place at the time appointed, and James came off the victor. The people, acquiescing in the result of this ordeal, ever after placed the greatest confidence in John Sullivan; and he soon became, and continued through life, their most beloved and popular citizen." — *Life of James Sullivan*, Vol. I., page 33.

The following extract from a letter of John Adams to his wife, dated York, June 29, 1774, throws light upon the early professional success and practical good sense of both brothers: —

" There is very little business here, and David Sewall, David Wyer, John Sullivan and James Sullivan, and Theophilus Bradbury, are the lawyers who attend the inferior courts, and, consequently, conduct the causes at the superior.

" I find that the country is the situation to make estates by the law. John Sullivan, who is placed at Durham, in New Hampshire, is younger, both in years and practice, than I am. He began with nothing, but is now said to be worth ten thousand pounds, lawful money; his brother James allows five or six, or perhaps seven, thousand pounds, consisting in houses and lands, notes and mortgages. He has a fine stream of water, with an excellent corn-mill, saw-mill, fulling-mill, scythe-mill, and others, — in all, six mills, which are both his delight and his profit. As he has earned cash in his business at the bar, he has taken opportunities to purchase farms of his neighbors, who wanted to sell and move out further into the woods, at an advantageous rate, and in this way has been growing rich. Under the smiles and auspices of Governor Wentworth, he has been promoted in the civil and military way, so that he is treated with great respect in this neighborhood.

" James Sullivan, brother of the other, who studied law under him, without any academical education (and John was in the same case), is fixed at Saco, *alias* Biddeford, in our province. He began with neither learning, books, estate, nor any thing but his head and hands, and is now a very popular lawyer, and growing rich very fast, purchasing great farms, and is a justice of the peace and a member of the General Court."

A few days later he says, " I dined with Mr. Collector Francis Waldo, Esq., in company with Mr. Winthrop, the two Quincys, and the two Sullivans, all very social and cheerful, — full of politics. S. Quincy's tongue ran as fast as anybody's. He was clear in it that the House of Commons had no right to take money out of our pockets more than any foreign state ; repeated large paragraphs from a publication of Mr. Burke's in 1766, and large paragraphs from Junius Americanus."

As Junius and Americanus were frequent signatures affixed by James Sullivan to his contributions to the press for the rest of his life, this conversation may not have been without some influence over their selection.

III.

ATTACK ON THE FORT AT NEWCASTLE.

There has been some controversy as to who planned, directed, and participated in this attack. Captain Eleazer Bennett, who died in Durham, 1852, at the age of a hundred and one, made the following statement : —

On the 15th of December, 1774, he was in the employment of General Sullivan, at his mill at Packer's Falls, when Micah Davis came up from Durham and told him he wished him to come down and go to Portsmouth, and to get anybody he could to come with him. The party consisted of about a dozen men. Their names were, so far as he could remember, Major John Sullivan, Captain Winborn Adams (afterward a colonel, killed in the war), Ebenezer Thompson (afterwards Judge Thompson), John Demeritt, Alpheus and Jonathan Chesley, John Spenser, Micah Davis, Isaac and Benjamin Small, Eben Sullivan, and himself. General Alexander Scammell, killed at Yorktown, John Griffin, and James Underwood were also of the party.

APPENDIX.

They took a gondola belonging to Benjamin Mathes, who was too old to accompany them, and went down the river from Durham to Portsmouth. It was a cold, clear, moonlight night. Stopping a short time at Portsmouth, they were joined by John Langdon with another party. They then proceeded to the fort, in possession of the British, at the mouth of Piscataqua harbor: the water was so shallow, that they could not bring their boat to within a rod of the shore. They waded through the water in perfect silence, mounted the fort, surprised the garrison, took the captain (Cochran) and bound him, and frightened away the soldiers. In the fort they found one hundred casks of powder and one hundred small arms, which they brought down to their boat. Again wading through the water, that froze on them, they made their way back to Durham. The arms were found to be defective, and unfit for use. A portion of the powder was taken by Major Demeritt to his house in Madbury; but most of it was stored under the pulpit of the meeting-house in Durham, on the site of the one that was taken down in 1848. This powder Captain Bennett understood was afterwards carried to Charlestown, and used by the patriots in the battle of Bunker Hill.

To the Honorable John Sullivan, Esq., Brigadier-General of the Continental Army.

SIR, — The Committee of Safety for the County of Hillsborough, in the Colony of New Hampshire, having in contemplation the great services you lately rendered the county in your civil capacity, and the great abilities you then exerted at the bar in their defence, at a time when the people were most cruelly oppressed by the tools of Government, pray leave to address and congratulate you on your appointment to the rank of Brigadier-General, — an appointment which, as it distinguishes your merit, so at the same time it reflects honor upon and shows the penetrating discernment of those truly eminent patriots from whom you received it, and of whom are composed the Continental Congress. Nor are we less sanguine in our expectations of the high advantages which must result (under God) to the public, by your military skill and courage, as you have been indefatigable in attaining the first, and have given a recent instance of the latter to your great honor and reputation, in depriving our enemies the means of annoying us at Castle William and Mary, and at the same time furnishing us with materials to defend our invaluable rights and privileges.

This, Sir, must be ever had in remembrance, and, amongst the actions of others our heroes of 1775, handed down to the latest posterity. That the Almighty may direct your councils, — be with you in the day of battle, — and that you may be preserved as a patron to this people for many years to come, is our fervent prayer.
July 19, 1775.

IV.

MILITARY ASSOCIATION AT DURHAM.

[New-Hampshire Gazette, March 10, 1775.]

Whereas some evil-minded and malicious persons have affected that a number of people in the town of Durham are about forming themselves into a company, in order to throw off all obedience to the militia officers, and set at defiance the laws of the Government, I desire you to publish the Articles of inlistment in your next paper, that the public may judge how little foundation there is for so scandalous a report. The articles are as follows : —

" We, the subscribers, do hereby agree to form ourselves into a company, and meet at Durham Falls on every Monday afternoon, for six months next coming, to acquaint ourselves with the military art, and instruct each other in the various manœuvres and evolutions which are necessary for infantry, in time of battle ; we also agree to appear each time, well furnished with arms and ammunition, and at our first meeting, to nominate and appoint the several officers who are to preside over us for the first month ; and then proceed to appoint others for the next month, — always avoiding to re-elect any that have served, until all the others have gone through their tour of duty as officers. And at any muster or field day we shall hold ourselves obliged to incorporate with the respective companies to which we belong, and yield all due obedience to the proper officers of the militia appointed by the Captain-General, and endeavor to instruct those who are undisciplined, in the best manner we are able."

(Signed by Eighty-two reputable Inhabitants.)

This is an exact copy of the articles, which any person that yet remains in doubt may be satisfied of by applying to me, and viewing the original, a sight of which may at any time be had;

and was there nothing more illegal and injurious in a late paper, signed by several persons in this Province, I believe the signers would not take so much pains in keeping it from the public view. But, whatever may be the purport of that, I rejoice in laying the contents of this before the people, that they may judge whether it has the least appearance of an illegal combination, or whether, on the contrary, it does not appear to be a well-concerted plan to promote and encourage the military art. I flatter myself that even malice itself could not adjudge this to be an unjustifiable measure, or suggest that any part of it looks like treason or rebellion; and I can account for the scandalous report concerning it in no other way but by supposing that these defamers expected to be rewarded for their slander.

Sir, I am your very humble servant, JOHN SULLIVAN.

DURHAM, March 4, 1775.

V.

LETTER OF GENERAL SCAMMELL.

Alexander Scammell was a student at law with General Sullivan. He entered the army at the commencement of the Revolution, and rose rapidly in the estimation of Washington and of the country. He was Adjutant-General at Yorktown, in October, 1781, when he was killed in an attack on the works of the enemy. He was warmly attached to Sullivan, who reciprocated his regard, and who was always pleased to have him in his command. The following letter, written soon after the battle of Lexington to Sullivan, absent in attendance on the Congress at Philadelphia, needs no explanation: —

HONORED SIR, — Your leaving New Hampshire at a time when your presence was so extremely necessary to cherish the glorious ardor which you have been so nobly instrumental in inspiring, spread a general gloom in Durham, and in some measure damped the spirit of liberty throughout the province. Nothing but the important business in which you are embarked permitted any degree of patience or resignation. When the horrid din of civil carnage surprised us on the 20th of April, the universal cry was, "Oh, if Major Sullivan was here!" "I wish to God Major Sullivan was here!" ran through the distressed multitude. April court, which was then sitting, immediately adjourned. To arms! to arms! was breathed forth in sympathetic groans. I went express for Boston by desire of the Congressional committee, then sitting at Durham; proceeded as far as Bradford, where I obtained credible information that evening; and next morning arrived at Exeter, where the Provincial Congress was assembling with all possible haste.

I reported the intelligence I had gained, that the American army at Cambridge, Woburn, and Charlestown was in more need of provision than men; that fifty thousand had assembled in thirty-six hours; and that the Regulars, who had retreated from Concord, had encamped on Bunker's Hill in Charlestown. The Congress thereupon resolved that the Durham company, then at Exeter (armed complete for an engagement, with a week's provision), should return home, and keep themselves in constant readiness; all the men being gone from the westward and southward of Newmarket, and men-of-war expected hourly into Portsmouth. It was with the greatest difficulty your Durham soldiers were prevailed upon to return.

Six or seven expresses arrived at Durham the night after our return; some desiring us to march to Kittery, some to Hampton, some to Ipswich, which places they said sundry men-of-war were ravaging. The whole country was in continual alarm. Suspecting that the marines at Portsmouth might take advantage of the confusion we were in, and pay Durham a visit, we thought proper to stand ready to give them a warm reception; and supposing that your house and family would be the first mark of their vengeance, although I had been express the whole night before, I kept guard to defend them to the last drop of my blood. Master Smith, being under the same apprehension, did actually lie in ambush behind a warehouse, and came very near sinking a fishing-boat anchored off in the river, which he supposed heaped full of marines.

Men, women, and children were engaged day and night in preparing for the worst. Many towns in this province have enlisted minutemen, and keep them under pay; and the Congress before this would have actually raised an army of observation, had they not waited for the General Court which sits to-morrow, in order to raise as much money as will pay the army when raised. I am extremely mortified that I am unable to join the army at Cambridge. But as I am honored with the management of your business, which cannot possibly be neglected, the dictates of duty and gratitude induce me to suppress every wish that may militate against your interest. Your family are all in health, and desire their tender love and duty to you. The particulars of the skirmish between the Regulars and the Americans will long before this reach you. In longing expectation, your safe, happy, and speedy return is hoped for by all your friends, but by none more sincerely than by

Your dutiful humble servant,

ALEXANDER SCAMMELL.

P.S. — Please to excuse inaccuracy, as I am obliged to conclude in the greatest haste. We have heard from you no otherwise than by Captain Langdon's of the 13th of April.

PORTSMOUTH, May 3, 1775.

VI.

CANADA CAMPAIGN.

Extract of a Letter from an Officer at Fort George, to his friend in New York.

[New-Hampshire Gazette, August 3, 1776.]

NEW YORK, July 14.

I never, never knew the fatigue of a campaign until I arrived at Canada. The most shocking scenes that ever appeared in a camp were constantly exhibited to view. When General Sullivan arrived in Canada, the army was torn in pieces by sickness and other unaccountable occurrences. A whole regiment was not to be found together. General Sullivan, with his usual activity and alertness, collected together a debilitated, dispirited army; tried the strength of the enemy, who were at least four to one, and performed one of the most remarkable retreats that was ever known. No person who was not present can conceive a tenth part of the difficulties attending it; the enemy at our heels, 3,000 of our men sick with the small-pox, those who were most healthy like so many walking apparitions. Al our baggage, stores, and artillery to be removed, officers as well as men all employed in hauling cannon, &c. Our batteaux loaded were all moved up the rapids six miles : one hundred of them were towed by our wearied men, up to their armpits in water. This was performed in one day and a half; our sick and baggage all safely landed at St. John's, and from thence at Crown-Point, with the loss of only three cannon, which were but poor ones. All this was accomplished, through the amazing exertions of General Sullivan, who performed what appeared to be almost impossible to have been done by mortal man! He is now on his way to New York.

VII.

THE LIVIUS LETTER.

The writer of the following letter to General Sullivan, Peter Livius, was, before the war, a resident " of Portsmouth, N.H. A member of the Council under the Royal Government, he was proscribed by the Act of 1778, and died in England, in 1795, aged, it is supposed, about sixty-eight years. Of the members of the Council of New Hampshire in 1772, seven were relatives of the Governor. Having been left out of commission as a Justice of the Common Pleas, when new appointments were made on the division of the Province into counties, and dissenting from the views of the Council as to the disposition of reserved lands in grants made by a former Governor, Livius went to England, and exhibited to the Lords of Trade several and serious charges against the administration of which he was a member. These charges were rigidly investigated, but were finally dismissed. Livius appears, however, to have gained much popularity among those in New Hampshire who were opposed to the Governor, and who desired his removal; and was appointed by their influence, Chief-Justice of the Province. But as it was thought that the appointment, under the circumstances, was likely to produce discord, he was transferred to a more lucrative office in the Province of Quebec. Livius was of foreign extraction, and, as would seem, a gentleman of strong feelings. He wrote to General John Sullivan from Canada, to induce him to abandon the Whig cause. The letter was published. Mr. Livius possessed a handsome fortune. He was educated abroad, but received an honorary degree from Harvard University in 1767."

The above account of Judge Livius is taken from Sabine's "Loyalists." It is derogatory to character even to be approached by a proposition to betray; but there appears nothing in the conduct or sentiments of General Sullivan to have encouraged confidence that such an attempt could have been, under any temptation, successful. The letter forms part of the history of the times and of his own.

SIR, — I have long desired to write my mind to you, on a matter of the very greatest importance to you; but the unhappy situation of things has rendered all intercourse very difficult, and has hitherto prevented me. I now find a man is to be sent for a very different purpose to you. By him I shall contrive to get this letter to you, a person having undertaken to put it in the place of that which was designed to be carried to you. You know me very well, and are acquainted with many circumstances of my life, and have seen me in very trying situations that might perhaps have been some excuse; yet I am sure you never knew me guilty of any ungentlemanly action. I remind you of this to convince you that you may safely trust what I say to you, as coming from a person who has never trifled with any man.

You know, better than I do, the situation of your Congress, and the confusion there is among you, and the ruin that impends. You have felt how unequal the forces of your own people are to withstand the power of Great Britain; and for foreign assistance I need not tell you how precarious and deceitful it must be. France and Spain know they cannot embark in your quarrel, without the greatest danger of Great Britain turning suddenly against and taking possession of their colonies, with so great a force already collected and in America; besides their fears of raising views of independence in their own colonies, to which they are much disposed. But why should I enlarge on this subject? I am sure you know the futility of all hopes of effectual foreign assistance, and that these hopes have been thrown out only to keep up the spirits of the deluded common people. You therefore will not suffer yourself to be deluded by them. The most you can expect from foreigners is, that they will help, at the expense of your countrymen's blood and happiness, to keep up a dispute that will ruin you, and distress Great Britain. It is not the interest of France and Spain that America should be independent.

But if it were possible you could entertain any thoughts that the hopes of effectual foreign assistance were well grounded, you cannot but know that such assistance must now arrive too late. The last campaign was almost consumed before the English army could get collected, and in a position to act in America; but now the campaign is just opening, the whole army in the greatest health and spirits, plentifully provided with every thing, most earnest in the cause I do assure you, well acquainted with the country, and placed so as to act briskly with the greatest efficacy. A few months, therefore, will probably decide the contest. You must either fight or fly; and, in either case, ruin seems inevitable. You were the first man in active rebellion, and drew with you the Province you live in. What hope, what expectation, can you have? You will be one of the first sacrifices to the resentment and justice of government; your family will be ruined, and you must die with ignominy; or, if you should be so happy as to escape, you will drag along a tedious life of poverty, misery, and continual apprehensions in a foreign land. Now, Sullivan, I have a method to propose to you, if you have resolution and courage for it, that will save you and your family and estate from this imminent destruction. It is, in plain English, to tread back the steps you have already taken, and to do some real essential service to your king and country, in assisting to re-establish public tranquillity and lawful government.

You know that I will not deceive you. Every one who will exert himself for government will be received; and I do assure you firmly upon my honor, — I am empowered to engage particularly with you, — that it shall be the case with you, if you will sincerely endeavor to deserve your pardon. It is not desired of you to declare yourself immediately, nor, indeed, to declare yourself at all, until you can dispose matters so as to bring the Province with you; in order to which you should as much as possible, under different pretences, contrive to send every man out of the Province from whom you apprehend difficulty, and to keep at home all those who are friendly to government, or desirous of peace. In the mean while, endeavor to give me all the material intelligence you can collect (and you can get the best); or, if you find it most convenient, you can convey it to General Burgoyne, and by your using my name he will know whom it comes from without mentioning your own name.

As soon as you find you can do it with efficacy and success, declare yourself, and you will find assistance you very little expect in restoring the Province to lawful government. If you do not choose to undertake this, another will; and if you continue obstinate on the ground you are now on, you may depend upon it, you will suddenly find it fail and burst under you, like the springing of a mine. What I recommend to you is not only prudent, safe, and necessary, it is right, it is honorable. That you early embarked in the Rebellion is true. Perhaps you mistook the popular delusion for the cause of your country (as many others did who have returned to their duty), and you engaged in it warmly. But when you found your error, you earnestly returned; you saved the Province you had engaged for, from devastation and ruin; and you rendered most essential services to your king and country, for which I engage my word to you, you will receive pardon, you will secure your estate, and be further amply rewarded. Your past conduct has been unworthy: your return will be praiseworthy. What is all this expense of human life for, these deluges of human blood? Very probably to get afloat some lawless despotic tyrant in the room of your lawful king. I conceive you must be surrounded with embarrassments. You may perhaps find difficulty in getting a letter to me. Possibly the fellow who carries this to you may be fit to be trusted. He thinks, indeed, he carries you a very different letter from this, and I suppose will be frightened a good deal when he finds the change that has been put upon him, and that I am in possession of the letter he was intended to carry; yet I have understood he has a family here, and will, I suppose, wish to return, and knows well enough it is in my power to procure him pardon and reward; and I imagine he thinks (as I trust most people do) that I am never forgetful of a man who does any thing to oblige me. You will consider how far you may trust him, how far it is prudent to do it; and you can sound him, and see whether he wishes to return, and whether he is likely to answer the purpose; and if you think proper

APPENDIX. 305

you may engage to him, that I will protect him and reward him, if he brings me safely a letter from you. I could say a great deal more on this subject, but I must close my letter lest it should be too late. Be sincere and steady, and give me an occasion to show myself —
Your sincere friend,
LIVIUS.

This letter was taken out of a canteen with a false bottom, by General Schuyler at Fort Edward, this 16th day of June, in the presence of us the subscribers.

BENJAMIN HICKS, Captain.
HENRY B. LIVINGSTON, <i>Aide-de-Camp to Major-General Schuyler</i>.
JOHN W. WENDELL, <i>Captain</i>.
JOHN LANSING, Jr., <i>Secretary to Major-General Schuyler</i>.</div>

I certify upon honor that this letter was taken out of a canteen; which I delivered to General Schuyler; which canteen I received from Colonel Van Dyck, who separated part of the wire from the false bottom, to see whether it was the canteen I was sent for, and who, after taking out this letter, and letting out some rum, returned it into the canteen, without breaking the seals.

BAR. J. V. WALKENBURGH,
Lieutenant.

June 16, 1777.

VIII.

VERMONT CONTROVERSY.

The following letter to Sterling, from Keene, Oct. 4, 1782, shows how far public sentiment in Vermont, as affected by her disappointment, endangered the general cause: —

I take the liberty of informing your Lordship, that last evening arrived in this town one Captain Snyder, who was taken, near Esopus, about three years since, and escaped from confinement, near Montreal, on the 10th of last month. He informs me that the British army were encamped on the Isle de Noix, on their way to Albany; that their numbers consisted of four thousand, principally German troops; that the Indians, under Johnson, were to move down the Mohawk River, and fall on Schenectady at the same time that the main army attacked Albany. He adds, that it was currently reported by their officers that the inhabitants of Vermont were to join them on their arrival at Crown Point; of which, from other accounts, there seems some reason to be apprehensive.

General Bailey also writes, by express, that he had similar accounts through other channels. I have conversed with an intelligent officer commanding on our frontiers, who confirms the account, and assures me that some of his party have reconnoitred the army at Isle de Noix, and find their number about four thousand, and, through a secret channel, have discovered that the army is commanded by Major-General Clark; that their object is Albany; and that they are in expectation of being joined by Vermont, — of which, from evidence I have this moment received, I have but little reason to doubt.

As your Lordship commands in the Western Department, it was thought proper, by the judges of the Superior Court, now sitting here, and all the officers in this quarter, to despatch an express with the foregoing intelligence, that you may take proper measures to frustrate the enemy's design. It is difficult to conjecture what may be their intentions. Possibly the plan of forming a junction of the two armies on the Hudson River may be again in contemplation; but making a diversion in that quarter to weaken General Washington, and then bringing him to action, is still more probable. There is, indeed, a possibility that their intention is to establish themselves on this side the Lake, secure, and bring over the inhabitants of Vermont, who are ignorant of the measures taken by their leaders, and may possibly attempt to make opposition when the plot is discovered.

If disaffection existed at the period in Vermont, it was by no means universal, and was probably less than the resentments, growing out of the controversy with the neighboring States, led to suppose. But, while it lasted, it was cause for solicitude, a source of danger; and, had the war been protracted, the presence of large numbers of disaffected within our limits would have proved an embarrassment.

IX.

MILITARY ORGANIZATION OF THE STATE.

[For the New-Hampshire Gazette.]

TO THE FREEMEN OF NEW HAMPSHIRE.

BRETHREN AND FELLOW-CITIZENS, — Conscious of having too small a share of military experience, I can only urge my late appointment to the command of the militia in this State, in excuse for addressing you upon a subject of such importance to the public, and of which my knowledge is so imperfect; but, were my talents even equal to those of a Frederick, I could do but little towards forming a well-regulated militia, without the countenance and aid of the people at large. You will permit me to observe, that, under a Constitution calculated to render a people free and happy, the mutual consent and joint efforts of all are requisite in some instances to bring about that reform which, in a less happy country, may be accomplished by the arbitrary dictates of a despotic prince.

With us, at this day, a slender excuse, a defect in the militia laws, or, at the worst, a small fine, may exempt a person during life from appearing in the field; but the despot issues his orders, and punishes the breach according to his own caprice; and as no person can conjecture the penalty, every subject fears to hazard the consequence of disobedience. Perhaps this may be one reason for the great success tyrants have had, in enslaving so great a part of the human race.

In Republican governments, people often turn their thoughts to that part of the Constitution which bequeathes them their liberties; but too frequently forget that they ought to pursue measures for securing them. We have already bravely purchased liberty and independence, and now make part of an empire where freedom reigns without control; but what will our late struggle avail, if we suffer the military skill which we have acquired, to be lost! and ourselves to sleep in seeming safety, till the avarice, the jealousy, or the ambition of some foreign prince rouses us from our slumber, and convinces us of our mistake?

We often please ourselves by observing, that this country is calculated for freedom and commerce, not for war. I sincerely join in the opinion, and most ardently wish it may ever remain such; but I have long since been convinced, that the only way to keep peace is to be prepared for whatever events may come. If we mean to keep our neighbors' sword in the scabbard, we shall whet our own.

As I flatter myself further arguments are not requisite to prove the necessity of disciplining and keeping up a regular and formidable militia, I shall proceed to offer some remarks for your consideration. It is not my province to dictate: I can only recommend. All important regulations must be ordered or approved of by the Commander-in-Chief, and even those orders must be consistent with the laws of the State. I shall, therefore, only urge upon the field-officers already appointed, to lose no time in nominating their captains and subalterns; and, in their selection, that they avail themselves of as much military talent and experience as possible.

I am far from wishing that no persons should be appointed but such as have had military experience; on the contrary, I am persuaded that some gentlemen who have never seen service have naturally excellent military talents, and bid fair to make great and good officers; but where one person has military experience, another none, all things being equal, it requires no uncommon share of sagacity to determine who should be preferred. I wish no person to be in office who is not likely to answer the purposes of his appointment.

Formerly, the man of wealth and family was sought after, without the least attention to capacity. I readily grant, that officers of every rank ought to be gentlemen and men of honor; if men of family, their advantages of education are generally greater; and if they are possessed of fortune, it is a most agreeable circumstance; but these alone can have but little weight, without other qualifications more essential.

The merchant will not hazard his ship to be navigated by a man, merely because he is a man of wealth and family; nor a gentleman his watch, in the hands of one unskilled in watch-making, barely because he possesses a large estate; and it is really surprising that the most unbounded and the most important science should be so lightly esteemed, as to intrust the teaching of it to persons totally uninstructed, and who have not even capacity to acquire a knowledge of it themselves.

But whatever appointments the field officers may think proper to make, I earnestly recommend that they be made as soon as possible;

APPENDIX. 309

and that the officers appointed, of every rank, use their utmost efforts to have the militia disciplined in small parties, without delay.

And here let me entreat the influence of every gentleman who wishes well to his country, to lend his aid in promoting a business so essential as the preservation of his own rights and those of his fellow-citizens.

The law of the State enacts, that every soldier shall be provided with a gun, bayonet, cartouch-box; but a uniformity of arms is much to be wished, and I cannot think it impossible to procure such as were used by the late American army. Many of them are now in the country, and many, I believe, for sale in the public magazines. If arms are to be purchased, I can see nothing but a little attention requisite, in order to have them of the same kind.

A uniformity of dress will be allowed, by every person who has the least military taste, to add lustre to the troops, to inspire them with military ambition, make them appear respectable in the view of spectators, and formidable in the eyes of their enemies; and this, in my opinion, is more easily attainable than a uniformity of arms.

I would only propose for consideration, a dress almost similar to that worn by the troops of the German Empire: a short coat of white woollen, and waistcoat of the same (of our own manufacture); the coat faced and half-cuffed, with blue, red, crimson, or any other color; the cape of the coat, and the front of the waistcoat, bound like the facing. A pair of linen overalls will complete the dress. A single minute spent in calculation will prove this a much cheaper dress than the militia now appear in. If a person keeps a suit for public days, I can see no good reason why he should refuse the cheapest; and if he is able to keep but one, I believe a moment's reflection will convince him that he will make a more decent appearance than in a suit which, by a single washing, may be ruined. If it should be objected, that it is not the fashion, my answer is, that if officers and men once adopt it, it will soon become as fashionable as it is now in Germany and Turkey, where the best troops almost in the world are clad with it.

If it should be objected, that this kind of clothing cannot be kept neat, the answer is, that even without washing, they are more easily kept so than any other. Whiting, flour, wheat bran, or chalk, used in the French army, and even in our own, kept white uniforms decent and clean, which would not admit of washing, and gave them a neater and better appearance than clothing of any color.

The operation which this must have respecting the balance of trade ought to be a powerful motive for adopting it. Almost the whole, if not all, the materials for this uniform may be manufactured among ourselves. If we allow twenty thousand militia men in this State, and this dress to cost each of them five dollars, and each suit to last a year, there will be one hundred thousand dollars kept among us, which, if we clothed in foreign manufactures, must be drawn out of the country. In ten years, a million of dollars will be saved to this single State. I am well aware of the argument too often opposed to this; viz., that if a man can purchase foreign manufactures cheaper than those of his own country, it is better for him as an individual. Admit this argument to be just, it only proves that people sometimes adopt, to serve themselves, what tends to ruin the society to which they belong; and that this must have that operation, will be discovered if we reflect on the fatal consequences, should every member in the community adopt it.

Our own manufactures would cease, idleness be introduced, and all our circulating coin be drawn away to pay for the labor and materials of other nations. No great force of reasoning is requisite to prove, that any country which imports three millions annually in foreign articles, and exports only two, will be one million in arrear; this balance must either remain unpaid, or the circulating medium of the country drawn away to discharge it.

This balance of trade against a nation, like a whirlpool draws off its coin, and leaves the people "poor indeed." This, among others, is a cause of the scarcity of money among us at this day, and is one principal foundation of our public distress. We feel the evil, and complain, although few attempt to discover its source. But I will now endeavor to demonstrate, that it not only tends to impoverish a nation, but even those individuals who conceive they are saving their interest, by purchasing foreign manufactures at a cheap rate.

If it has a tendency to distress the nation at large, to drain it of its coin, and leave poor debtors with their effects at the mercy of the rich and powerful, or rather in the hands of foreign merchants, or their agents here, how much will the pretended saving avail them? Their real and personal estate will be reduced in value; and, in order to raise what is needed to pay for articles they fondly conclude are purchased upon advantageous terms, double the quantity of money actually paid for them will have been lost.

If, therefore, a great saving must be made to the State, by clothing our military force in uniforms of our own manufactures; if individuals will feel the advantage, and the corps appear more respectable, would not the militia of New Hampshire do themselves high honor in adopting a measure which, while it adds brilliancy to them as troops, will contribute largely towards enriching their country?

Having proposed this subject for your consideration, I shall now address myself to the gentlemen of talent and capacity, who may have the offer of commissions. Some, perhaps, may decline because they have ample fortunes, and wish to enjoy life in ease and tranquillity. Others will allege their having held equal, or even superior commissions in the army or elsewhere; and many may urge the expense attending an office, as a sufficient objection against holding it.

If the first of these arguments had been adopted at the commencement of the late war, we should not at this moment have even the shadow of liberty to defend: if the second was to prevail, I think no person could urge it with better propriety than myself.

The third objection is only rendered formidable by a practice, too common in America under former Constitutions, which I trust will never take place under the present.

Formerly, in many of the United States, a muster day often presented a scene of feasting, and not of military exhibitions. The principal officers, instead of attending to the duties of the day, were employed in preparing and ordering expensive entertainments for spectators and officers: while the soldiers were left to burn their powder to no purpose; to march without order; to be the spectators of an untimely feast; to return home without acquiring any other knowledge than that which arose from seeing the near resemblance between a general muster and a riot.

I am far from wishing muster days to be considered as days of feasting, either for officers, soldiers, or spectators. They are days for exhibiting military skill; for acquiring a knowledge of manœuvres; and not for feasting and revelry. Judicious spectators will be better pleased with a display of military acquirements, than with a feast, without having a sight of the performances they came to view. Officers will have less trouble, and be able to perform their duty with ease, and less confusion. Soldiers can be more regaled by having refreshments provided for them to partake of, at proper intervals, than by seeing the most luxuriant tables in which they can have but little share; and will undoubtedly be better pleased, to have their time taken up in the business of the day, than in that which has no relation to it. If the militia mean to become soldiers, they must act the part of such, in acquiring the necessary knowledge. If they wish to become the strength and safety of their country, they should avoid practices, however ancient, which have a tendency to prevent their obtaining the object in view. If the plan herein recommended should be adopted, the objection relative to expense will in a great measure lose its force.

Many people suppose a militia can never be equal to troops in a regular standing army; and, therefore, will not hazard an attempt which they suppose to be vain. But stubborn facts destroy the supposition. The militia of the Swiss Cantons are equal, if not superior, to the standing forces of their neighbors. And the Prussian army, so formidable in Europe, is nothing more than a well-regulated militia. The voice of the Prince calls them to the field; three months are taken up in disciplining them, and in passing the reviews; they are then furloughed for nine months of the year, during which time they work at their respective occupations, without being called upon, unless in case of invasion or actual war.

I know so much time of the yeomanry in this country cannot be spared; but much more than has ever yet been spent might be devoted to a business so important, without being sensibly felt; and I cannot avoid urging this in the most pressing terms at a time when, however desirous we may be of a lasting peace, war does not, in my view, appear at a great distance. If any gentleman should differ from me in sentiment, and can assign a satisfactory reason for the British refusing to give up the important posts on our frontiers, ceded to us by treaty, I shall then with pleasure change my opinion, and my fears on that head shall be at an end.

In order to prepare for every event, if in each neighborhood the officers and soldiers were to assemble one or two hours in a week, to practise the use of arms, and regularly attend on the proper muster days, they would soon become expert in the art of war, be a terror to every ambitious power, and render themselves able and skilful guardians of those liberties purchased by the blood of their brethren, and the treasures of their country.

JOHN SULLIVAN,
Major-General.

DURHAM, January 27, 1785.

APPENDIX. 313

[For the New-Hampshire Gazette.]

To the Gentlemen of Family, Fortune, and Education in New Hampshire.

GENTLEMEN, — While the ambitions of princes, the jealousy of States, and the avarice of unprincipled Courts have an existence, national contests will undoubtedly take place; and as no earthly tribunal has an acknowledged right to redress the injured, or to punish the aggressor, an appeal to arms is the only remedy.

It therefore becomes the duty of every people, to prepare for making this dread appeal, with some prospect of obtaining reparation for injuries received, or defending themselves against the attacks of an ambitious or insulting foe.

We have lately emerged from the shade of tyrannical power; have established an empire to which the fertility of our soil, the extent of our territory, salubrity of our different climes, invite the industrious and oppressed of every nation.

America has now become an object to excite the envy of other powers, and to fire the resentment of those restless tyrants who may justly dread an increase of numbers in a country where their own subjects can be protected from their lawless domination. We should therefore take the proper and necessary measures for defending ourselves against every attempt which envy, ambition, or unjustifiable resentment may stir up against us.

Common prudence dictates, that more attention is requisite for guarding treasures of great value, than things of small account. A rich and valuable country is more likely to be attacked, than a barren and uncultivated desert; a defenceless town, than a fortified city; a careless and undisciplined body of men, than an army conversant with the evolutions of war.

I confess myself to be one of the number that experienced too great a share of the fatigues of the war, to wish ever to see America involved in another; but, to conclude that an event will not take place because we are averse to it, betrays a weakness that will not admit of an excuse; and to postpone the preparations for war until the moment of attack, is a species of national suicide. If a man was at this time to predict a speedy war in America, he could expect no better treatment than Ahab gave the prophet who foretold his fall at Ramoth Gilead; because we are no better reconciled to the one than

Ahab was to the other; but it surely cannot be amiss to say, that considering the conduct of Great Britain, the spirit she discovers in withholding our posts, the war that has been lately kindled in Europe, the nations that there may be involved in it, and the disposition of some of them respecting America, it is at least possible that we may, even against our inclination, be drawn or driven into it. As it cannot be denied that this event may take place, let me ask whether it is not our duty to prepare to defend ourselves in case of necessity, and whether the time of peace is not more proper for those preparations than the time of war.

I have already taken the liberty to address the people of this State in general upon the subject; and, if my endeavors have the desired effect, the train-band of New Hampshire will soon be able to act the part of soldiers when the safety or the interest of their country calls them to the field. But my zeal for the security and honor of the State compels me to call upon you in particular; and, lest it should be made a question for whom this address is more especially intended, I will explain myself, by saying, that it is designed for gentlemen of family and fortune; for persons of the most reputable and honorable positions; for gentlemen who have received academical honors, and are by law exempted from appearing in the field; and for those who have formerly held civil or military commissions; and the first part of it particularly for such of them as are in the bloom and vigor of life.

You, gentlemen, will readily grant, that, in time of invasion, the whole force of the State should be called forth, if necessary, to repel the attack; and that this force, in order to insure success, should be well instructed in the use of arms. But many circumstances have hertofore operated against our having gentlemen of the first talents and capacity in the field, to acquire this necessary knowledge. The thought of serving on foot, and doing duty with persons of inferior rank in life has, perhaps, induced many to submit to the fine imposed by law, and others to excuse themselves by the exceptions in the militia acts. Yet I will venture to assert, and call upon your own feelings to justify me, that, in case of invasion, your bosoms would glow with patriotic ardor, a military zeal would instantly possess every breast; and that you would then wish to be in the place, however great the danger, where you could render the most essential service to your country. But believe me, my dear friends, the most consummate bravery, without that knowledge which is acquired by practice, will be of but little advantage ; the most heroic valor cannot supply its place, or undaunted courage serve as a substitute.

The man who means to fight his country's battles must before the day of action be accustomed to the use of those weapons with which he intends to annoy its enemies; lest he should, like the Israelitish hero, be compelled to lay aside what he had not sufficiently proved. I know that the law ranks many, in whose valor and activity the country would place the highest confidence, with the number that compose the alarm list; but I am persuaded, that the active and aspiring souls of many among you would suffer a species of imprisonment in that kind of service, among persons, many of whom (although of the most respectable characters in life), yet borne down with the weight of years, and only enjoying the feeble remains of a military spirit, have not a sufficiency of bodily strength to carry their wishes into execution.

You will pardon me, therefore, if I take the liberty of pointing out to you, my much-esteemed friends, the posts of honor, the place for exercising all your talents, and where you can be of the most essential service to your country.

The Legislature has established a regiment of light-horse, and the executive authority will undoubtedly appoint some gentlemen to command it whose talents and reputation will do honor to the corps. Permit me to mention some part of the duty of this body.

They are, in case of invasions, to scour the country, to watch the motions of the enemy, to observe their movements, judge of their designs, and give intelligence.

They are to have the charge of all important despatches, and to be intrusted with the most secret and interesting messages. In time of action, they are to cover the flanks of the army; to attack every force which attempts to surround it; to charge any part of an enemy thrown into confusion, and complete their disorder ; they are to pursue and harass a flying enemy, and make prisoners by cutting off the retreat of such of them as may separate from the main body in their flight.

Much more might be said upon the utility of this important corps ; but enough has already been hinted, to prove that this post offers the fairest field for a display of military valor, and for reaping the laurels of heroic merit.

I am not unmindful of some objections which may be made by some among the characters I have taken the freedom to address

APPENDIX.

Having commanded formerly as officers, and now acting as privates, is among the foremost with one class; and, perhaps, serving under officers who have no better talents or pretensions than themselves, will have its weight with another. But, however fashionable the first objection has become in modern days, it had no weight with the virtuous citizens of ancient Rome. The greatest commanders that the world ever produced, when their command expired, cheerfully served under those who but the preceding year were subject to their orders.

With respect to the second objection, I can only say, that my earnest desire is, that each man in this important regiment may have all the qualifications of an officer; and that the corps may become one of the most respectable in the world, on account of the worthy characters of which it may be composed; but, as all who have merit cannot be in commission, some must act as privates. But here let me ask, whether these objections, and every other, which can possibly be raised, will not lay with greater force against joining the alarm list. You will there have to do duty on foot, and probably with persons brought up in a very different line of life; but in this corps you will avoid the fatigues of serving on foot, your duty will be separate from that of the infantry, the persons acting with you will be gentlemen of your acquaintance, the companions of your social hours, whose fortunes and reputations are equal to your own.

If examples were wanting, a very striking one presents itself in Pennsylvania, where the first gentlemen of family and fortune in the city of Philadelphia serve as privates in the light-horse. And the advantage of having such gentlemen, acting in that capacity, in time of danger, is almost inconceivable. With how much more safety can an army repose, or a country rest, when they know that the motions of the enemy are watched by gentlemen of vigilance, judgment, and fidelity, than if only observed by persons who have not talents to judge of their designs, or perhaps capacity to realize the importance of their own trust! With how much more certainty can we rely upon their intelligence, than upon that which we receive from persons of inferior abilities! And with how much more confidence can we commit secret messages and despatches to gentlemen of the first reputation, than to persons whose want of fidelity may lead them to desert, or whose want of attention or capacity draws them into the snares of a vigilant and artful enemy! By these hints, however imperfect, you will see very great advantages which your country may receive from your services; and as I am convinced that neither former commissions, or exemptions by law, can stifle the patriotic flame in your bosoms, or keep you from the field in time of danger, let me entreat you to join that corps where you will do the highest honor to yourselves, and be of the most essential service to your country.

Your fortunes will enable you to equip yourselves in a proper manner, and to devote the necessary time to training your horses, and acquiring a knowledge of manœuvres. Every meeting will be an agreeable interview between friends and acquaintances of the first rank and fortune; every parade day will give delight to your fellow-citizens; and, on the days of battle, victory will hover over your standard, and your own conduct proclaim you the terror of your country's foes.

Having offered my sentiments to those gentlemen who are in the bloom and vigor of life, I now take the freedom to address that very respectable class of citizens, who compose the alarm list, — a body consisting of persons between fifty and seventy years of age, of whatever rank in life; of military officers, who have served with great credit; civil officers in the highest esteem; gentlemen of the first wealth and reputation who have passed the meridian of their days; and of those men possessing the greatest literary talents. These are the characters which make up this venerable band.

To you, my much respected and worthy friends, I can say nothing for your instruction. Many among you possess military knowledge in the highest degree, and know from experience, that every thing that has been, or can with propriety be said upon the necessity of disciplining troops, and accustoming them to the use of arms, applies as well to your corps as to others, although many of the individuals need no instruction. I therefore flatter myself, that those gentlemen who have had military experience, will use their endeavors to teach those who are not instructed.

Many of you whom the law ranks in the alarm list, I am sensible, have held very important military commissions, and are now capable of acting with honor and reputation in any office or department; but either from inclination, from advanced life, or, perhaps, from unavoidable neglect, are not now in commission, and, consequently, in the time of danger, must appear in this respectable body. Permit me, therefore, to entreat your assistance for the public good. Let me request you to assemble, and nominate your officers, and recommend them to the President and Council for commissions. This is nearest the mode which the law has pointed out, and I can see nothing in the Constitution that renders it objectionable.

If you should think proper to assemble frequently for exercise, it will afford me the highest satisfaction; not because I suppose all need to be instructed; but because those that are experienced will impart their skill to others; and the example will have the most salutary effects.

Your own judgments will direct you whether to adopt a uniform or not; and, if you should, whether cloth of our manufactures will not do most honor to you and be of the greatest advantage to the State.

I beg leave to assure you, that every measure which you may adopt to advance military knowledge shall by me, while in office, be acknowledged with great gratitude; and must, in my opinion, be viewed by all your fellow-citizens as so many marks of your attachment to that country which you helped to make free.

JOHN SULLIVAN,
Major-General.

DURHAM, February 24, 1785.

To the Learned Gentlemen charged with the Education of Youth in New Hampshire.

GENTLEMEN, — As the profession of arms is in every country esteemed honorable, even when the science of war is learned with a view of extending conquests over unoffending nations, it must be infinitely more so, when taught for the purpose of national defence, and for the security of dear-bought freedom.

Permit me, therefore, gentlemen, to entreat you, if it will not interfere with the plans which you may have laid for diffusing literary knowledge, to set apart some hours in the week, for the youth under your care to amuse themselves in learning the manual exercise and military manœuvres. If this proposal should meet your approbation, your own wisdom will dictate the best method for carrying it into execution. If relaxation from studies is necessary, perhaps none can be so useful; and I am convinced, that, in a short time, none could be more pleasing to your pupils. You will then have the pleasing satisfaction to see the youth, whom you have learnt to converse with the sages of Greece and Rome, to admire the heroes

APPENDIX. 319

of ancient and modern times, and to value that freedom for which they have fought and bled, made, by your care, proper champions to defend those natural and national rights, which you have taught them to hold in the highest estimation. JOHN .SULLIVAN,
Major-General.

DURHAM, 27th Feb. 1785.

X.

WASHINGTON'S VISIT TO NEW HAMPSHIRE.

In Brewster's "Rambles about Portsmouth" is a minute detail of the incidents of this occasion, and an extract from Washington's journal giving his own account of it. The gazettes afford other particulars.

On Saturday, Oct. 31, 1789, President Washington was met at the State line of New Hampshire by General Sullivan, President of the State; Langdon; Wingate; several of the Council; Colonel Parker, State Marshal. Escorted by "several troops of cavalry in handsome uniforms, and also by many militia officers in white and red uniforms, of the manufacture of the State," he proceeded to Portsmouth, where he arrived before three o'clock, and was received at the State House. He was conducted to the Senate Chamber, and addressed, on behalf of the town, by Mr. John Pickering; to which he made a response. A review then took place of the horse, infantry, and artillery; and Washington was conducted to his lodgings, at Colonel Brewster's, by Sullivan, Langdon, and Parker. In the evening, the State House was illuminated, and rockets fired from the balcony.

The following day, Washington was conducted to the Queen's Chapel; and, in the afternoon, attended church at Dr. Buckminster's. On Monday, an excursion was made down the harbor, to inspect the forts; and Washington drew from the water a cod, which had been hooked by Mr. Willey. A visit was paid to the Wentworth mansion; and, on their return, the party dined at Governor Langdon's. On Tuesday, Washington called on General Sullivan, and on Mrs. Lear, the mother of his private secretary. About two o'clock, he received a formal address of welcome from General Sullivan, on behalf of the State authorities, and dined with them at the Assembly Room, "one of the best he had seen anywhere in the United States." In the evening, he attended a public ball given in his honor, and, the next day, proceeded to Exeter. Sullivan had invited him to dine at Durham, but it was probably too far from his route for the invitation to be accepted.

Printed in Dunstable, United Kingdom